Adventure Travels in the Himalaya

JOHN ANGELO JACKSON
(Jacko)

Sketches by
GEETA KAPADIA

Foreword by
HARISH KAPADIA

W0007272

INDUS
PUBLISHING COMPANY

Published by
INDUS PUBLISHING COMPANY
FS-5, Tagore Garden, New Delhi-110027
Tel.: 25151333, 52133022
mail@indusbooks.com
www.indusbooks.com

ISBN 81-7387-175-2

Printed at
B.B.N. Printers, Najafgarh Road Indl. Area, New Delhi

Foreword

You can't kill the spirit
Its like a mountain
Its old and strong
It goes on and on
    –Willie Unsoeld

Few months ago we had organized a lecture by John Jackson, Jacko to friends, in Mumbai. While arranging his transparencies he was murmuring about the voltage of the projector little lower than his liking and we were wondering he may be too meticulous and particular. But no sooner he started his presentation one could see that his pictures span more than five decades and it was very high voltage stuff. He regaled the audience with a wide kaleidoscope of events, different regions, and incidences from his life.

John Jackson has been in mountains for as long as one can remember and particularly he has been lover of hills and Himalayan range of India. He started almost immediately after the Indian Freedom in 1947 and his last visit was this year in 2005. One can imagine the range of areas and timeframe that he has covered, allowing him to witness the changes in the range. After that lecture he literally cajoled audience to ask relevant questions and like someone who is used to replying any queries, dealt with them appropriately.

This is the second facet of Jacko. He had been the Director of Plas y Brenin in Wales, a major outdoor institute, for several years. His experiences while dealing with students and novices is what makes him an exact person. Under him several students have learnt how to enjoy hills and be good at it. During his early days Jacko climbed in Kashmir and the Sonamarg area, in particular and was teaching several para-military forces in India about skiing and safety in mountains.

I happened to meet Jacko in Delhi as he was on his way to Darjeeling for a trek. He had both hips replaced and he was tattering around as he picked up a large plate from the buffet of the Indian food. Looking at him I marveled at his independent nature and chemistry to handle the rough with good. As we said goodbye, I simply mentioned that "Jacko you may be staying over in Darjeeling" implying that he will not be trekking. Looking at me he replied quite routinely, "Why Darjeeling, I will be trekking with everybody?" Rather sheepishly I asked, "But with your kind of hip, would you be able to manage a trek?" He made a gesture, "I got two sticks and with this I can go anywhere" and with a chuckle he added, "Don't worry, I limp but I limp quite hard and quite fast". You cannot suppress a person with this spirit and enthusiasm to be in the hills.

Jacko has been a regular contributor to the *Himalayan Journal*, and as the editor, I have exchanged much correspondence with him. He dug up his store of memories and always came up with something useful to print. His association with leading mountaineers of his generation is a storehouse of knowledge. Talking with him about Tom Longstaff, Noel Odell, Eric Shipton and Bill Tilman, with whom he has rubbed shoulders, is a liberal education. He was the member of the successful Kangchenjunga expedition in 1955 and as we know, no summit is climbed without teamwork and Jacko played an important part. For the Everest 1953 expedition led by Lord Hunt, Jacko was in the reserves but he has no regrets for any missed opportunities. Hills have given him plenty and he accepts them with grateful thanks.

Eileen, his energetic wife, should get much credit for doing almost everything that Jacko has done. She has accompanied him to hills every time, looked after him when John was not well and stayed with him through thick and thin. The present book is just a part of John's larger experiences with Eileen, which he calls it "The Dreams We Won". John has dreamt with eyes wide open and has made them come true.

It is indeed my good fortune to know Jacko, and I count him amongst my friends. Quite rarely a person, whom you admire and who is your hero, becomes such a good friend. I have though one complaint against him. Many times when I return from an unknown area, and having gone into different valleys, as I talk to Jacko, he makes a hole in any ego that I may have gathered. Like recently, I returned from Assam Himalaya and Jacko promptly said that "Well, I was there in 1940s". Such is this man and such is his experience.

HARISH KAPADIA

Mumbai
15th April 2005

Acknowledgements

I would like to acknowledge the enormous amount of help and assistance that has been given by Harish and Geeta Kapadia in the production of the book. Without it, it is doubtful if it would ever have seen the light of day. To Geeta also go my grateful thanks for the wonderful black and white drawings she has done for me. They are so beautiful. I would also like to thank my wife Eileen who typed the whole of the manuscript.

JOHN ANGELO JACKSON

To a normal man, any high place is an invitation. Of course, not all men can become mountaineers. And though the calculating and practical man of the world has little use for the exploits of the mountaineer, the world owes little to its practical men, whereas great is its debt to its adventurers.

Contents

9

Introduction

"Your glance is kind as we step slowly forth from
your valleys. We are always welcome at your feasts.
We have loved you well and you have rewarded us."

–Julius Kugy

The following selection of memories span a period of sixty
years and are intended to give an insight to the fascination
and immense satisfaction of expeditions and travel in the Himalaya. My companion with whom I have shared many of the
journeys for over fifty years is my wife Eileen. They are some of
the "dreams we won".

In the millennium year, we left footprints on the plains of
Rupshu in south-east Ladakh. Geographically it is a part of Chang
Thang where the harsh winds whip through the dry grasslands
creating a very cold environment.

We camped at 15,000 feet by the shores of Tso Moriri—a lake
that is a glittering blue diamond surrounded by rolling whale-
backed mountains of snow and ice. Nearby is the village of Karzok
inhabited by rugged semi-nomadic Changpas. Because it was mid-
September and the start of their long harsh winter, flocks of goats,
sheep and herds of Dzo and Yak were being rounded up for shelter.
Harvest time had ended, so each morning a steady line of Karzok
inhabitants walked past our tent to visit the local monastery where
at this time of changing seasons, a visiting Rimpoche gave each

of them his blessing for a future of peace and plenty. It was the year of our golden wedding and fitted well with our mood, so we named our journey the 'Golden 2000'.

Once again the Himalaya with its rich diversity of people, cultures, religions and environment gave us its own blessing for the present and the future.

It has always been so and the writing of this book will have been fulfilled if you, the reader, agree with the truth of those lines of the poet Edward Thomas.

"Often and often it comes back again
To mind, the day I passed the horizon ridge
to a new country."

JOHN ANGELO JACKSON
Anglesey

1

Burmese Hills and Kashmir Himalaya

(May 1944)

"From here on up the hills don't get any higher
But the valleys get deeper and deeper."

–Folk song

THE BEGINNING

Up draughts of hot humid air made the aircraft buck and bounce as it lost height and the dark green jungle of Burma seemed to be reaching for the aircraft in which five of us were quietly working. But all was not quiet for every extraneous sound was drowned by the pulsating throb of the two giant piston engines of a DC3 taking us to our rendezvous. Tree-topped hills skimmed by and we sank yet lower. Then soon we could see hill-paths like snail tracks twisting and spiralling down into the enveloping depths of tropical vegetation. Fleetingly we caught a glimpse of a clearing and of many tiny ant-like figures rushing away from newly prepared and clearly marked DZ—dropping zone. The aircraft banked and turned tightly lining up on the DZ and inside there was a great activity as air gunners and navigators heaved and stacked supplies by the open door. These were jute sacks filled with rice or sugar, *atta* or *dal* and weighing 100 Pounds apiece.

Red light on!—get ready—green light on—heave—and the pile of sacks offloaded 100 feet above the ground hurtled to the earth at high speed. For over half an hour the operation was repeated until all the supplies were dropped to the isolated detachment of a long range penetration force in the Chin Hills. Finally we made a last flight round the clearing, waved from the door and dipped a wing in friendship and support to the gesticulating figures below. We climbed higher and on reciprocal course set off back for the air strip several hundred miles to the west in steamy Bengal.

By now down in the dark and deep cut valleys it was already night but at 12,000 feet the sun still shone and lit up the surfaces of clouds that in this cooler part of the day were condensing and forming along the ridges of the mountains. Katabatic air currents caused the silvered surfaces of the clouds to curve and flow into huge greying streamers of mist that seemed like gigantic waterfalls, their veils of spray pouring down into the jungle. Over in the east, the sky was darkening to a deep Prussian blue with a base of yellow greens and lilacs, whilst in the west the sun sank to the horizon and changed from gold to a blood red orb that was rapidly being eaten by the devouring earth. At first the propellers and the leading edges of the aircraft wings held a glint of burnished copper, followed by a fiery red that was finally quenched as the sun disappeared and the mountains, valleys, jungle and low-lying mist slipped into the cool embracing arms of night. Very high cirrus clouds still caught the rays of the sun and once more reflected back the colour changes—pale gold, changing to orange and bloody crimson whilst inside the aircraft a blue fluorescent glow from instrument panels provided a small but encouraging area of light. Following the half hour burst of furious activity at the DZ we again worked quietly, oblivious to the roar of engines, content with the success of the mission, and pleased that back in the Burmese jungle, men would be cooking nourishing meals over tiny jungle fires because of what we had done. I knew that my companions were glad to be leaving the hills behind. For them the hills were not friendly but a constant threat. They knew that within seconds, they could render our giant craft and its powerful engines of many hundreds of horse-power into a screeching tearing mass of mangled metal.

None of us wanted to be a part of that! Even so, I felt sad that my companions could not feel as I did about the hills. For me, they were friends not enemies and the evening sunset among the Chin Hills had been a beautiful and inspiring end to a successful mission. I found it to be the same on all such flights so that the mountains of Burma became familiar friends that regularly uplifted my heart with their interesting shapes, complexity of ridges and dark mysterious depths of valleys. Time and again they held out a promise for the future and longed for journeys along dusty trails in unknown lands.

The journeys began for me on September 3rd, 1939. Several of us were climbing on the gritstone crags at Widdop on the Bronte Moore when Midgley Barrett, the water bailiff at the reservoir walked across the embankment and called up to us that war had been declared. At the same moment a drone in the sky made me look up to see a lone aircraft heading east. Where was it going? Where would we all be going? That was a question among so many that filtered through my mind and I felt bewildered, wondering if I and my companions were soon to part, never to see each other again. Having discovered the freedom of the mountains and the moorlands it seemed such a waste of time at the age of eighteen to have to go and fight in a war, but I treasured that freedom and so felt defiant. Perhaps that aircraft overhead had been an omen, for early in 1940 I joined the R.A.F. Volunteer Reserve and became a Wireless Operator/Air Gunner.

Eventually, I flew in Burma and on finishing my first tour of operational flying was granted a short leave and went to Kashmir. There I first looked into the Great Himalayan range.

My view point was from a 9000 feet hill named Chergand from which I looked down on to Dal lake in the Kashmir valley and across to the Pir Panjal mountains to the south. North of me line after line of snow-clad peaks stretched far away and beyond Nanga Parbat sixty miles away.

Watching the clouds that in the late afternoon were disappearing below ridge after ridge I was reminded that in a few days I would once again be flying over the Chin Hills of Burma. These peaks and valleys were different to those jungle-clad mountains but they stirred my mind in similar fashion.

Here were areas where perhaps man had never trod and for me there was a strong pull at the heart and in the mind. A cold land maybe where in the evening the snows would be turning pink then suffusing into purple shadows and I longed to trek into them, to get to know their environment and come to know the people who lived among them. That is what it was like seeing the Himalaya for my first time and I knew immediately I must return.

I have done so many times on treks and expeditions and on most of them with the best companion of all. This was my wife Eileen. Together we shared so many adventures and experiences and what follows is a part of the "The Dreams We Won".

2

Overland to India:
Facets of a Journey
(February 1976)

"Let us probe the silent places
Let us seek what luck betide us
Let us journey to a lonely land I know.
There's a whisper on the night wind
There's a star agleam to guide us
And the wild is calling, calling....
Let us go."

–Robert Service

For many years my wife Eileen and I planned to return to India and the Himalaya and finally decided we would travel overland in our own transport. This we did by buying a second hand petrol-driven Ford Transit Caravanette which once overhauled was made safer and more useful by making three important additions. The first of these was a large and immensely strong luggage rack made of wrought iron that extended from the roof of the cab and out over the front bonnet. In addition to carrying tents, skis, climbing equipment, spare wheels, tyres and extra clothing, we found that in the Far East, the rack gave us welcome relief from the heat and glare of the sun. Secondly, we added extra springs to absorb shocks on the roughest of tracks. The vehicle never let us down. The third addition was made after a conversation we had with two friends (the doctors Peter Steel and Drummond Rennie) during a 'Mountain Medicine' Symposium held in North Wales. Both insisted that a very loud and piercing twin horn was almost as important as brakes—invaluable advice that proved to be absolutely true. We visited many places during our travels which as well as the journey overland to India, included driving to Nepal, Kullu, Kashmir and Ladakh. We never broke down, suffered but three flat tyres—and quickly gave the name of 'Juggernaut' to the Transit because it never stopped for anything.

Looking back years later, I realise that as we travelled from North Wales, we lived life to the full and though I haven't written about many facets of the journey (because at the time I merely thought of it as a means to an end) it was really an end in itself.

The Journey Begins

"It is obviously going to be your lucky year." These encouraging words were included in a letter to Eileen by Batchelor's Foods who having donated two cases of soups and diced apples for our journey, had in error sent us four. She pointed out their error but they asked her not to return the excess and finished their letter with the above comment. To both of us it seemed a good omen.

Eileen had taken on the task of organising most of the special foods for the nine months we would be away, which included rations for Sherpas as well as Himalayan porters for a period of at least ninety days. When I stacked the nineteen boxes of food inside the Transit the night before we started the journey, I felt sure there would be enough to eat—and there was.

We began our travels on the first day of February. The weather was cold and grey and though it remained so throughout the day, we travelled with a feeling of lightness and good cheer having had a heart-warming send off, from friends in the village of Dwyran on Anglesey and Capel Curig in Snowdonia.

Istanbul—Gateway to the East

Long before we arrived in Anatolia we became acclimatised to the cold and reconciled to the knowledge that the temperatures would be exceptionally low. At Frankfurt am Main, a New Zealand driver of a much battered T.I.R. lorry gave us lurid accounts of snow-blocked passes in north and central Turkey, of icy, rutted tracks, freezing diesel fuel, and even of freezing petrol in temperatures down to -45° centigrade. Prospects for the future seemed daunting.

In Austria we met our son Robin who was with the British ski team, and with him for several days we watched events at the Winter Olympic games. At Seefeld, the temperatures outside the 'Juggernaut' fell to -20° centigrade, and later at Hohentauern in Steirmark the thermometer dropped even lower. After the games ended, Robin returned home whilst we continued our journey east through Yugoslavia and Bulgaria, where there was less snow but it was none the warmer.

It was on reaching the outskirts of Istanbul that we caught the first glimmer of a warming sun and during a two day stay with friends Otto and Rosi Ther, we built up a sunny kaleidoscope of impressions. Crossing the Galeta Bridge over the Bosphorous, we looked up towards the Golden Horn absorbing the sounds of the busy bustling cosmopolitan population. These sounds mingled with the hoots of frantic traffic, the warning blasts of ship's klaxons, and the exhorting cries of fishmongers who at each end of the bridge stood among trays of strong smelling fish. People sitting quietly drinking small cups of strong Turkish coffee were a contrast to darting vociferous moneychangers and noisy, pugnacious traders of trinkets. Women with the flat-faced features of people in the Balkan countries shared seats with us on the train from Yesilkoy into the centre of Istanbul. Poor but proud, their hands were hard and cracked and tough blunt fingers constantly smoothed out the creases of the neat clothes covering their small frames. Their shoes, though old and worn, were cared for, headscarves were brightly coloured and when parting from the older women, the young showed respect by placing their hands to their foreheads and giving a slight bow.

At the old bazaar in Istanbul, all the colours and the splendours of the orient were on display—artifacts of gold, silver, bronze, turquoise, and utensils made of copper reflected the rich warm glow of the metal. The shops laid out a dazzling array of antiques, fine clothing, leather goods, ceramics, and carpets from Anatolia, Armenia, Persia, Nuristan, India and far away Kashmir. It was contact with an old world—seemingly timeless—and a total contrast to the younger people outside in the streets playing volleyball and football, or to the excitable students shouting slogans and spraying walls with political text.

At dawn in the morning we left Istanbul. We were awakened by the clattering wheels of a railway train, followed by the cries of the Imam from the mosque calling the devout to prayer.

Graveyard of the Lorries

A grey and hostile landscape blanketed with wind-drift snow began to glow soft and pink at sunrise on the morning we drove to the joint Iranian and Turkish customs post at Bazargan. Condensation crystals sparkled by the side of the rutted icy track and showers of ice diamonds winked their way to earth from a clear blue sky. There was a sparkle to the world, and a promise of more sun with increasing warmth and colour to come; a welcome promise after the previous days of crossing the bleak and treeless plateau of Anatolia where night temperatures had fallen to -35° centigrade. This the ancient land of the Hittites lay deep with snow, and untidy clusters of flat-roofed, mud-walled dwellings were grimly silent, as their occupants remained within doors seeking warmth from smoky fires of damp wood and burning dung. The narrow mountainous road, potholed and ice rutted led over higher and yet higher passes, the Kopdagi Gecidi 7841 feet on to the Tahir Gecidi 8122 feet and eventually to Agri Dagi (Mount Ararat) near the border.

The first day we named the route the 'Graveyard of the Lorries'. Frequently we came across trucks that had skidded off the road, overturned, or jack-knifed then burned out, and several had rolled down the steep mountainside. Twice we found a cluster of lorries that, unable to avoid each other, had simply battered and bumped their way together to a level spot where they remained seemingly inextricably intertwined. On a section of thirty kilometres, we counted over one hundred lorries that had met one or the other of these fates. Finally on the night previous to reaching the border we stopped at a small wooden shack near Taslicay—a shack where a solitary pump gave promise of fuel for the Transit. When we finally stopped it was late, winds were strong and bitingly cold; the 'Juggernaut' sheeted in ice was heavy, running sluggishly, and in the dark our halting place, welcome though it was, appeared to be at the end of the world. A boisterous and mottly gang of grubby youngsters swept out of the dark shrieking incomprehensibly, and surrounded the vehicle. One, taller and older than all the others beckoned us inside the wooden shack. Inside we sat on orange boxes beside a roaring and almost white hot diesel stove drinking beer out of the neck of a bottle with an Italian and an Hungarian lorry driver. "They're a hard, tough but good people," said the Italian, "and you are welcome". "You want coffee?" queried one of the youngsters. We both relaxed, impressed by the quick warm friendship shown to us in such a remote and seemingly inhospitable spot. Within the hour we were back inside the 'Juggernaut' and fast asleep.

Turkoman!

Cheese with flatbread (*nan*) and *chai* without milk or sugar became our diet as we traversed the mountains, then rolled on across an open monotonous plain between Tabris and Tehran. "Whatever you do avoid arriving in Tehran at 5 o'clock in the afternoon". Peter Boardman had warned us, but inevitably it was right on 5 o'clock when we arrived, and that ultimate in chaotic experiences, though now joked about, left an indelible impression. To use a modern idiom it was 'mind blowing' and when finally at dusk we extricated ourselves from the bedlam of Tehran, we sped on and over the Elburz mountains as if pursued by demons.

After a few hours sleep, we were off again at dawn, driving down the last few miles of a bare and craggy defile and across the rice-growing plain to Sari. North of us stretched the Caspian Sea, and the wooded foothills of the Elburz mountains lay to the south. By mid-day, we were well into the Steppe country where snow covered the wooded hills almost down to the plain. Here in the land of the Turkoman nomads we frequently stopped to watch the shepherds and their tough looking dogs slowly moving flocks of sheep to areas of fresh grazing. At one stop, a car drove by then screeched to a halt, and the sun-tanned occupant, wearing a bright red sweater, pointed to our skis, then enquired if we had been skiing at Ab Ali in the Elburz.

"No we haven't," I told him "but we do intend to ski in Nepal".

"If that is so, you must be going to bring back hashish," he replied laughingly, but stopped laughing when I asked him if he was an Iranian ski instructor. He drew back his shoulders, lifted his chin, then replied with pride— ·

"No, I am not an Iranian, I am a Turkoman!"

Systems and Souls

Before arriving at any customs posts, we had a system that we hoped would help us cover all formalities quickly and allow us to move on as soon as possible. An hour or so before arrival, we used to wash down the 'Juggernaut' and following this, I would have a shave, then we would wash and put on clean clothing. Documents and information required varied slightly in different countries so always we had the following material ready in a zip folder— passports, visas, green card, carnet or other vehicle insurance, international driving licence, number of chassis, number of engine, list of spares, typed lists of equipment, and medical documents which included inoculation and vaccination certificates. Carrying the zip folder, a pen and hardbacked notebook, I used to present myself to the police and complete all the necessary formalities, then move on and do the same for the customs. At least for us the system worked well and both going out and on return we were delayed for more than one hour on only one occasion. This was on the return journey at the Afghan/Iranian frontier. On the Afghan side, we sat for several hours whilst a Landrover owned by four unkempt French lads was systematically taken apart in a search for drugs. They had been to Swat in northern Pakistan, a notorious place for 'pot' but none was found. The young Afghan customs official then beckoned me to drive the Transit on to a ramp and spoke to me in French.

"Sorry, I'm British," I said.

"Oh! Then take everything out and put it on the tables," he replied in English.

By the time I had opened the rear doors he had noted our names on the side of the vehicle 'John and Eileen Jackson'.

"Mr. John. Do you have anything you shouldn't have?" he asked.

"You mean things like drugs, or guns and ammunition?"

"That's right," he said. On my replying "No" he put out his hand and asked "Will you shake on that?" We did. However, as he made out the clearance note for our move on to the next border he asked me to read and mark well the sign above the door of the customs shed. It read as follows:

'If you have any guns, ammunition, or drugs, declare them now for if you don't we will find them.'

There was then a break in the sentence followed by the telling rider,

'And if we don't the Iranians will.'

But it was the final ominous prayer that really hit the mark— 'And if the Iranians do,—May Allah have mercy on your soul!'

Into Afghanistan

Space—a land of almost limitless space was our first impression of Afghanistan. It seemed an empty land though it was soon evident that it was far from empty. A cold wind swept constantly across the road (built by the Russians between Kandahar and Herat) and along it long lines of slow-moving camel trains carried trade goods to and from remote settlements. Bearded Afghans, backs to the wind squatted patiently by the roadside, waiting— forever waiting—as if life for them stretched into eternity.

Small and nimble donkeys laden down with loads of *lakri*

(wood) trotted steadily over the stony barren ground. These were followed by their wood collecting owners who, having walked and searched huge areas for the precious fuel in a seemingly bare and treeless land were bringing carefully garnered bundles to pick up trucks waiting at the roadside. Sometimes we stopped in what seemed a really deserted spot to see in the distance the movement of sheep, goats, donkeys, camels and the groups of nomadic peoples who owned them.

Occasionally we passed by flat-roofed fortified houses built of mud and straw, or further away from the road we could see little clusters of small black tents (yurts) out of which spiralled blue-grey smoke providing evidence of habitation. From them savage dogs looking huge and shaggy often came bounding towards us, anxious to protect the few belongings of their masters. Once, in the middle of the afternoon there was a shimmering, a mirage, giving the road an appearance of being almost underwater. In the distance a tiny mounted figure came slowly towards us and I was reminded of the film 'Lawrence of Arabia' and the Bedouin mounted on his camel coming out of the desert to visit his water-hole—but this time as the figure came nearer, we recognised it for a young Afghan on his modern Honda motorbike!

Then there was the wind—always the wind—and rolling balls of tumbleweed flittering in ghostly fashion from stone to stone, or trundling eerily along the road.

Oranges, Eggs and Rice Pudding

The road between Kandahar and Kabul, built by the Americans, makes a gradual ascent through the valley of the river Tarnak to Ghazni.

All along this valley we had clear views of picturesque forts, and mud-walled villages, all of them enhanced by a strong sun shining onto the surrounding 'whipped cream' snow. Again there were people—walking, sitting, sheltering, smoking or talking—and outside the small village shops young boys dressed in European fashion were selling baskets of fresh juicy oranges and clusters of fresh or hard boiled eggs. These we bought. The fruit and eggs were very cheap and a welcome supplement to our daily diet, and throughout our stay in Afghanistan we had an abundance of such fresh foods. Beyond Ghazni the snow again lay deep and we crossed a treacherous pass at 9000 feet, but then there was an easy descent to Kabul where the first sign we saw augered well. It read.

Sigis Hotel—Restaurant

Good Food and Rice Pudding

Later in the Steak House in Chicken street (I wonder if it is still there) we met Theresa and Jonathan Hewat who were on the last leg of a three year drive through Africa, South and North America, the Far East and India. They were full of joy when we gave them two tins of Tate and Lyle's Golden Syrup—a commodity for which they had been longing for sometime. An impressive map showing the route of their journey was painted on the back of their Volkswagon Kombi and for anyone wishing to emulate their travels, the book they wrote and published later *Overland and Beyond* is well worth buying.

So much has happened in Afghanistan since we were there. We met many fine people and had many satisfying experiences but now as the country goes through the agonies of civil war the memories are tinged with sadness.

On a happier note, at Sigis Hotel, not only did we have rice pudding but found bottles of Italian wine which we bought for a few Afghanis, but were amused to find that another label on the back of the bottle told us it was *produced* and *bottled* in Afghanistan!

We stayed in Kabul for two days, then moving on I continued writing my diary each day to Delhi.

March 4th, Evening

"No one is allowed to travel through the Khyber pass between sunset and sunrise," says 'Buster' Goodwin "and the man who came to sit with you when you had your coffee by the roadside at noon would be a guard. Many Pathan families still fued with each other and it is a potential danger that travellers become embroiled in their activities".

'Buster,' who wrote the book *Life Among the Pathans* is a mine of information, and whilst I write this diary, he and Eileen are having a great time together with Eileen inundating him with questions. We arrived here in Rawalpindi a couple of hours ago finding 'Buster's' house in Peshawar road quite quickly. As well as being a retired army colonel of the North West Frontier Force, 'Buster' is also the Himalayan Club Secretary for Pakistan and we've discovered that we have many mutual friends and acquaintances. They are mountain people who have stayed with him in the past—Mike Banks, George Garratt, Hamish McInnes, Wilfrid Noyce and so on—but he is extremely pleased to have news of 'Nobby' and Arthur Clarke. 'Nobby' quite clearly made a tremendous hit with him. 'Buster' (who is 81 years of age!) resembles an older Don Whillans (of whom he's also glad to have news) or reminds me of the statues of a benevolent Buddha.

This morning after a minor delay trying to get a water pump to work we left Kabul just after dawn and descended through the Tangi-Gharu gorge. Rays from the early morning sun slanted down from serrated rock ridges differentially lighting up the dark recesses of the gorge. Once we were away from the deep cut defile we crossed a warm and fertile plain from which we had crisp clear views of the snow-covered outliers of the Hindu Kush. After a short stop at the border we wound up and through the gears and through the bends of the Khyber pass stopping at times to take photographs but more to absorb the atmosphere and get a feeling of the history of this ancient route. Many straw and clay forts dotted the mountain sides, whilst below us down in the defile, along the old and dusty trail, trains of mules and camels carrying a variety of trade goods wound their way slowly between Kabul and Peshawar. It is how it must have been for centuries.

March 5th, Evening—'Battle of the Horns'

Today the journey has been very varied following a reasonably early start at 6.30 a.m. After leaving Rawalpindi we crossed the rivers

Jhelum, Chenab and Ravi in that order before arriving in Lahore. There we asked for directions to Ganda Singhawala from three engaging and beautifully clothed Pakistani girls. For reasons we now well understand they seemed puzzled by our insistence that we wanted to go to Ganda Singhawala. Being a most polite people they eventually gave us the information and their initial reluctance to give it was only made clear on arrival at Ganda Singhawala where we discovered that as a border crossing point it had been closed since 1971. However, the extra ninety miles of driving did take us through some of the most peaceful pastoral country we've yet travelled—a splendid contrast to the noisy dusty road between Pindi and Lahore. On that part of the day's journey we found the public carrier vehicles played a disconcerting 'chicken game' with each other seeing who would waver first then drive off the tarmacadam road and onto the brown earthen bullock tracks. As part of the 'chicken game' the PCV's made much use of their motor horns. These varied remarkably in range and scale but were all of a similar intensity. Some kept up a high shrill shrieking hoping to impress with their continuous production of maximum decibels, whilst others more of a middle range, gave intermittent blasts both long and short. Some would sweep by using a shattering mixture of the two types, but without doubt the most successful protagonist was a bottom of the scale, reverberating bass horn that sounded not like the oncoming of a truck or bus, but of a slow-moving cargo ship in the middle of a Mersey fog. Whenever it was necessary, we added our own quota to this constant cacophony of sound and rightly we've called the day the 'Battle of the Horns'.

March 6th, Morning

Last night we eventually stopped and stayed outside a police station some ten miles from Wagah, the border between Pakistan and India. Despite a long and tiring day, we were kept awake for a time and also reminded of the 'Battle of the Horns' by the infuriating buzzing and whining of hundreds of mosquitoes. We again took our Nivoquine anti-malarials and will repeat the dose every three days for the next eight months until we return back home.

Evening

By 10 a.m. this morning we had completed formalities with the Pakistan customs at Wagah, and were then quickly through the Indian customs at Attari Road and into India. It has been a relaxing day driving quietly along the Grand Trunk (G.T.) road through the Punjab and Haryana to Pipli where we are now staying.

Despite the big cities with their millions of inhabitants India is a rural country and it has been good to take so many photographs of village life—such as the old man and his son watering their buffalo by the river and not many yards away the women of the village washing and combing their hair then collecting water for the home in shining brass *chattis*. We are now staying at the Green Parakeet—one of the rest houses (or caravan-*serai*) belonging to Haryana Tourist Complex. The food is good and amazingly cheap—for less than 8 rupees (50 pence) we had a well-spiced curried chicken with rice, cream caramel and a cup of instant coffee! Even more surprising is the luxury we can have for 50 rupees (£ 2.50) for the night for the two of us. Our double room is air conditioned with its own bathroom and shower—a welcome luxury after two and a half weeks of living in the 'Juggernaut'.

March 7th, Evening

Up at 8 o'clock! It seemed like afternoon as we have usually driven a hundred miles or so by then. After a leisurely breakfast we had a stimulating morning and afternoon meeting many people and visiting a variety of places. It being a 'Holi' day many were visiting the temple of Hanuman, the Monkey God, or the temple of Lord Krishna where a heady aroma of incense permeated the rooms which then seemed to follow us to the most sacred Banyan tree where Lord Krishna wrote the Bhagavad Gita. Most of the people wore clean pale yellow robes and were quiet and graceful. Beneath the shade of the Banyan tree we sat and talked with the chowkidar from the Green Parakeet who explained that the sacred tanks (man-made lakes) nearby are being strengthened and enlarged in preparation for the important holiday on April 29th when there will be an eclipse of the sun. Up to 2,00,000 people are expected to travel from all parts of India to bathe in the tanks and wash away their sins.

Its a land of contrasts—and we felt it more when we arrived back into modern India at our hotel and rest house which is absolutely first class.

March 8th

Delhi at last! We broke the siesta of our friend Harish Sarin, who I think was surprised as we arrived in Delhi on the day we forecast. He arranged our stay at the India International Centre (a superb place) where we met John Lall, the Director, who is a friend of Charles and Denise Evans, and the man who was the political officer in Sikkim when we went to Kangchenjunga in 1955.

'Horars Cops' and Preparations

The day after our arrival in Delhi we made arrangements for a journey by train to South India, and in Connaught Circus also booked a train to Calcutta for a visit to Darjeeling and Kalimpong that we intended to make later. The 'booking office' owned and run by Lil Ram—a Congress man, and Ramesh, a fortune teller— was the most amazing 'booking office' I've ever used. It was actually the space beneath the bottom stairs of a multi-storey building and at the entrance a large placard described the proprie- tors as "property dealers, astrologers and numerologists, menders of typewriters, bicycles, and travel agents". Lil Ram, who proudly told us he was a member of the Delhi Jail Committee got me to phone the railway booking office to book our seats, then most charmingly charged me an extra 30 rupees for doing my own booking!

When we were leaving, he gave us a card which read as follows:

Annual Horars Cops	Rupees 80
Complete Life History by Indian Method	Rupees 500
Complete Life History by Western Method	Rupees 800
To ask any questions	Rupees 10

He was so friendly, anxious to help and delightfully naive.

I wondered what he would have told us in our 'Horars Cops' before we started our journey overland to India.

3

The First People: Kashmir

(September 1976)

At the present time Kashmir is an unhappy land in the grip once again of terrorists of a particular religion and political persuasion. Throughout its history, it has so often been a place of turmoil in turn occupied by Buddhists, Hindus, Moghuls, Sikhs and others.

Srinagar—'City of the Sun' is the capital and overlooking the city with its lakes and river is a temple hill we have visited often. This is called Takht-i-Suleiman by the Muslims and to the Hindus it is Shankaracharya. Yet it was first sacred to the Buddhists who around 200 B.C. at the time of the great Indian Emperor Ashok used it as a place of meditation. The temple is still there, seeming to defy man's inhumanity to man but when the first people came to live by the lakes, it was long before there was any evidence of mankind on the hill. Through the years we have sought to find out more about those first migrants to the Vale of Kashmir. In doing so we have come to know it well and in every way we have been in agreement with the sentiment of the Moghuls.

"If there be a Paradise on the face of the earth, it is here, it is here, it is here". This comment is attributed to a Moghul Emperor of the 17th century and significantly the assertion 'it is here' is repeated three times. The rulers of the Moghul Empire were not used to repeating themselves and to be asked to do so was such an affront that there were terrible consequences for those who asked. In this way, the Emperor, by making his own trio of assertions left no doubt about his feelings for the Vale of Kashmir. All the companions, Eileen and I have ever been with to Kashmir have found no reason to quibble with the comment and have particularly enjoyed the peace and tranquillity of the many gardens designed and built by the Moghuls. A feature of these gardens are the marble pavilions and rippling cascades set amongst terraces lined with Chenar trees (*Platanus orientalis*) which provide a dappling of sunlight and shade by swift flowing water channels and quiet pools.

Away from the gardens, placid lakes and running waterways irrigate lush green rice fields that contrast with distant rugged ravines cut deeply into hill slopes by swift flowing glacial torrents. Sweeping weeping willows and neat ranks of stalwart Lombardy Poplars edge the roadways and line the banks of the winding Jhelum river. Small groups of barefoot women wearing wide-sleeved cotton gowns (the *pheran* made of cotton or wool is the standard dress) hustle in and out of houses built of a mixture of wood, plaster, and red sun-dried bricks and a broad sweep of snow and rock peaks, the Pir Panjals, form a majestic undulating backing for these peaceful pastoral scenes.

On Dal lake local fisherfolk paddle shallow *dungas* (dug out boats) from one fishing ground to another followed by kingfishers (Pied and Blue) that skim among the acres of water lilies and tall flowering lotus blossoms. In late geological times it was a much larger freshwater lake that filled the oval-shaped valley, one that was some 84 miles in length and varied from 20 to 25 miles in width. Eventually for reasons unknown, the lake broke through the surrounding mountain barrier and drained away leaving behind a flat fertile plain. At present the flats, several hundred feet above the plain, indicate the levels to which the waters of the lake had risen at one time. Additional evidence of these differential lake levels is provided by the many shells of water chestnuts and the remains of freshwater animals to be found.

Several times during the past few years we have been to such alluvial flats taking the road from Srinagar, for sixteen miles along the road that winds eastwards and to the north around the shores of Dal lake. There at a place called Burzahoma we have found the local people growing crops of Indian corn and other vegetables and using the area for grazing cattle—a distinct contrast to the gently terraced rice fields spread out on the plain below.

It is on the alluvial flats above the plain where some of the earliest inhabitants of Kashmir first lived over four and a half thousand years ago. They were part of a wave of migrating people that came from the north and west, through areas we now know of as Iran and Afghanistan and who began their wanderings in the 4th millennium B.C.

Sometime around 2300 B.C. a part of this Aryan-speaking intrusion into India established dwelling sites on the flats. These earliest settlers were neolithic people, who put up structures of massive stones, megaliths, that are in evidence today and are one of the reasons why during the last decade there has been a partial excavation of the site. These huge silent monoliths of stone, some lying on the ground, others rearing starkly into the sky against a backcloth of the Chergand hills make immediate impact on arrival. They provide direct and powerful evidence of a people's driving force and spirit—a people whose knowledge and culture made evident through their artifacts straight away gain your attention and hold your respect.

During excavations there have been finds of polished stone axes, bone harpoon heads, awls, bone polishers, arrowheads and of flared neck flasks along with other hand-made pottery. Deep excavation pits have been dug revealing several different levels and times of occupation, and the more you look among the pits the more evidence you find of the one time dwellers at the site. Black carbonised (charcoal) layers show where fires were lit for warmth and for cooking, whilst pieces of animal bone amongst broken pottery provide further insight into the life-style of the people.

On recent visits it has been clear to us that during further excavations, remains of human burials have been discovered as well as skeletons of other animals. More dwelling pits as well as landing steps have indicated the high levels to which the lake used to rise in relatively recent times. Whilst searching the pits and photographing the megaliths we have found that local children and womenfolk watch us curiously and we often wonder just how much of a folk memory they have of their ancestors. Sometimes one or another of them gives a piercing shriek and points out a sherd of pottery to us but generally it is we, the visitors, that are of greatest interest to them and not the ancient artifacts. Many of the children scramble amongst the megaliths, which they use as a playground and encourage us to take their photographs, then hold out their hands for *buksheesh*.

We wonder what they, and their parents would think of the thrice repeated statement made by the Moghul Emperor Jahangir. And we wonder too what did the first people whom we know of because of their axeheads and hand-made pottery think of the valley with its huge expanse of lake and surrounding snow-clad mountains?

We will never know, for all that remains of them are a few of their artifacts plus those huge stones, the megaliths; and they are silent.

4

Sonamarg and the Valley of Glaciers

(September 1976)

Eileen shouted "I'm freezing," as a fierce blast of cold air blew across the pass at 14,000 feet.

"And the weather's worsening," I called but my reply was lost as vivid forked lightning lit the gloom, to be followed almost instantaneously by an enormous crack of thunder. Curtains of hailstones the size of small peas swept across the glacier from the rock cirque above. Each stone that hit bare skin stung venomously and the rest having fallen to ground ran and rustled in ever broadening streams over the bare ice.

"See that big rock Eileen? Let's shelter under the overhang".

"OK. Beat you to it" and Eileen with anorak wipping in the wind and ice-axe at the ready ran neatly over treacherous ground before flinging herself beneath the rock lip. I joined her within seconds but none too soon as more massive veils of hail hissed and swirled around us. Each and every time jagged lightning presaged the onslaught of wind and hail and savage cannonades of thunder rolled and reverberated among the mountains of Thajiwas in the Kashmir Himalaya. We crouched together for warmth not knowing how long the storm would last. A few of the hailstones clung to the woollen neck of my sweater then rolled down over the bare skin of my back and nestled at the crack in the seat of my trousers. Though only mid-morning it was already almost as dark as night and it was more than the discomfort that was raising the hairs and the goose lumps on my skin. "Listen!" Eileen's fierce whisper made me concentrate and immediately I heard an ominous humming sound I'd heard before on other mountains. "It's from the ice-axes," I shouted and picked them up, then scurried over the glacier ice to lay them down safely some distance away. As I ran back towards the boulder the humming and whining increased and there was a distinct crackle as the bared hairs on my hands and neck rose stiffly with the static. The danger seemed to be too great and I slid awkwardly to crouch beneath a second rock. Time and again for the next hour or more, the lightning flashed and the elements raged around us, then gradually the storm abated.

From my rock I looked across at Eileen who grimaced, and I knew what she was thinking. "We can't climb anything now," she said.

Earlier in the morning it had been sunny and relatively warm as we walked over mountain meadows filled with Gentians, Geraniums, Corydalis, Immortelle, Edelweiss and a multitude of other Himalayan plants, that carpeted our way. "No we can't, but we will another day—perhaps tomorrow," and the next day we did. We climbed 'Valehead Peak' at the head of the valley on the 21st July. It was Eileen's birthday.

The Thajiwas valley runs south-east to north-west and joins the Sind river below the village of Sonamarg in the 'Golden Meadow'. Two very different types of rock form its boundaries. On the left looking up the valley is the soft lime and sandstone of cretaceous age whilst opposite on the right, the high peaks and rocky buttresses of Thajiwas are made up of a tough igneous rock of the Punjab volcanic series. Sycamore, Spruce, Blue Pine and Deodar cover the lower limestone slope of Zabnar and eventually at 11,000 feet these give way to straggly stands of wind-riven silver birch. Above the treeline grassy slopes lead to Zabnar summit which is a good walk from Sonamarg and provides one of the best viewpoints for the mountains of Ladakh to the east. Opposite

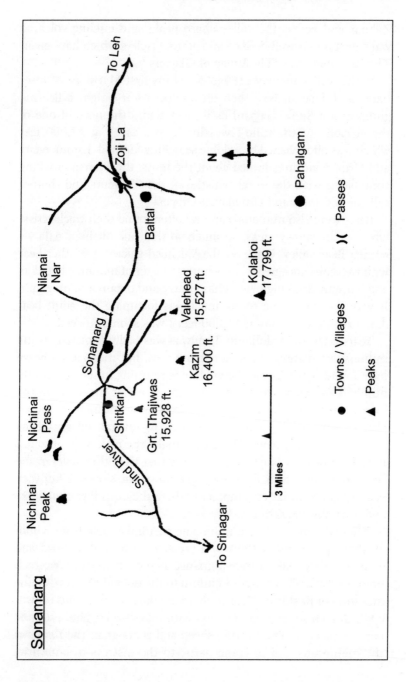

Sonamarg

To Leh

Zoji La

Baltal

Pahalgam

N

Nilanai
Nar

Sonamarg

Kolahoi
17,799 ft.

Valehead
15,527 ft.

Kazim
16,400 ft.

Nichinai
Pass

Shitkari

Grt. Thajiwas
15,928 ft.

Sind River

Nichinai
Peak

To Srinagar

3 Miles

● Towns / Villages

▲ Peaks

)(Passes

● Passes

Zabnar and across the valley sharp peaks and circling volcanic walls enclose six well-defined and active glaciers which have given Thajiwas its name, 'The Valley of Glaciers.'

In this valley many years ago, I saw my first Marmots, Mousehares and Tibetan Fox, then on one occasion caught a fleeting glimpse of a Snow Leopard as it sped across the neve of one of the glaciers. At the time I was living in a camp at 12,000 feet which was often visited by wildlife searching for food. Lammergeirs and Griffon vultures lurked about the tents, their harsh croaking contrasting with the sweet whistles of the Marmots and sharper calls of Redstarts and Himalayan Dippers.

Bears were also numerous and we often found their tracks crisscrossing the snowy areas, so much so that one offshoot nala we named Bear valley. Once on the Valehead glacier, a mother bear with two cubs appeared from behind a cluster of morainic boulders and without thinking I gave chase to try and obtain a photograph. It was a stupid thing to do and I was fortunate the adult bear didn't turn on me, but at 14,000 feet I was soon outpaced.

Years later, the wildlife in Thajiwas was badly depleted during military occupation of the Sonamarg area, but more recently we have found that high up the wildlife is retuning in its variety and numbers to when I first camped there. It is not the same in the lower reaches of the valley where, each year, numerous Indian tourists journey on foot or horseback to several old snowbeds below the Arrow glacier. There they make the rock walls resound to their shrieks of laughter as for their first time they revel in the snow and shy snowballs or toboggan down the slopes. Later they visit a nearby Gujar encampment where they can buy *chapatties* and warming mugs of tea.

These Gujars are a semi-nomadic pastoral people from whom all the gypsy races of the world are said to have developed and each year they make a transhumance as they drive their livestock from the lowland pastures of Jammu to the upland *margs* or alpine meadows of Kashmir. Most of them are dark skinned and brown-eyed, though some are to be seen with rosy cheeks, blue eyes and fair complexion. Their cattle, sheep and goats graze the flanks of the mountains and in some parts, to the distress of botanists, graze away the rarer alpines and create a coverage of more typical meadowland flora.

Fortunately this was not the case at the campsite from which we climbed 'Valehead Peak.' Our tents were pitched on a shelf that we had levelled out of a steeply inclined but lushly flowering *marg* which some fifty yards below us disappeared beneath a broad swathe of old snow. In this short distance between the snow and our camp, a profusion of flowers provided us with multi-coloured carpet on which to tread and the aromatic aroma of Wild Thyme and Lavender saturated the air as we crushed them under foot. We walked through thickets of Purple Crane's Bill (*Geranium wallichianum*) and clusters of Kashmiri Harebells then trod carefully to avoid damaging rosettes of Kashmir Gentian that seemed to reflect the deep blue of the sky. Tall golden Globe flowers (Trollius) grew next to even taller yellow flowered Lousewort (*Pedicularis bicornata*) whilst Corydalis, yellow and spurred, vied in beauty with the dry petalled Pearly Everlasting or Immortelle.

Whilst drinking hot mugs of tea by the tent doorway, we could reach out and touch yellow or orange flowered Potentilla (*Potentilla argyrophylla*) and clusters of globula flowered *Primula denticulata* mixed with orange-eyed Asters. A few yards away in amongst the igneous rocks, tiny stations of *Primula rosea* hid shyly in the shadows and thick succulent leaves of Stonecrop (*Sedun ewersii*) with their small star-like flowers, spread themselves out from each soil-bearing crack and cranny. Earlier in the day, on our way to the mountain, we walked over wind scolloped snowbeds where patches of red and rose-coloured snow attracted our attention. These patches, bathed in the soft light of early morning were near to the edges of the snow mantle and we realised we were looking at good examples of snow algae (*Chlamydomonas nivalis*) which give rise to this phenomenon of red snow. Soon we stepped off the snowbeds to traverse a steep grassy bulge where once again, as at our campsite, we found an abundance of Immortelle, Gentians, blue and white Anemones, water-saturated cushions of Androsace (*mucronifolia*) and an astonishing profusion of velvet-petalled Edelweiss (*Leontopodium*).

Once beyond the grass bulge we were back on snow and traversing the Valehead glacier below the mountain. We struck up the glacier and gained the Pinnacle Buttress by cutting steps over a steep and icy traverse as thickening clouds and wisps of snow gave warning of rapidly deteriorating weather. It was cold on the ridge and quite exposed difficult climbing, but still we found time to enjoy seeing the vividly coloured lichen and again the green and pink cushions of Androsace. Clumps of fleshy-leaved Roseroot (*Sedum*) grew profusely in soil-filled cracks and a single station of Giant Sausserea, looking as if a spider had spun its web around the leaves, trembled violently in the wind. Beyond the rock buttress all difficulties ceased and wasting no time in the worsening conditions we descended quickly from the summit and back down the ridge to the col and the glacier. We were back in our mountain camp by mid-afternoon having had an exhilarating ten hours. In the evening sitting round a crackling campfire, we watched the last light bathing the tops of our Thajiwas mountains, then to the north the sun finally touched the tops of lonely mountains beyond the Zogpu Dhar and Nanga Parbat.

Over the years, I have had many such days in the valley for with its steep glaciers, high rock peaks, varied flora and fauna and the annual influx of nomadic pastoral Gujars it is a place well worth the visiting. Do go there!

5

Himalayan Traders and a Blue Poppy
(1983)

"More than anything, the mountains teach us to look into ourselves and beyond and give a sense of oneness with our Universe.
   Each one of us is alone and yet so much a part of the whole."

–Indira Gandhi

Earlier I quoted a few lines from the Welsh poet, Edward Thomas in which he was remembering days when he passed over from one valley to another to reach a new country or environment. Passes do have the magical property of opening up new vistas and each time following an ascent there is a feeling of excitement prior to discovering what lies on the other side. Such moments are never forgotten. The first time Eileen and I crossed the Khardung la in Ladakh at 5600 metres (18,300 feet) we were immediately greeted by a magnificent panorama of the mountain ranges to the north. To the fore were the peaks of the Saltoro Kangri range and the Saser Mustagh. Beyond them rose the Karakoram giants, Gasherbrum and K2 with a cloud plume streaming from its summit. Beyond the pass we descended to the Nubra valley and part of the big bend of the Shyok river. Here the climate was much milder than that of the Indus valley around Leh from whence we had come.

On another occasion we crossed from the Dhauliganga to the Rishi Ganga via the Duransi pass in Garhwal. Lammergeirs soared serenely overhead whilst Yellow Billed Mountain Choughs 'chacked' vociferously amongst the crags. The scenery was impressive and I remember taking a photograph of our companion, Mike Leask whilst he admired the tall rocky spires of the 'Curtain Wall'. Soon we were looking down into the depths of the Rishi Ganga and catching our first glimpse of the Nanda Devi summits within the 'Sanctuary'.

There have been many passes with similar kinds of memories ever since. Once, with three others, I wrote a section of the *Climbers Guide to Sonamarg, Kashmir*. This was published by the Himalayan Club. The area of which I wrote was Zaiwan and Liddarwat each of which lie in separate valleys—the Sind and the West Liddar.

To the north and east of the village of Gund in the Sind valley of Kashmir, there lies a group of limestone peaks rising to almost 16,000 feet in height. You can cross these mountains via the Yem Har—the pass of the goddess Yem, at the foot of which the semi-nomadic traders of Central Asia have for countless centuries stopped and made a brew of tea in thanksgiving for a safe crossing. A tiny lake or *sar*—Yem Sar lies at the foot of the pass supplying cool, clean water to the many streams that irrigate the surrounding richly coloured and delicately scented 'alpine' meadowland. There, among the angular glacial boulders and in the damper areas of ground surrounding the Yem Sar you can find the Blue Poppy. It was here, after a lone trek from the resthouse at Liddarwat that I found my first Meconopsis just a single isolated plant, its colouring enhanced by a black backcloth of shade provided by two arching rocks. It was sturdy with many blooms and the green of the leaves was the green of emeralds with a texture of velvet. Overall there spread a delicate glinting mass of golden prickles. Sunlight was shining directly on to the almost transparent flowers. Centrally, a five-lobed style stood proud of the single green ovary surrounded by an orange ring of stamens and this bright centre-piece was set against the blue background of the four overlapping petals. They were not a primary blue but a delicate, barely hinted at Royal Purple. I had often heard it said that the blue was the blue of the sky in early morning but I felt this description to be too simple. For me at that moment by the Yem Sar, the only similar delicacy of colouring, almost indescribable, was that of the blue-purple haze rising from distant Himalayan valleys at dawn. A peregrine falcon, wings ripping through the air as it dived, distracted my attention. My eyes returned from sight of bird, glare of sun and dark hue of lake and once again I was impressed by the breathtaking beauty and strength of the flower. Like the Central Asian traders, I brewed tea in thanksgiving for a safe crossing of the pass but remembered also to include thanks for my first find of the Himalayan Blue Poppy.

6

Yatra: A Pilgrimage

(1976)

"Thou art a star behind the hills and
I am a passerby upon the road."

—Rabindranath Tagore

For thousands of years pious Hindus have travelled immense distances on religious pilgrimages to sacred shrines of India. Their journeys have taken them to the temple of Vishnu at Badrinath in Garhwal, the shrine of Krishna at Dwarka on the Bombay coast, or to the sacred lake of Ganderbal at the foot of Haramukh and many other remote places. One such pilgrimage of which the origins are said to go back as far as 1000 years B.C. is to the cave of Amarnath in the East Liddar valley of Kashmir. The cave is where Lord Shiva is said to have explained the secret of salvation, and inside it, there are several *lingams* or phallic symbols of ice which are said to wax and wane in size at the time of the full moon. Amarnath cave is at 12,000 feet and all around it peaks on the Kashmir-Ladakh border rise to almost 18,000 feet —a rugged cirque of snow, rock and ice. To reach it, the traditional 'Pilgrim Road' starts in the East Liddar valley at Pahalgam and is a well-graded track. Each year in late July and August, thousands of pilgrims make the six day return journey, but in 1976 fierce storms and heavy rains had damaged the track causing landslips. Worst of all, the lower part of the Liddar valley was heavily flooded and for a time, there was no access from Pahalgam. In August, the main period of the Amarnath *Yatra* (pilgrimage) the *yatris* (pilgrims) sought a different route via Baltal. When several decades earlier four of us wrote a guidebook to this area of Kashmir and Ladakh, no pilgrim route existed from Baltal. It would have been too difficult.

Harry Tilly who wrote the Amarnath section described the route as follows:

"From Baltal in the Sind valley, ascend up the difficult nala (gorge) of the Upper Sind which is only accessible for about 3 miles. The track then crosses a small stream and soon afterwards becomes indefinite, traversing very steep slopes of mud and detritus in which steps may have to be made (with ice-axe). In places projecting rock buttresses enforce a crossing of the river though the rock buttresses can be passed (rock climbed) if the river is in spate".

On August 9th, an increasingly large number of *yatris* began to pass through Sonamarg to reach Baltal, so we decided to join them. Eileen thought the *yatra* would be a good experience for us too. In addition we could check out the route for I felt that the above description in the 'Guide' must surely need revising.

In the evening, we camped by the Sind river at Baltal and for several hours watched the hordes of ardent pilgrims arriving for their last push to the cave the next morning. An early start was essential and everyone was up and away before the dawn. Many rode ponies, one was carried in a palanquin, others sat in *dandis* (basket seats) carried on the backs of porters, but most people were on foot and travelling at various speeds. Orange smocked *Sadhus* (holy men) jostled with modern young bloods dressed in western garb; clearly the one group there for reasons of piety and the other mainly for curiosity. Fathers, mothers and anxious young children made way for noisy groups of 'sky-clad' (naked) *Sanyasis*, who had their painted faces and bodies smeared with ash. Several tiny and fragile old ladies pressing determinedly on to their goal were a contrast to the many portly and unfit middle-aged men who huffed, puffed and sweated along the track. Soon a wealthy Hindu couple passed by on riding ponies and behind them a retinue of porters carried wooden *charpoys* (beds), chairs commodes, canvas tentage, heavy marquee poles and an abundance of varied foods. The urgent desire of all those we met on the track was to reach the cave of Amarnath before the end of the day. Our own wish was to make the return journey of approximately twenty miles by the evening. No doubt some of the pilgrims wished to do the same and there was no reason why they shouldn't.

The *rasta* (track) had changed a lot since Harry Tilly wrote his first description for the 'Guide' and beyond the three mile pony point (now jeepable) the Indian army had carved out an undulating path above the true right bank of the river. Most of the time, the river was hidden by snowbeds of old avalanche debris and from them at frequent intervals a breeze lifted cooling wafts of air that brought relief to the hundreds of overheated *yatris* as they toiled along the dusty path. We soon began to leave the main throng behind, catching up to other pilgrims who had left Baltal the night before, no doubt benefitting little having had to spend the hours of darkness in uncomfortable shelters. Steep sections rising over and above the rock buttresses increased in number and length so that eventually at over 13,000 feet we stopped for a mug of tea at a watering place named Sangam. A family of enterprising Gujars had erected a rough shelter and from it in chipped enamelled cups, they sold tea, hot sooty and sweet, but welcome and refreshing. Ahead from Sangam, the view opened out and beyond the cave of Amarnath the twin-headed peak of Nichhang 17,862 feet, its rocky north-west face festooned with hanging glaciers, presented an inviting and formidable challenge for the mountaineer. Beyond Sangam as we continued the journey, we left the track so that the *yatris* could visit Amarnath in peace. It seemed the right thing to do and we moved up onto the flanks of the mountain rising above the shrine. There, bathed in warm sunshine and lying amongst a profusion of Himalayan flowers, we dozed for a while, then collected handsful of wild strawberries, small but tasty. An hour or so later, feeling that our own pilgrimage had been fulfilled, we began the return journey along the track meeting many pilgrims still aiming to reach Amarnath and stay the night. Others for whom the journey had already proved too much had dispiritedly turned back for Baltal, but there were some in high spirits who had successfully completed their *yatra*—a culmination of their desires. Fortunately the day had been dry and warm, for many pilgrims were badly clad and unprepared for harsh weather. On a wet day, the path would have been dangerously greasy and slippery. On return to camp we found that a lady riding a pony was missing and two days later her body was found beneath the snowbeds where she had been swept after a tumble down the steep hillside. From Baltal we returned to Sonamarg that same night and the following morning I revised the *Climbing and Trekking Guide* as follows:

"At Baltal, it is now possible to go a further 3 km by jeep to the point where the Sind river takes a sharp bend to the southeast. From here a good path, steep in places, heads to Amarnath cave and to the Amarnath and neighbouring peaks. The path could become very slippery in wet weather and here, as in all walks written about in the Guide, it is stressed that good footwear is essential. *Chaplis* and bedroom slippers are dangerous! This route is likely to become of increasing importance to pilgrims and already some refreshment is available at Sangam during the summer months".

With the present state of the troubles in Kashmir during the second millennium, we wonder if the pilgrims still use this route. We do know that twelve years after the first *yatra* from Baltal, it was still being used. We like to think that our revision comments contributed to the safety of the *yatris*.

7

Canadians in Kashmir

(August-October 1987)

In the Ziwan and Liddarwat area of the mountains of Kashmir, the West Liddar river trends north-west and there is a gradual rise to 9000 feet as you follow its course for fifteen miles to reach the camping grounds and forest hut at Liddarwat. It is a beautiful place surrounded by fir-clad slopes and with jagged pinnacle ridges springing out in all directions of the compass. From here a rough track used by the semi-nomadic Gujars of Jammu follows the river to its main source, the larger northern glacier of a mountain called Kolahoi. It was in this valley of West Liddar and on that mountain that the Canadians had their expedition. As leader I ensured that Liddarwat was used not only as an acclimatisation and rest camp but also as an area for environmental study. A base camp was placed on a small *marg* near the snout of the northern glacier and here the mountain dominated the scene. On first arriving there I sat down and let my mind dwell on memories from the past forty-four years and on some of the history of the mountain.

Kolahoi—the mountain is a massive block of volcanic rock that rears majestically to the sky for 5425 metres (17,830 feet). Over many thousands of years its pyramidical shape has been created by glacier ice plucking and grinding at the rock, whilst the constant action of freezing and thawing has sharpened and etched its ridges. The name means 'Wreath Stream' and is descriptive of the large carving north glacier. No one knows who first called the mountain Kolahoi but I felt sure the explorer brothers, Doctors Ernest and Arthur Neve could have thrown most light on the matter. Some of those early explorer mountaineers liked to name it the 'Matterhorn of Kashmir' because of its likeness to the mountain in Switzerland but of the names I preferred that given to it long ago by the local people and the Gujars—'Gwashi Bror' (Goddess of Light).

I had first crossed its northern glacier in 1944 using a tent pole in lieu of an ice-axe and reached a height of 15,000 feet. It was my first glacier, an exhilarating and mind-blowing experience. There had been several returns to Kolahoi since and once with Eileen having crossed the Yem Har we descended to the West Liddar and camped by a group of deserted Gujar huts. There was much dead wood lying around and despite having our own cooking stoves, the ponyman Rasool built a huge fire. "I am unable to sleep," he said "and I am frightened the bears might come". He continued to burn logs throughout the night and at dawn had a kettle of water boiling from which we made hot coffee, then broke our fast with toast and marmalade. Later we walked by the river to the glacier snout noting on the way that many Dippers and White-capped Redstarts were busily flitting from rock to rock. Large clumps of yellow-flowered Corydalis made a bright splash of colour against the milky glacial water, whilst Marmots whistled their alarm calls when we approached each patch of mountain meadow. These meadows, the grazing grounds for the sheep and goats of Gujars, were carpeted with Mountain Asters, Gentians Immortelle and Primula.

Soon the early morning clouds had begun to clear and the sun shining on the new snow upon the mountain made it glisten and sparkle with refracted light. Mid-morning, we walked down to the forest bungalow at Liddarwat enjoying the sound of the rushing glacial river, and the pungent smell of pine in the forest. It rained later so we stayed in the bungalow. No wet tents to pack the next day!

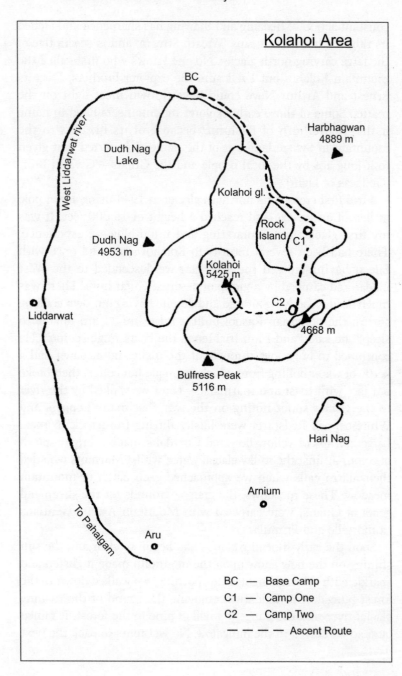

Kolahoi Area

BC

West Liddarwat river

Dudh Nag Lake

Harbhagwan 4889 m

Kolahoi gl.

Rock Island C1

Dudh Nag 4953 m

Kolahoi 5425 m

C2

4668 m

Liddarwat

Bulfress Peak 5116 m

Hari Nag

Arnium

To Pahalgam

Aru

BC — Base Camp
C1 — Camp One
C2 — Camp Two
– – – – Ascent Route

The *Chowkidar* (caretaker) was glad to see us and made a fresh brew of Kashmir tea flavoured with cinnamon and cardamons—sweet, tasty and hot. Then, because it was our final evening in the mountains, we had a last stroll up the valley before rolling into our sleeping bags for the night. There was no glorious sunset, just a peaceful soft evening and blue veils of smoke spiralling slowly from the *chowkidar's* cooking fire. We wondered if we would ever return.

The following year we had been invited to the Laurentian University in Canada where I gave a lecture on mountaineering and mountain environments based on my book *More than Mountains*. The lecture triggered off the idea for a Canadian expedition to Kashmir. We were both invited to join and I was asked to be the leader. Though living thousands of miles from Sudbury in Canada (we live in Wales, UK) we still played a major part in coordinating travel arrangements for trekking, climbing, field work and a final cultural journey to Ladakh. Twenty people were taking part which should have been twenty-one. Eileen who knew that area well and who had done so much to bring the expedition plans to fruition had to withdraw at the last minute.

She had a detached retina which was successfully operated on a few days prior to departure but the medical advice was that she should not fly. She was very much in my thoughts as I sat there at base thinking of all that had gone before, then my mind switched to the present as ponies and porters arrived with food and equipment. Raghu (N. Raghuriathan), at the time a lecturer at Delhi University came with them. He was a splendid liaison officer who became a most important member of our mountain team. Other members of the expedition followed and Gerald Courtin, our Professor·of Botany, quickly began to assemble a portable computerised meteorological station. This automatically measured wind speeds, humidities, maximum and minimum temperatures and solar radiation. Interesting measurements of the variable Katabatic air currents flowing down Kolahoi and even the north glacier were also made possible. This and other data provided much interesting information about the area. The long hard winter had served to retard the growth of flora so that Courtin with his group felt disappointed at the sparsity of botanical specimens. He was to declare later that he felt the Kolahoi and Thajiwas valleys were becoming botanical deserts because of the excessive grazing of goats and sheep brought high by the Gujars. It was a relief when the following year Eileen and I led a botanical trek in the same areas which we called the 'Valleys of Flowers' trek. Our findings clearly showed that once the snow melts and the high sun warms the soil, the Himalayan arctic-alpines flourish abundantly. We felt sure that valley beyond the Sonmus pass so richly carpeted by Himalayan flora could be likened to the Bhyundar in Garhwal.

Whilst the botanists continued their investigations, David Pearson the geologist and Peter Beckett a lichenologist made a general survey of the geology and moraine sequences above base. Their work on the patterns of the Little Ice Age advance and retreat was important and could be of assistance in establishing some form of global synchroniety. Peter's lichenometric survey was made using the lichen *Rhizocarous geographicus* found growing on the rocks of the moraines. This work provided some chronological dating of the Little Ice Age that took place from the

17th to the 19th centuries and we found the areas above our base camp were good for such research. The moraines below the north glacier and on the mountain Harbhagwan were also investigated. All this field work was going on whilst forward camps were being placed on the mountain.

The Ascent of Kolahoi 5435 metres (17,830 feet)

In 1912 when Kolahoi was first climbed by Dr. Ernest Neve and Professor Kenneth Mason, the ascent was made by the north glacier to the col, thence to a couloir (later named the Neve-Mason couloir) which led to the east ridge and summit. Forty years later following an expedition to Garhwal, two of us climbed Kolahoi by the same route. We were very fit and well acclimatised to altitude. From a Gujar encampment at 9000 feet we reached the summit and returned, thus completing 18,000 feet of ascent and descent in the day.

I knew such a 'tour de force' would not be possible for the unacclimatised Canadians and early in the planning decided that the modern approach of circumnavigating the rock island to the east of the north glacier and setting up two camps would be preferable for the party. All expedition members could be involved with load carrys to establish and supply the camps during which, and afterwards, they would make many of their environmental observations.

The day following the setting up of base, four of us worked out a cairned route to the rock island, then because late winter snow greatly facilitated progress, we placed our Camp I on the neve-field below the icefall. The height was at around 3900 metres (13,000 feet). All the women team members were pressing me to let them loose on the mountain (I don't think they felt the men could feed themselves properly) so Heather Baines the doctor, plus Lynette Bernier and Merlyl Zuliani led by Raghu, our liaison officer, took further supplies the following day. It was as well for during the next seven days the weather was very variable with sudden snow squalls and storms involving thunder and lightning. Snow-slides and small avalanches on the higher steeper ground were frequent and care had to be taken when placing Camp II at 4550 metres (15,000 feet). I quickly decided that our initial route using fixed ropes would become too dangerous because of possible snow and rock avalanche. A safer way was made straight up the glacier. Jacqueline Mitra, Roger Couture, Lubomir Lehocky and I then carried heavy loads to the camp and stayed overnight so that all four could climb the mountain the next day. We were away by 3 a.m., quickly heading for the Neve-Mason Couloir. Striding across the glacier by the light of a full moon was stunningly beautiful and surface ice-particles resembling flakes of napthalene, reflected the lunar light. Soon however, just before the dawn, heavy clouds began to form but we hoped that later they would soon disperse in the hot sun.

For the first four or five hundred feet the couloir is at an angle of 45 degrees, then the route takes to the rocks as the angle steepens. Danger from snow avalanching down the couloir is normally high but on this day the hard snow-ice was ideal for front pointing in crampons, and this enabled us to continue upto 60 degrees angle in the couloir making greater height at good speed. Mitra's clip-on crampons had come off several times even whilst crossing the glacier and already I had cut steps for her for most of the way. Now as the ice steepened, I put her on the rope and sent Couture and Lehocky ahead. After several rope lengths the thickening clouds began to hide the Kishtwar peaks, it began snowing and wicked gusts of wind whipped spindrift over steps in the ice and into hand holds whenever we traversed rock sections. It became bitterly cold. At approximately 5100 metres (17,000 feet) the wind increased in strength and visibility deteriorated. We decided to turn back. Mitra had climbed with real courage in the conditions. Lehocky and Couture had last been seen higher up the couloir at perhaps 5300 metres (17,500 feet) and we wondered if they might have tried to reach the summit but the weather had beaten them also. A roll of thunder greeted our return to Camp II some five and a half hours later. The storm continued unabated putting down half a foot of snow in the first hour. Spindrift began to settle in the tent, then by 2 o'clock in the afternoon there came a lull and we were able to descend safely to our lower camp on the nevé. There we found Pearson, Bernier and Zuliani in residence and they greeted our arrival with hot mugs of tea and billy cans of soup. Lehocky descended to base but the rest of us stayed on drying out our clothes and resting. No one came up from base camp where rain and sleet had flooded the tents. Our only visitors were flocks of yellow-billed Mountain Choughs, a Giant Honey Bee (*Apis dorsata*), two Yellow Coster butterflies and several small spiders that seemed to live quite happily on the glacier.

The stormy weather had not only slowed progress up the mountain but the field work too had been brought to a halt. Fortunately, the various disciplines seemed happy with what they had already achieved and everyone was pressing hard to be taken up the mountain. Steve Varieur, Eberhard Berrer along with Roger Couture, Pearson and the two girls Bernier and Zuliani took extra loads to Camp II.

Success at Last!

I remember the day well. It was July 15th and I was determined to have as many Canadians as possible ascend to Camp II. On the same day Couture and Pearson with the two girls in support would make a final attempt to reach the summit of Kolahoi. They left the camp in calm weather at 3.30 a.m. but an hour later lightning followed by peals of thunder presaged a sudden blizzard that lasted for over ninety minutes. Numb with cold they returned to the camp to thaw out, then once more the weather changed abruptly. Two hours later in bright sunshine and very determined, they set out again. Previously I had seen that new snow had avalanched down the couloir, so I encouraged Couture and Pearson to take to the rock ribs as soon as practicable. This they did. Again the weather was fickle and shortly after mid-day they experienced snow squalls and cold winds. Later there was thunder and lightning and a static that caused their ice-axes to sizzle and sing, but against odds they continued to climb. Because of fatigue and cramp, Pearson had to stop the ascent some 200 feet short of the summit but Couture persisted alone until his ice-axe pushed through the summit cornice overlooking the unclimbed north ridge. It was 6 p.m. and it had been a brave climb. Eventually both climbers returned safely to the camp in the dark by 9 p.m. It was a great effort in the conditions. Fortunately for the rest of the expedition members who had ascended with me to Camp II by mid-morning it proved to be a glorious few hours in hot sunshine before we returned to base. Indeed, one or two suffered from glacier lassitude but all were elated and amazed at the mountain scene. Peaks of the Kishtwar seemed but a stone's throw away covered in blankets of whipped cream by the fresh snow. Nun Kun, cloud-topped appeared imperiously high, whilst the nearby peaks of Amarnath and Thajiwas stood as sentinels to Kolahoi truly deserving its native name 'Gwashi Bror' (Goddess of Light).

All camps were evacuated from the mountain the next day. This was not the end of the expedition for we then continued on to Ladakh and met up with those remarkably friendly Buddhist people of the land of passes. Geologically, the sorting out of rocks that mark the suture zone of India and Asia created the greatest interest. These rocks that had been deposited on the ocean floor created a colourful and exciting melange between Lamayuru and Mulbek as well as at the gorge of Khalse. Patrick Demeyere and Bob Rogers were very involved with the cultural aspects of the visit to Ladakh and they devised a series of visits to places of special interest. Bob, who was the Director of Outdoor Education at Laurentian University, was also my deputy throughout the Canadians' visit to Kashmir and Ladakh. In Leh he arranged a visit to the Tibetan refugee village on the south bank of the river Indus. Leh Palace, a magnificent structure impressed even more. Though partially destroyed in the Dogra War of 1836, this example of monumental architecture had been built in the 17th century by the fifth Dalai Lama. All admired its situation and particularly enjoyed the view across the Indus to the extensive Stok range of mountains over in Zanskar. Many Buddhist *gompas* were visited, but what impressed most of all was the dignity, humour, faith and industry of the people of the country.

Final Thoughts

Kolahoi is not a high peak by Himalayan standards but it is a peak of some quality. Its accessibility and the surrounding environment proved ideal for the expedition requirements. Yes, the Canadians set up their camps and climbed the peak as well as made their investigations in the valleys and on the mountain. In doing these things, they had much fun and most importantly gained great satisfaction.

That is what going to mountains is all about.

8

Pass of the Goddess Zoji
(1945)

The time was 45 million years ago. Vast tectonic plates converged and the huge Indian and Asian continents collided. As one plate, the Indian, subducted beneath the other the Himalayan mountain belt began to form. No sentient creature existed to record the event but aeons later came man who investigated the phenomenon and in so doing began the exploration of the largest physical feature of the earth. The Great Himalayan axis curves down from Nanga Parbat in the north-west to Nun Kun in the south-east, then continues through to the Satluj, Garhwal and beyond to Nepal, Sikkim, Assam and eventually to China. Two subsidiary mountain ranges run either side of the Himalaya between Nanga Parbat and Nun Kun. These are the Zanskar range to the north and the Pir Panjals to the south. Altogether they constitute an extensive area of mountains and valleys which are very varied in character and of immense interest to the trekker, mountaineer and traveller.

When continents collide, they suture themselves together to form a longer continental mass. There is no better area than Ladakh to study such a zone and a pass out of Kashmir leads you to it.

Eight miles up the Sind valley from Sonamarg lies the village of Baltal and here the river divides. The tributary to the northeast cuts its way through a spectacular gorge of crumbling slates. This is the Zoji Nar. The low pass at the head of the gorge has the name Zoji la—the Pass of the Goddess Zoji.

The name comes from an ancient legend of Western Tibet which tells of a remote valley to the north of Leh wherein lived the goddess Zoji who had fallen in love with a local god. Several jealous demons or djinns (Ladakh abounds with such creatures) fearing the union of the god and goddess turned the pair of lovers into beautiful white snow-pigeons. Undaunted the pair of lovers planned to escape by flying into Kashmir—the young god to fly round by Nanga Parbat, and the goddess to fly over an unnamed pass into the Sind valley. All seemed to be going well, then at the last moment the demons realised what was happening and as Zoji reached the highest point of the pass, they changed her into a large block of slate in the shape of a woman. From this block of rock which can be seen to this day, the pass got its name.

The Zoji la at 11,556 feet is one of the lowest passes in the Himalaya but it is also one of the most dangerous because of avalanche and sudden storms. Because of this, the pass becomes closed from November to May but even so, there are those who are caught out at the beginning of winter. Without doubt the worst disaster came at the start of the winter of 1986/87 when over 300 people lost their lives on the Zoji la because of storm and avalanche. At the start of a snowfall there was a disasterous delay in allowing a convoy of vehicles to cross from Dras in Ladakh to Baltal in Kashmir. Inevitably the road, never a good one, became blocked with snow, and buses, cars, taxis as well as military vehicles, now unable to move, were overwhelmed by avalanches that roared down the steep flanks of the mountains that soar above the pass. In the August of 1987, when leading a Canadian expeditions to Ladakh, I saw that some of the transport was still buried and the long dead occupants still waiting to be disinterred. This reminded me of one of my first crossings of the pass long before any road was built.

Early one May, I was trekking with a group through to Mulbek in Ladakh. There was still much snow on the pass and along the alignment of the Gamru river which flows gently towards Matayan, the snow had cracked open, frequently leaving vertical cliffs of hard-packed snow some fifteen to twenty feet in height. A trader from Baltistan must have been attempting to cross a few months earlier, for we found the carcasses of thirteen ponies and at the last, the body of a man and a boy. Probably father and son. This was in the days when the track was known as the Ladakh Treaty road, though it was no road, merely a pony trail—the chief trade route between Kashmir and Central Asia. It was in 1975 that the Indian Army engineers completed the construction of a tar macadam road between Srinagar and Leh and this enormous feat of road building is why each year so many people are now able to visit Ladakh. The crossing of the 'Pass of the Goddess Zoji' will always prove to be one of the highlights of the journey.

The slates of the pass change as you move further eastwards to more metamorphosed mica schists and eventually to dramatic scarps of Triassic Limestone. The transformation is startling for the mountain scene, treeless, rocky and barren in Ladakh is in strong contrast to the sweeping tree-clad and lush grassy slopes of the Kashmir valleys. Not only is the Zoji la an environmental divide but an ethnographic frontier as well, and one of the joys and much of the charm of the country to the east lies in the change in the people, their customs, clothing and religion, but first let me tell you about the *Mi-Go* so that you can keep a look out for him/or her, when next you make your journey to Leh.

When I lived in Sonamarg, I sometimes used a porter to carry loads for me to Nichinai, or up into the camp in the valley of Thajiwas. He was the old man (*Buda*) of the village and during his long life he had many interesting experiences. In 1934 he had carried as porter, over the Burzil pass, to the base camp of Nanga Parbat for the German expedition. On other ventures, either as porter or ponyman he had travelled extensively throughout Kashmir and Ladakh. He was a wonderful man to have known, kindly, cheerful and in his simple halting way a raconteur.

Once he told me of having seen a hairy creature wandering across the base of a boulder-strewn nala (gully) above the Zoji la.

He became quite excited as he told me it was walking on two legs, and was of a fierce appearance. Clearly and genuinely he had seen some strange animal which he said was the *Mi-Go*. This is the name used in Tibet and the Western Himalaya for the Abominable Snowman, and in his efforts to describe the creature I wondered if he had let his imagination run away with him. "There are plenty of bears in Kashmir and you probably saw one of those," I said, but he stuck to his story and was sure the animal he had seen was not a bear but some other unusual and frightening creature. It was the first time that at first hand I had heard of the 'Snowman', and later I often thought of it when I was a member of the largest expedition ever to go to the Nepal Himalaya in search of the animal. If only I could have seen the *Mi-Go* on the Zoji la! Perhaps you will. Certainly by crossing the pass you will enter a land of *chortens*.

9

Little Roof of the World: Ladakh
(1945 and 1976)

"The soil considered as rock, links common
stones with the atmosphere and the dead dust of
the earth with the continuity of life."

–G.A.J. Cole

Little roof of the world—Ladakh—land of painted mountains,
the place of chortens. This country has been given many
descriptive names. Ladakh is the highest inhabited area in the
world with most of its population living between 11,000 and
15,000 feet above sea level. The people, mainly of Mongolian
origin, are stocky and compact, diligent and hard working. It is
they who through hard work and skill have created many green
and fertile oases out of the barren and ascetic landscape. There
you not only find cultivated barley, buck-wheat, lentil peas and
other legumes, but also orchards of apples and apricots, hedges
of wild roses, stands of Poplars and lines of Willow trees providing shade for irrigation streams. It is a land of rich and rare
experiences and to reach it there is now an Indian military road
linking Srinagar in the Vale of Kashmir with Leh. By speeding up
the journey it has made a big difference for travellers who in a

short time are able to pack in a whole kaleidoscope of impressions and experiences. Having made the journey on foot through to Mulbek and beyond on several occasions, I realised the difference when with Eileen I first drove out of Kashmir into lower Ladakh, or Purig as it is called, and on to Kargil. In Purig the majority of the population are Dards or Dogpa people, an Aryan Indo-European race similar to those who live in Hunza. Unlike the Hunza who are now Muslim, the Dards have mainly remained Buddhists though in recent times the Muslim population has been increased by migrants from Kashmir. Kargil is the main administrative town of Purig province.

At Matayan

When we began our journey the unmetalled Zoji la track was particularly bad following late winter and spring avalanches and the only way I could complete the ascent was by turning the vehicle round and driving all the way up in reverse!

Beyond the pass our first stop was at Machoi where at one time there was a small rest house and a *dak* (post) runner's shelter. Remnants of the building are still there and from it we made an ascent upstream to the Machoi glacier and the base of Machoi peak. This easy walk up the left lateral moraine is well worth doing if there is time, and for those with experience, opportunity and equipment there are several fine peaks of varying difficulty for climbing.

Returning to the vehicle we drove round the corner from Machoi and almost immediately the deep cut and narrow valley of the Suweke Nar came into view. Its river drains the snows of several large glaciers emanating from a group of rugged mountains rising to 18,000 feet in height. Extensive grassy slopes lie beneath the glaciers which is where the Gujars graze their stock in the summer months. We passed many large groups of these nomads on our way to Matayan and some, instead of taking the Suweke Nar track were settling in for a stay on a large flat stretch of meadow bisected by the road. This is Mini Marg which has been a grazing area for sheep and goats for many centuries. The road also detours round the small village of Matayan where, when I first knew it there was a small Buddhist monastery and a rest house (caravan-*serai*). Both have gone, and the monastery building has been replaced by a Muslim mosque, the Dardic population having moved on or been converted to Islam.

The Gamru river has its source at the Zoji la and hitherto has been flowing northwards but beyond Matayan it turns to the east until its confluence with the Muski river just before Dras. Its course is probably decided by the geology of the area which is similar to that at Sonamarg where there is a junction of Dras volcanic rocks with Triassic limestones and sandstones. The rugged eroded scarp features impressed us—tier upon tier of looming rock walls rising thousands of feet above the village.

As I said to Eileen "there is plenty of evidence of the mountain building forces responsible for the uplift and creation of the Great Himalaya, and it is here that Gordon (Gordon Whittle, geologist and mountaineer) first explained it to Wilfrid Noyce and me years ago."

Certainly it is most dramatic country.

Polo in Dras

Though other traffic was speeding on to Dras we stopped at Matayan and once across the stream entered the flat-roofed village. The flat roofs were a reminder that by crossing the Zoji la we had also crossed the Himalayan watershed and entered a land of little precipitation. Even so, late in the year I have seen when cloud masses have built up and snow has fallen with ominous persistence. It is a time of avalanche, and a time too when the Gamru becomes sloppy with a mush of ice and snow, then flows sluggishly along the flat valley floor until it becomes hidden in a world of swirling snow flakes. Ladakh in winter can he a stark and unfriendly land where little life stirs in the villages.

It is then the inhabitants crouch over carefully nurtured fires to keep warm, and to further sustain life cook meals from stored grain and root vegetables. We thought of these things as we sped on to Dras, another cold village, which has been recorded as the

second coldest place on earth inhabited by humans. The confluence of the Gamru and Muski form the Dras river which has
actively cut through the sedimentary and igneous rocks. This has
created steeply rising rock flanks on each side of the valley which
in winter rarely receive the sun. Katabatic airflow pours down the
deep cleft enveloping Dras in an intensely cold blanket of air.
Though it sounds drear and austere, Dras can be a busy village
and when we arrived, bus loads of travellers were already at the
one time caravan-*serai* which was being used as a refreshment
stop and restaurant. Most were drinking from cartons of Kashmir
apple juice or eating freshly-cooked *samosas* whilst some of the
more energetic members, having had refreshment, were kicking
a football along the narrow street.

Years earlier the caravan-*serai* would have been filled with
traders from Kashmir, Lahaul or Baltistan and it was in Dras that
I watched my first game of polo. A group of Baltis had been
challenged to a 'chukka' by the local Ladakhis. In quick time the
wild tangle of horsemen were charging up and down the one
narrow street from one end to the other hitting a rounded stone.
Loud yells, and triumphant shouts echoed from the soaring rock
walls and each scratch team played the game to its limit. That
was a game of polo being played as it must have been played for
centuries in Central Asia. In Ladakh it is still the central game
and one that we have been fortunate to watch on occasion at the
national stadium in Leh.

Kargil and a Mission School

Once our passports had been checked in Dras we sped on our way
to Kargil where there are many hotels and restaurants. More
importantly, for people driving their own vehicles, there are petrol
pumps. The outskirts of the town have become important to the
Indian army as an area of military depots, a reminder of the
continuing troubles with Pakistan and China. Everywhere there
was evidence of change.

A few decades earlier all traders were welcome in the town
whichever country they came from and of whatever religion they

might be—Hindus, Muslims, Buddhists, Christians or Animists—but many of the ancient trade routes are no longer in use and the frontiers have closed. Now the local Ladakhis and Muslim traders from Kashmir smiled at potential customers—Americans, Germans, French, British and travellers from the antipodes—people who had just arrived on the express bus. This is the biggest change in human population, for prior to the partition and later troubles, the town buzzed with a cosmopolitan throng of peregrinating traders—aggressive horsemen from Hunza, turbanned and avaricious money-lenders from Afghanistan, wild looking tall men with blue eyes and ruddy cheeks from Chang Thang or Northern Tibet, industrious Lahaulis from south of Zanskar, shepherds from Kangra and Kullu and humble *numdah*-carrying porters from Baltistan. Once an important trading town, Kargil is now the halfway stopping point on the way to Leh.

"Where was the Bergers' Mission School?" asked Eileen. Looking for it without success, I had to admit I couldn't say.

Daniel Berger and his wife were missionaries at Kargil when I first met them, and they had been there for eleven years. Their mission built of mud and lathe, was square and two-storied in the traditional style of Western Tibet. Within it, they housed and cared for twenty or more orphaned Ladakhi children aged between six and sixteen years, and the older girls who were at the giggling stage had the straight backs, long black pigtails and rosy high-cheeked beauty of Tibetan girls. They were the ones who first made butter tea for me. They began by shredding brick tea into a shallow pan then covered the tea with about a quarter inch of water. Once the water had boiled, crude carbonate of soda was added and when the tannic acid of the tea and the alkali of the carbonate reacted the whole mass bubbled and frothed like a small volcano. They repeated this process several times and eventually stirred the remains into a pan of boiling water. Whilst one girl stirred the pan, another pounded butter in a brass bound bamboo tub. Soon the tea was poured in the tub, another blob of butter was added and the pounding and possing continued. Finally a handful of salt was thrown in to taste. The resultant liquid is not at all like western tea and is definitely an acquired taste. Usually we sat crosslegged during the tea drinking and sometimes a plate of *tsampa* (barley, ground and roasted) was passed round. *Tsampa* mixed with butter tea is the usual breakfast for the lamas in the gompas and it was the same at the mission. The tea and the *tsampa* having been mixed together is then rolled into wholesome and nourishing sausages. Often the *tsampa* may be mixed with a small amount of butter and sugar which makes it a little more interesting and this mixture too is rolled into *tsampa* balls. Daniel told me once I had enough, I could put the rest in my pocket as it was Tibetan etiquette to put spare *tsampa* balls or sausages into the large fold (*ambag*) of a smock (*chuba*). Apparently this can be a life-saver for a visitor who on returning home at night might be chased by demons, devils or djinns. Well-loaded with the sausages he could run away throwing them over his shoulder as bait. Hopefully the demons would then stop and eat the sausages at the expense of losing a tasty Ladakhi!

On my last visit to the Berger's mission the whole group of orphaned children plus Daniel and his wife and three children turned out to wave goodbye. Daniel held his youngest daughter in his arms whilst the rest of the mission softly sang a Ladakhi song of farewell. Three years later they were all dead. The Berger family and all the children of the mission were massacred by Muslim rioters. A brutal, senseless and evil slaughter of the innocent and good.

Eileen was sorry not to find the site of the mission and though we have looked again for it on revisits to Kargil, we have never found anyone who could remember its position. Probably its foundations have been absorbed into the many new buildings that have been constructed in recent times.

Certainly we didn't linger long in Kargil but found the petrol pumps, refuelled and then continued to drive along the military road towards Mulbek.

Once through the narrow winding gorge beyond Paskyam, I looked constantly for the winding pack pony trails along which we used to have to travel, and Eileen was most enthusiastic when I pointed out the many Buddhist stone carvings and the ancient chortens. The Suru river provides ample water for irrigation at

Mulbek where there is a broad and green oasis. On arrival we found Ladakhis, both men and women busily gathering in their crops, winnowing the barley, or filling baskets with ripened apricots. Rising above this energetic scene was the impressive Mulbek gompa on top of its high rock aiguille.

But certainly there were changes for though all was quiet and peaceful at the monastery. We discovered on return to our vehicle that local children had stolen the red perspex reflector plates from the rear. I was reminded of the old lama of Mulbek (now deceased) and of a strange prophecy he once made and wondered if he had ever foreseen the day when a red box on wheels bearing the sign of the red dragon (not of Tibet but of Wales) would trundle through the village.

Whenever I have revisited Mulbek, I have told people about his prophecy, so why not now?

10

Prophecy of the Head Lama of Mulbek Gompa

(1945 and 1987)

The bus rumbled along the Ladakh highway and in it, Dave Pearson (Professor of Geology from Ontario) was, as usual, in an ebullient and informative mood.

"Look at the rocks Jacko, we're right on the Indus Suture zone".

"The what zone Dave?"

"The suture zone, the fracture line showing where the ocean floor between Asia and India was lost. We're at the edge of India, where it drifted, and collided with Asia. Terrific, isn't it? Its a major line of reference in the Himalaya".

Dave's enthusiasm was infectious and I looked with interest, for the rock environment he was pointing out was dramatic—a stark and harsh lunar type landscape, sometimes called the land of painted mountains. The 'paint' is made up of sedimentary and volcanic rocks that have been sheared and crushed during the collision of the continents. They made up a line of coloured melange that we had been seeing all the way along the road between Lamayuru and Mulbek. On the way we stopped to photograph a group of Ladakhi children at the Namika la, and I remembered that once with Eileen, I had scrambled to the top of the massive rock pinnacle above the pass.

"That must be a much tougher, more durable rock Dave. What is it?"

"A good question, Jacko. It is a dolomitic limestone, a chunk of rock that probably fell from the continental shelf at the time of collision. Probably during one of many earthquakes. We will see more and for instance the *gompa* at Mulbek is built on top of such a block of dolomite".

The *gompa* of Mulbek! I knew it well. It seemed incredible to think that the massive block of rock on which the *gompa* was built was a limestone laid down over 200 million years earlier, when the subcontinent of India was close to Antarctica and slowly moving northwards in the Tethys sea.

"Dave, I'll tell you and the others a true story about the Head Lama of Mulbek when we get there, but first read this. It is something I wrote about the *gompa* when I first went there many years ago".

I had a copy of *More than Mountains* with me so produced the pages that described my first visit to the monastery and I wondered what Dave might think of my final sentence relative to time.

The path, which is steep and lined with prayer-flags, winds behind the back of the aiguille, and before I arrived at the door of the monastery, two of the monks, or lamas came out to greet me. They were Red Hat lamas, members of the sect which practise a lamaism less strict than those who wear the yellow hat, for they still retain some of the customs of the earlier Bon religion of Tibet. Their long robes were the colour of old red wine, and on their feet they wore a special type of *cratpa* (felt boots) with turned-up toes and calf length uppers of brilliant crimson colour. Neither spoke Hindustani and no method of communication was possible, but their gestures were friendly, their faces all smiles and I followed them into the flat-roofed building.

Light filtered into passages through narrow wood-framed slits and lit up rows of wooden. prayer-wheels, wooden drums with a central spindle round which the drum can revolve. The hollow drum is filled with carefully folded papers on which have been printed many Buddhist prayers. A light touch of the finger causes these to revolve, and each turn of the wheel is the equivalent of saying many thousands of prayers. Wheels vary greatly in size, type and colour and some which are little larger than a bobbin are held in the hand. This type have drums made of copper embossed with lively Lotus patterns, figures of Buddha and the prayer *Om Mani Padme Hum*. As the band rotates clockwise the drum turns and a chain with a piece of lead attached swings outward, helping the rotation by centrifugal force. Larger wheels, some of them twenty feet high are turned by water-power. Bright colours are popular, though sometimes in the monasteries, age and neglect have turned them to a dull brown. From Ladakh to Sola Khumbu and beyond they are the same in construction and meaning, and like the torcho or the chorten symbolise to the traveller the high mountain and plateau country of Central Asia.

The passageway led off into a room smelling strongly of rancid butter which was burning in small brass goblets—a tiny wick giving forth a small amount of light. Clothed Buddhas and idols were placed side by side in rows, one above the other—the clothes there to keep them warm. Cymbals, drums, flutes and huge ten-foot trumpets (*Saung Daungs*) littered the floor. *Thankas* and ceremonial masks covered the walls. It was a dusty room conveying an atmosphere of great age.

The drone of a voice attracted me to another small ill-lit alcove. Again butter lamps were burning, this time by a small table on which was propped a *gompa* book. A sharp-eyed, bald-headed monk sat cross-legged by the book, reading aloud at tremendous speed. His was a chanting voice that maintained one note, dropping only slightly at the end of a sentence or a page. Occasionally there was a bubbly, sucking noise; the monk swallowed, paused for a moment, and then the rustle of paper indicated the turning of a page. Here time was of no importance.

Knowing the age of the rock on which the *gompa* was built, Dave had felt my final sentence to be very apt but later, like the rest of the Canadians wanted me to tell my story about the Head Lama. It concerned a prophecy he had made to two friends of mine, Harry Tilly and Gordon Whittle. In the prophecy he had foreseen the future with uncanny accuracy and the fulfillment of it came at a time when I finished my operational flying in Burma and returned for a second time to the Air Force Mountain Centre in Kashmir. The story had begun in the previous year.

On a day late in October of 1944, I was with a group of fighter pilots on the Ladakh side of the Zoji la. A cold and biting wind blew straight down the valley, rattling the wooden shutters of our caravan-*serai* where a pine log fire warmed the main room. The wind whipped down the sooty chimney frequently filling the dwelling with smoke, making eyes smart and shed salt tears. A good strong smell of frying eggs and soya links was mixed with that of wood smoke, damp clothes, steaming leather boots and body sweat. Outside the wind was increasing in its strength and ferocity, blowing great globs of snow almost horizontally to the east from whence appeared a line of pack mules and many men. With heads down against the cutting wind and cold of snow they forced their way along the track to the rest house at Matayan. When the line of travellers arrived, I was delighted to recognise Harry Tilly and Gordon Whittle who were returning with their party from a journey to the Wakka-chu and to the Buddhist *gompa* of Mulbek. Quickly we fed them and provided steaming hot mugs of tea. Information passed rapidly to and fro and then Harry told us of their visit to the *gompa* and of their meeting with the Head Lama who was a prophet. Whilst in a trance he had told them that in the following year (1945) the war in the west would end, with the defeat of Germany. A less credulous part of the prophecy was that the war in the east would also end in the same year and most dramatically, with the use of a weapon that would be catastrophic in its power. It was a strange story and one not easy to believe. Even so, Tilly's description of Mulbek, of butter tea and *gompa* books, devil masks, incense shrines and images of Buddha, made me want to visit that distant place and meet the man of prophecy.

I did so on several occasions, but it was in August 1945 when I had returned to Kashmir again that the improbable prophecy came true. I had been with Bill Starr on a mountain reconnaissance in the Matayan area of Ladakh. We had been attracted by a beautiful pyramidal-shaped peak at the head of the Matayan nala. It drew us like a magnet, something about its purity of line and the virgin innocence of its snows. We climbed it by the north ridge and despite the lack of gripping technical problems, each foot of ascent sent our spirits soaring. Strangely, that day we both felt an exceptionally strong sense of freedom and exhilaration, then finally at the summit a peace that all mountains of age, durability and isolation can give. We also found a cairn built by Gordon Whittle and Ralph Stokoe and realised that this was none other than 'Cumberland Peak' of which they had made the first ascent the year before. To the north we could see the Karakoram, the highest points disappearing into a cloud base at some 24,000 feet and were elated at making this second ascent. The first by the north ridge. Quietly we added stones to the cairn that linked us with our friends and reminded us of days shared with them on other mountains.

A few days later on the 19th August we sat cooling our feet in the cold glacial waters of the Sind river below Gund. A pale-faced group of young men, air crews fresh out from Britain walked along the dusty track towards us.

"Hi! What's the latest news of the war?" we asked, having been a week away in Ladakh.

"Don't you know?" they exclaimed, "the war ended four days ago!"

"But that's impossible! How?"

"A bomb! Enormously powerful. Catastrophic! At one blast it destroys whole towns or cities. Two cities, Nagasaki and Hiroshima have been totally demolished in Japan and the Japs ended the war before more could be used. Yes—its all over!.."

It was a hot summer's day in the Sind valley with the sun blazing down from a clear azure sky, but I felt the hairs curl on the back of my neck. I remembered the evening in Matayan the previous year and the recounting of the prophecy as told to Harry and Gordon by the Head Lama of Mulbek. Suddenly it was cold as if a chill wind was blowing out from the barren lands to the east.

"Which was the day the war ended?" I asked.

"On the 15th of August," was the answer—and I realised it was the day we had climbed 'Cumberland Peak' and experienced such a great sense of freedom and peace.

I have told the story of the prophecy to many people both before and after I told it to the Canadians and it has never failed to impress.

It should. Though inexplicable, it is true!

11

Zanskar: A Journey in Time
(1983)

There are five *tehsils* or regions of Ladakh. Purig lies between Kargil and Zoji la; Nubra is to the north of Leh and leads into the Karakoram; Rupshu is a high plateau area to the southeast of Leh and the Indus valley, and Upper Ladakh, of which Leh is the capital. The fifth *tehsil* is Zanskar (sometimes written as Zaskar) the so-called hidden kingdom. When in 1945 I first looked across the valley to the Zanskar range from the top of the *gompa* at Mulbek, they had an immediate magnetic appeal, and I decided that someday I must visit that little explored mountain region. It lies at a general altitude of 4000 metres (13,200 feet) between the valley of the Indus and the Great Himalayan range and a variety of routes are available for trekkers.

For the non-trekking traveller it is possible to make a journey to Padum, the capital of Zanskar, by taking a truck, bus or jeep along the new road built in 1980. This road goes from Kargil over the Pensi la via Ringdum *gompa* and is partly surfaced as far as Parkutse. Many climbing expeditions use the first part of this route to gain a quick access to the base camp site of Nun Kun, and trekkers also use the transport to Ringdum then trek the last few days to Padum. The summer and early autumn are the best times for travelling and trekking as in winter and spring, it is extremely cold and the country can be quite isolated from the outside world.

When I did trek through Zanskar, it was after I had been back to Ladakh many times and was in need to recapture the atmosphere of earlier days. It was to be a journey in time, a description with a double meaning, for Zanskar is changing fast.

Autumn 1945—Central Asia—Cold! A harsh and icy gale was blowing in the north-east bringing with it tiny flakes of snow which increased in size and number as we leant into the wind, and pressed on to the caravan-*serai* at Kharbu. Soon the shape of the low Dak hut loomed out of the greyness caused by the swirl of spindrift and the lateness of the wintery day. Laden sweating ponies stopped their steady plod, snorted, and with heads down waited patiently by the stable railings for their burdens to be removed.

Ponymen whistled cheerfully and laughed with pleasure at the timeliness of their arrival. There was activity and bustle everywhere. Nailed boots were thumped on rough wooden floorboards to remove clogged snow, and ice-axes rattled as they were stacked by the swinging door. Blowing on my hands for warmth, I turned to shout for my head ponyman to bring me *lakri* (wood) to make a fire, and there he was—Rajbah, his skull cap black with grease, soot and grime crowning a dirty, dark and lined face from which peered two red rimmed smoke inflamed eyes. He was grinning with pleasure, anticipating mine, and in his hand he held a mug filled with dark brown liquid from which steam curled slowly. *Garam Chai Sahib* he said, and it was, very hot, salty not sweet, thick and fatty, unlike western tea, but I was cold, and it was just what I needed. I had had it before, seen it made—Tibetan butter tea. For people of the west its taste needs to be acquired but on a windy and fiercely cold day at the end of a twenty-four mile trek in Ladakh, it seemed any man's drink, though the aircrews and paratroopers who were with me, didn't quite agree.

Later in the evening whilst everyone slept, the fire of wood and dried pony dung died away to glowing embers, the wind ceased to rattle the wooden slates of the roof and the huddle of silent dwellings at Kharbu were enfolded in an intensely gripping frost. Winter had begun.

Autumn 1983—the overladen bus bounced and rattled past Kharbu on the Ladakh military road and I reflected that 40 years before there had only been a narrow winding trail. Ladakh or Western Tibet had seemed incredibly remote and would surely remain an unchanging land. That next morning in the autumn of 1945 as we moved off from the Dak hut to walk to the *gompa* at Mulbek, the track worn out of stone over centuries of time, was only occasionally revealed as wisps of wind whipped away the spindrift and ponies and men picked their way precariously above the ice edged Indus river.

Now the bus sped over tar macadam, frequently slowing dramatically to avoid lines of pot holes or to allow lines of army trucks to pass us on their way to Sonamarg in Kashmir. Eileen and I had found it to be the same in 1976 when having driven overland to India and Nepal we had later also driven through Ladakh to Leh. Changes in the land had been abundantly evident and then, because of our mode of transport, we could not free ourselves of the feeling of guilt because we too were a part of that change. Perhaps we can return, we had thought, and once again journey entirely on foot, as I had done so often several decades earlier. I knew that if we could, we would live life to the full and at each day's ending know that on the morrow we would have the satisfaction of discovering what lay beyond the next horizon. 1983 was to be the year.

During the pre-planning back home, I didn't expect that I could recapture the feel of those earlier days, for Ladakh seemed to have changed too much. As it happened, at times, I did recapture the feel by making a journey through Zanskar *tehsil* from Lamayuru to Padum. At first we had hoped to traverse the whole of Zanskar perhaps over the Umasi la to Kishtwar, or over the Shingo la to Lahaul to reach Manali in Kullu. Time was not on our side and we consoled ourselves that earlier we had trekked from Kullu over the Rohtang la and into Lahaul. We had descended the Chandra-Bhaga and above Keylong ascended to over 17,000 feet on an outlier of the Gangstang peaks. Thus we knew some of the route to the south of Padum and we could forego the satisfaction of making our first crossing of the Shingo la to another time. As it

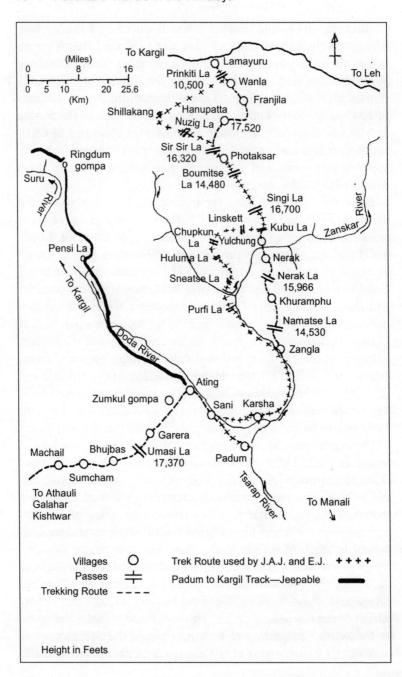

Villages ○
Passes ╪
Trekking Route – – – –

Trek Route used by J.A.J. and E.J. ＋＋＋＋
Padum to Kargil Track—Jeepable ▬▬▬

Height in Feets

turned out, our journey entailed the crossing of a dozen or more passes, mostly at heights varying from 14,000 feet to 17,600 feet and of all the various possible routes, our eventual way took us on sections of Zanskar that I had not seen described before. As is usual in Central Asia, the country was vast, rugged and barren, dry and hot through the day, yet freezing each night, and our tents plus equipment were frequently sheened with frost in the early morning. Four of us (Jeremy and Gillian Naish were our companions) left Lamayuru in the mid-morning; the worst and most dehydrating time, but the walk over the Prinkiti la to Shilla took only three hours. With a dawn start, this part could readily be added to the next day's journey but Lamayuru is at 12,000 feet and a short first day is a sensible approach to acclimatisation. Besides we would have missed staying the night in our ponyman's house which was typically Tibetan in style, with a flat roof, two-storied and the traditional verandah made out of wood. He really made us welcome and his *chang* (barley beer) was some of the best I have ever had.

Apricots, apples, pears and grain crops were ripe and all the people of the village were busy at the harvesting. It was the same at other villages throughout the trek and mid-September to October probably provides the best opportunities for purchasing food on the way. Another benefit of travelling at this time of the year became abundantly clear as we ascended the Shillakang gorge the next day. From Shilla a dusty trail led us past a line of wind-eroded chortens and into a wild canyon of smooth vertical rock walls, massive overhangs and a profusion of jagged soaring spires that reminded me of Yosemite. Twenty-four times that day we crossed the swift flowing river that flows through the gorge. Three times we crossed by bridges and twenty-one times by wading but because of the time of the year the river was low and only on a few occasions did the water rise above our knees. We camped at the end of the gorge by the confluence of two streams and the following day had a long haul up and over the Nuzig la at 17,520 feet. Descent from the pass to Spangtang—an uninhabited and desolate spot—was an easy walk over sandy terrain, sparsely sprinkled with cushions of cinquefoil, mountain asters, and edelweiss on which flora a handful of yak and dzumjok managed to graze. After striking camp at Spangtang we again had a river crossing several miles below the Sir Sir la (16,400 feet). This time there was a greater depth and power to the water, making the crossing more difficult but the ponies and donkeys laden with tentage, food, clothing and cooking gear took the river in their stride. Throughout the entire trek, it was on the higher passes nearing 17,000 feet on which they had a tough time and the ponies in particular would blow hard and take frequent rests. The donkeys didn't seem to mind, carried just as much, cost only two-thirds the amount of money, foraged better and never wandered away at night.

In comparison to the previous two days, our campsite by the bridge above Photaksar was a garden of Eden. Soft springy green turf and a nearby clear water stream made for ideal camping. A bonus was that a mile or so down the valley, beyond the fields of millet, peas and barley there clustered a group of flat-topped Ladakhi houses at which our ponymen, Pangma Wantak and Sonam Thondup, found us all a source of refreshing *chang*. By morning it was much colder, cloudy, with fresh snow on the mountains and small white flakes danced along the fabric of the tents. Lingshot *gompa* and the village of Lingshot lay two days walk away across many passes. First the Boumitse la at 14,480 feet was followed by a gradual ascent to a campsite on the north side of the Singi la, a pass of 16,700 feet. 'Singi' is the Tibetan word for lion, and above the pass to the west the 'Singi Peak' 19,440 feet in height, truly fitted its descriptive name. A variety of walls, cracks, rock gendarmes and hanging glaciers made up its formidable defences and that evening the sunset on the rugged heights glowed fiercely red. Our walk to Lingshot the next day proved to be a lengthy one making ascents and descents of many passes including the Kubu la. But it is the Singi la which will linger longest in memory. A cold and exhilarating breeze plucked at the skin on our faces when we topped the pass, marked at its highest point by weathered chortens bristling with *Lung Ta*—bamboo poles with prayer flags attached. Each of the ragged flags complete with sacred texts crackled crisply in the wind and even in that vast and arid landscape they seemed to provide evidence of man's determination to improve his mark in the next round of existence. The unclimbed Singi Kang still towered above us for thousands of feet then our eyes moved on to the stony trail where our ponies and donkeys were resting. At the very beginning of the day it had proved a hard ascent for the ponies and the rest plus the subsequent descent must have been a welcome respite.

A relative abundance of flora festooned the edges of the track—Gentians, Ox-eye Daisies, Dog Rose, Cranesbill, Delphiniums, seeding Anemone and Primula. A striking contrast to the rest of the dry and stony environment. A final long ascent followed by an undulating traverse and descent led us to the cluster of houses that surround the *gompa* of Lingshot. We could have camped on stony ground well above the dwellings or have risked dysentery by camping in the tiny fields below the monastery but it was dark on our arrival, and instead we took the alternative of staying at the importantly named 'Tachan Hotol' (their spelling error) run by the lamas of the *gompa*. This hostelry consisted of a large grey yurt-shaped tent with an adjacent canvas-covered cook-house. Thirty pence (5 rupees) a night was all it cost to stay and there was room enough for us to sort out all our gear, label films, heat up hot water on our primus stoves, and hang up our washing. We found Lingshot to be a fascinating and enlightening stop over for a day and a half and we were particularly impressed by the busy life of the lamas and the laity at harvest time.

Already the small fields of barley and split peas had been harvested and near a swiftly flowing leat below the *gompa*, the cut crops were stacked and drying in the sun. Some of the grain and pulses had been collected into V-shaped baskets and at one section of the leat, a group of lamas were washing and rewashing this produce. The system was to make a gap in the leat and release the water into a sack lined trough. Here a couple of lamas 'paddled' the water as others fed in large quantities of barley or of split peas—whichever had to be washed. Eventually the lip of the trough (mostly sacking) was lowered and the contents plus the water poured out into a fine-meshed basket. The water escaped whilst the fresh washed produce remained, later to be carried off and once more laid out in the sun to dry. Nothing was wasted and each cupful of crop would be vital for survival throughout the long hard winter to come.

At 7 o'clock the next morning we entered the courtyard of the *gompa* and whilst examining the exterior of the building, heard and saw a lama blowing the *gyaling* (silver trumpet) to call the monks to prayer. Certainly no travellers should miss the early morning *puja* in the *gompa*, where during the morning prayers, we ate *tsampa* and drank hot butter tea along with the lamas. The interior of the *gompa* was dark, smelt of a mixture of rancid butter, incense and the dust of ages. *Thankas* covered the walls, many Buddhas sitting crossed-legged on the symbolic lotus blossom ringed the room and the frequent tinkle of a *dorje* bell punctuated the rapid chanting of the monks.

Outside the monastery the glare of the sun was intense and when the *puja* was ended, we set out for the yak grazing grounds at Sneatse beyond the Chupkun la and the higher Huluma la at 15,500 feet. Again there was much gaining and losing of height along the way and the descent from the final pass for many miles was by a steep and often narrow gully frequently filled with beds of old snow. Route descriptions tell you that these are glaciers but don't be taken in by this, or by much of the other information put out in various books and pamphlets. Sometimes the timings and descriptions are so inaccurate that you have to wonder if the authors ever made the trek or merely read the map—and that not too well. Because of our late start, we camped the night within the narrow confines of the gully about one hour above Sneatse. Cold, katabatic air flowed down the steep gully throughout the night and in the morning the stony ground was frozen hard. A most unusual sight was the ice ribbons that had formed round dead flower stalks just above the stream. Though I have several times photographed ice-flowers, I have never seen such ribbons before nor seen illustrations of them either. They must be caused by the super-cooled air being saturated with water vapour despite the freezing temperatures and by a process of sublimation then formed as the air flows over the flower stalks.

Once again there were numerous old snowbeds frozen hard

following the cold night, over which we had to walk, but the four of us made good progress in the early morning. Soon we were at Sneatse and the yak-man sold us *lobo*, a mass of delicious yak curds that in flavour resembled a strong tasting cottage cheese and was somewhat similar in appearance. It was a very tasty and welcome addition to our diet. A little beyond Sneatse, the Zanskar river or Tsarap Lingti chu (chu—a river) to give it its Tibetan name had cut a tremendous chasm through massive layers of rock and the river so far below looked quite tiny as does the river in the Grand Canyon. At times the pathway became non-existent, then at others where it was just a few inches wide, it meandered above great vertical drops of thousands of feet and we felt relief that the ponies and donkeys were sure of foot. We took care ourselves on the loose gravelly track. From above the great chasm, a descent wound down to a bridge across the Oma chu and then a steep ascent led us across the Purfi la, the last of the passes on the way down to Padum.

It was here we met the French party, a mixed group of sixteen people, followed by thirty-six laden ponies and half that number of camp servants and cooks. Such a large retinue must make a tremendous impact on a sensitive environment but it was a small party compared to many climbing and trek groups in the Himalaya and it is good to know that more and more small expeditions are going for climbing as we used to do in the past. Descent from Purfi la led to the true right bank of the Zanskar river which we followed to Padum for the next few days. It was a tedious walk over flat ground and we took our time along this last section but we found relief from the monotony with the frequent glimpses of the glaciated Zanskar/Kishtwar peaks, many of them unnamed and most unclimbed. A real problem was the heat and dehydration. A well-filled water bottle was a boon and the one or two lateral melt-water streams were a blessing providing opportunity for a naked lie-down in the icy water, cold but exhilarating. Villages such as Hanomil, Pidmu and Pishu were excellent places, providing us with an insight into the daily way of life and the culture of the people.

In late September, each village was a hive of industry. People were threshing and winnowing grain, others sorting animal fodder, carrying loads of fuel, stacking cakes of yak dung, weaving thick cloth for the winter or wherever possible using the flat roof-tops of the houses for storage. Livestock are stabled in the bottom floor and their body heat rises. People live on the next floor and above them the stored materials provide insulation. Thus the population of the village is neatly sandwiched between two important warmth-giving layers and the Zanskaris are better able to last out the long hard winter.

Padum was a disappointment, though it is said improvements are on the way because of the road being extended between the township and Kargil. Certainly the open drains could go, and perhaps some of the better rather than the worse aspects of life in the western world might appear. At the time, we felt that the indigenous population had gained nothing and lost much. It was sad to see the too rapid changes that had taken place in the township and because of them, the disintegrations in the way of life of its simple kindly people. I prefer to remember the previous night at Karsha as our final evening. The harvest festival was in full swing and for much of the night, a golden harvest moon shone down on our tents, lighting up the fields of stubble and frequently groups of Zanskari girls, arms linked, ran singing through the campsite. For them the granaries were full, and at that time of abundance, the whole wide world they knew held great expectations.

The journey through Zanskar *tehsil* did help to recapture the atmosphere of earlier days in Ladakh and in particular that part of the journey via the Shillakang gorge over the Nuzig la to Spangtang and the Sir Sir la. That is a wild and uninhabited tract of land that gives you the full flavour of the vastness and loneliness of Central Asia. On the trek we were not to experience its like again.

We left Padum by truck at 5 o'clock in the morning, taking the Indian Army 'road' to Kargil. We had paid off our ponymen and given them the remainder of our rice, cooking oil, *dal* and various valuable containers. We lay down in the back of the truck as best we could and at the end of the day we all agreed it was the noisiest, bumpiest and the dirtiest journey any of us had ever made. The only relief was the mugs of tea we had in a teashop we found at Ringdum *gompa*, and the occasional glimpses of the peaks of Nun Kun seen through mid-morning mist. Snow was falling in Zanskar as we made the crossing of the Pensi la. Winter had begun.

12

Kullu: 'Valley of the Gods'
(1976)

A part of the Lesser Himalaya called the Dhauladhar lies to the south of the Ladakh-Zanskar ranges. Several large rivers drain the snows of the Dhauladhar and their valleys were at one time part of several separate Himalayan kingdoms. They are now brought together as one Indian state—Himachal Pradesh, which is comprised of the areas of Chamba, Kangra, Kullu, Lahaul & Spiti, Kinnaur, Mandi, Shimla, Solan, Sirmour, Hamirpur, Bilaspur and Una. These areas are predominantly Hindu, except for Lahaul & Spiti, which for a long time have had strong trading links with Tibet, where the population is mainly Buddhist.

There has been road access to Kangra and Kullu for a long time, but only since 1975 has it been possible to drive through Lahaul to Leh in Ladakh. Travelling on foot in Lahaul is always the first choice, if maximum contact with the people and experience of the environment is desired, but if time is short, a motor safari across the country on the second highest motorable road in the world is well worth taking. The route crosses several high passes beyond the Rohtang la and includes the Bara Lacha la 15,500 feet and the Tang Lang la at 17,500 feet. Overnight stops can be made at Keylong, Jispa and the old Central Asian grazing ground of

Sarchu *Serai*. It is a marvellous painted landscape of purples, ochres, pinks, yellows and browns with backdrops of pure white snows and marbled glacier ice. This is a happy contrast between the lush greens of Kullu and the more stark and rocky terrain of Lahaul. Such a safari can now be extended beyond Leh over the Khardung la to the Nubra valley. This has been opened to visitors since 1994.

Shimla (Simla) famous since the days it was a hill station and summer capital in the times of the British Raj is now the capital and the main gateway into Himachal Pradesh. Buses regularly travel from Delhi via Chandigarh to reach Shimla and it is the route Eileen and I took on our first visit when we drove our own Ford Caravanette. On another occasion we varied the journey by taking the early morning broad gauge railway train from Delhi to Kalka. At Kalka we transferred to a narrow gauge line on the train known as the 'Himalayan Queen'. It then took us on a slow but fascinating journey to Shimla. It is a train journey of great interest to railway buffs and in our case was made even more interesting when we met the train driver—B.S. Gill. His own water colour paintings of the railway and its surrounding environment were on show and for sale—and he is quite a salesman!

From Shimla, the road takes a winding route to Mandi on the Beas river and then continues north to Kullu. The road north-west of Mandi is one we used on the return from our first visit to Kullu and Lahaul. It traverses through Kangra and Chamba via Dharamsala and Pathankot and in this way we journeyed on to Jammu & Kashmir. The camping, climbing and trekking (and increasingly the skiing in Kullu) in all the areas is quite superb and they are much less frequented than in other parts of the Himalaya.

We have been to most of them on different occasions and whilst trekking or skiing in Kullu and Lahaul have came to know the Kangra shepherds (known as Gaddis) very well. When eventually we went to Kangra town and to Dharamsala it was good to see and to discover, something of their homeland.

Tibetans and Kangras

"Why are there so many people here?"
"Because it is the Dalai Lama's birthday".

This was the answer given to us several years ago when we arrived at Dharamsala in the Kangra valley. The one time British hill station seethed with people, mostly Tibetan refugees who had settled there after the Chinese invasion of Tibet in 1959. It is now looked upon by the exiles as their capital and is the main residence of the Dalai Lama.

By mid-afternoon the special ceremony to celebrate his birthday was over and taking our cue from the Dalai Lama who had returned to his home, we escaped from the noise and bustle of the town and sought out the peace of the hills. We chose a narrow dirt track that took us to an opening in the pine forest and in the evening when the clouds cleared, the lights of the township winked up at us from across the re-entrant. Above us the rock

ridges and old snowbeds of the high Kangra peaks caught the last days of the sun and glowed serenely golden. It was humid in our forest opening and the frosted areas of rock and snow seemed invitingly cool but frustratingly remote.

When it darkened at the clearing the surrounding pine forest became alive with flashing fire-flies pursuing their evening nuptials and below us the main square in Dharamsala glowed red from many log fires. Like the Sherpas of Nepal, the Tibetans love to sing and their songs are similar for they are of the same race. For several hours we listened to them, their cheerful voices rising from around the log fires, then echoing from ridge to ridge of the hitherto silent hills. Long before midnight the singing ended, the fire-flies ceased their searchings and we found it was cool enough to sleep.

Lying south-east of Jammu & Kashmir and west of Kullu, the Kangra valley is a part of the mountain state of Himachal Pradesh. The high peaks which were above our forest clearing, flank Kangra to the north and are a part of the Lesser Himalaya range known as the Dhauladhar. Though Dharamsala is now inhabited mainly by Tibetans, the rest of the Kangra valley is populated by a race of people who arrived in much earlier times. These are the Kangras, the shepherds of the hills. In the dry season they are content to stay in Kangra but prior to the coming of heavy monsoon rains that saturate the hill slopes and flood the 'paddy' fields, the shepherds begin to move their flocks. It is an annual transhumance that takes them to the drier mountain areas of Kullu, Lahaul and Spiti to the north. Having seen many of these hill shepherds over the years we have come to admire their sturdy independence. During the 4th century B.C. the huge army of Alexander the Great moved out of Europe and into Asia. Having traversed the Anatolian plateau they crossed Persia, Afghanistan, into northern India including Kashmir and eventually into the Chamba and Kangra valleys. The present day Kangras are said to be the descendants of the remnants of that great army, and certainly their traditional clothing is intriguingly similar to the classical costume of the Greek guards. When you compare them you see there is no difference in the costumes except in the material of which they are made.

Living rough with their flocks on the high mountain slopes in all weathers, these hardy shepherds maintain traditional pastoral customs that go back thousands of years in time. Their way of life is much the same as that of the shepherds in the Pindus mountains of Greece. In similar fashion each tend their stock with care and friendliness, knowing each and every one of their flock and each animal's character. We have met with many of them each time we have been to Kullu and the 'Valley of the Gods'.

Journey to the 'Valley of the Gods'

A wind like the hot blast from a furnace raised curtains of dust across the narrow road when we trundled our way out of Delhi towards Kangra and Kullu. Even in the hills the day temperature rose above 100 degrees Fahrenheit during the next two days. Hot winds blew strongly out of the plains to the south, and a rising pall of dust creeping nearer and nearer day by day proved to be a harbinger of yet higher temperatures and greater trials to come. From Mandi the road to Kullu and the 'Valley of the Gods' was under reconstruction, its track rising sinuously above the massive river Beas—a surging powerful mass of grey-brown water heavy with glacial silt. For long distances road gangs made up of local men, women and children were breaking hardcore and spreading a narrow carpet of angular rocky rubble along the route. Always, a low layer of ochreous finings hung above the rubble and frequently a swiftly moving cloud of dust ahead forewarned of oncoming traffic. Soon we were edging a passage with wheels churning at the brink, and poised thousands of feet above the swift-flowing Himalayan torrent. We descended to the confluence of the Beas and Parvati, and one mile higher at Bhuntar, a local Kullu man swept down the river on the back of an inflated buffalo skin. His legs trailing the surging waters acted as rudders and with practiced ease he was able to ferry glide from one bank to another. The powerful river flowed at a rate of many knots and an error could have been fatal. Huge waves rolled back from obstructions hidden beneath the torrent and as if revelling in the challenge

the man ferry glided sideways into the white-topped standing
rucks and swept swiftly down to the confluence where the clean,
cold green ice-water of the Parbati melded with the grey-brown of
the Beas. Probably he was merely shopping and having bought
red hot peppers at a village on the true right bank of the river,
was now ferry gliding to the true left. There at another village he
would perhaps buy salt and grain before deflating the skin and
placing it on the back of a bullock cart or even on a bus. In this
way he would return to his home in the valley of Kullu; a fruitful
valley of orchards where grow apples, plums, cherries, apricots and
peaches. Before the township of Kullu, the valley opens out and
we soon caught exciting glimpses of distant snows supported by
the coniferous-covered flanks of the lower Pir Panjals. An unexpected and very interesting aspect were the numerous small state
quarries and the slate-roofed houses of Kullu that reminded us
of Wales and home, for this slate-roofing mixed with a more alpine
style of house construction seemed a strange Austro-Welsh mixture of ideas marooned in another world.

Though Manali and Kullu are the main towns of the valley,
we at first stopped in Raison and stayed at Jimmy Johnson's
Orchard. Jimmy and his wife Bala were tremendously helpful and
hospitable as well as having a great knowledge of the area. Their
orchards in which grow apples and various stone fruits such as
plums and peaches are set above and along the valley floor through
which flows the famous glacial river Beas.

We stayed in their old house—a huge wooden structure with
fine big rooms and a large verandah. There was a cool relaxing
atmosphere, and outside all the shades of green contrasted with
the colour of fruit and blossoms set against a backcloth of snow-
covered Himalayan peaks.

For the next few days we explored the region which has been
a happy recreation area for fishermen, *shikaris*, trekkers and
mountaineers since the 19th century. Even so it still retains its
own cultural identity. Hindu temples with the pyramid-style
roofing are typical and Buddhist monasteries are on the increase
since the influx of the Tibetan refugees. Walks are numerous and
later at the Manali Orchard owned by John Banon, we discovered

a splendidly descriptive guide to local walks written by Deana Pettigrew. It is more than just a local guide, for it also describes journeys to the high passes and to the glacier of the Solang nala. We found Kullu to be a land of light, shade, shape and colour, a paradise for photographers, and for travellers in general an ideal area for meeting a cheerful cosmopolitan population in an ancient Himalayan region.

But how does the valley get its name? In October at the time of the festival of Dussehra, hundreds of Hindu gods ate brought out from the many temples in the Kullu valley. These are then taken to the green and grassy Dhalpur maidan south of the town. Throughout India the festival of Dussehra celebrates the victory of Rama over the demon king Ravana, but in Kullu there is an extra dimension in that homage is paid to the god Raghunathji and all the other gods.

Throughout the general festivity there is much music and dancing until on the 7th day Ragunathji is returned to his temple. This gathering together of the many hundreds of temple icons at the time of Dussehra make it an extra special occasion from which the area gets the name 'Valley of the Gods'.

13

Skis in the Kullu Himalaya

(1976)

People have been skiing in the Himalaya over a long period of time and the Ski Club of India was first formed in 1926. Presently the most definitive book on skiing in that part of the world is *Skis in India* written by Major H.C. (Charles) Bagot, later Lord Bagot who was Chief Instructor of skiing at the R.A.F. Centre in Kashmir when I was Chief Instructor of Mountaineering.

Whilst trekking and travelling in various sections of the Himalaya, Eileen and I, whenever possible, have also skied. This has been on the glaciers in the Everest area, on the flanks of Trisul in Garhwal and in Thajiwas, the 'Valley of Glaciers' in Kashmir. We were also fortunate to ski with the Indo-Tibet Border Police on the Kullu Lahaul divide and later to be involved in the running of the first Kullu Summer Ski Festival in the Rani nala.

One outcome of that involvement was that later we suggested to Harish Sarin that a National Ski Federation of India be formed. Through his influence it was and for many years now it has been affiliated to F.I.S. (the International Ski Federation). During a recent visit to Kullu, we again met several of the skiers from the Indo-Tibet Border Police and the mountaineering institute with whom we skied and ran the ski festival. It was good to discover that since that time, government finance had helped with ski developments in the Solang valley above Manali. In addition in the 1990s Swiss and American firms have developed Heli skiing on the Rohtang and the Hampta la. These are big changes from the earlier times when we had to carry our skis from Marhi to reach the passes.

Camping at Marhi

Following a stay at Jimmy Johnson's orchard, we went to find the Western Himalayan Mountaineering Institute in Manali. Harish Sarin, President of the Indian Mountaineering Foundation was keen that we met Harnam Singh, the Principal of the institute and see something of the buildings of the new centre. Fortunately, as it turned out, we were given incorrect information on how to find the W.H.M.I. and when we arrived at the waterfalls of Rahla beyond Manali, we realised we were a long way astray. We decided we might as well carry on despite having to frequently negotiate the rubble of recent landslides, and the angular hardcore of the road repairs that were in operation. Up and up we went continuing to twist and turn along the road to the Rohtang la. In several places the road had been completely swept away by avalanche leaving rutted boulder-strewn sections that threatened to turn us back. At one desperately steep and rocky turn we lost three mud-flaps, a reversing light and our backstep, but on we went. Soon we began to edge our way through narrow snow cuttings and as the sides of our vehicle scraped the snow, we gazed up the sides of the cutting rising fifteen feet above us. This already narrow and dangerous route had been made more difficult by frequent meetings with large flocks of sheep and goats (bakra) tended by the Kangra shepherds who kept us waiting poised over frightening depths whilst they moved the animals to one side.

"Let's turn back" suggested Eileen and I agreed we would, if after the cutting there was no improvement. When we did finally emerge, the improvement to the road was negligible but the improvement to our morale immense.

This was because on the snow slopes that rose eight hundred to a thousand feet above the true left bank of the river, two separate groups of people were skiing. This was totally unexpected. Going over to the first group we found they were an advanced ski course from W.H.M.I. Manali. A little higher up the slope, the second group of skiers were performing some elegant up-unweighted Christianas. This was a party of Indo-Tibet Border Police from Garhwal Himalaya, there to gain further experience in the mountains of Kullu. Bhagat Singh, an Inspector of the Police, told us that his party, and that of the W.H.M.I. were camped a few hundred feet above at the village of Marhi. "There is plenty of room. Do camp near us". This invitation became almost an entreaty when he found we had our skis with us and off we went to set up our tent.

Above us was the Rohtang la, the boundary between Kullu and Lahaul, said to have been created by Lord Shiva who smote through the mountain barrier to create the pass. William Moor- croft, a surgeon from Liverpool, who eventually became an indefatigable Himalayan traveller and explorer first calculated the height of the Rohtang when he crossed it in 1820 and built a stone cairn to mark the source of the river Beas.

By road distance Marhi is 21 kilometres from the top of the Rohtang la and at the time it was the furthest that any vehicles could go. The pass was still blocked by heavy winter snows and did not open for normal traffic for another seven weeks (mid July) long after we had left Kullu. Even so, this superb snow area around the Rohtang 13,050 feet and the Hampta la 14,100 feet became our mountain home for the next two weeks.

Snowbeds were melting quickly on the 'alps' around Marhi, a small village of a dozen or so stone dwellings. Already roofs of corrugated iron were replacing those destroyed by avalanche earlier in the year. Where we camped, a fresh green spread of short grass contrasted with the clean snows of the Pir Panjal mountains, and whilst we sat drinking tea the increasing warmth of the sun seeped into our bodies. We realised that here we had found a place of peace and beauty. A soft murmuring of running water emanated from a dirty white bed of snow nearby and clumps of pink primula pushed through the snow to reach for the sky and light of day. Within days our 'alp' was profusely carpeted with an abundance of other Himalayan flora—purple iris, white anemones and the rich gold of burgeoning sulphur-yellow wind flowers.

Rohtang la and the Rani nala

Our first ski with the W.H.M.I. and I.T.B.P was very interesting as we side-stepped and herring-boned up a steep slope. We paused momentarily then swooped down to the Beas river as gracefully as we could. Mostly it was old snow made bumpy by wet avalanche sloughs and in places narrow, so that I used a variety of turns—mainly short swings in the narrows and Welen technique in the rough to absorb the bumps. Straight away both ski groups were intrigued and keen to find out as much as possible about us and our different way of skiing. Wedeln, short swings and Welen they had never seen before.

"What do they call this way of skiing?" asked Ran Singh.

"How can we learn?" queried Misra.

"Do show us," demanded Bhagat Singh—and so for the next two weeks I did.

Each day, either at the snowbeds, sometimes in the two mile long avalanche nala, the Rani, or on the top of the Rohtang la, I gave two or more hours of instruction. This was to the Indo-Tibet Border Police. I derived immense satisfaction from teaching such fine mountain men. Most had climbed to the summits of some of the world's highest mountains—Saser Kangri, Shivling and Nanda Kot to name but a few. I still feel great satisfaction that during our stay in Kullu I was known as the 'Guru' or 'Guruji,' the teacher. In the afternoons following the tuition, we free-skied the magnificent slopes of the Pir Panjals and on the third day we were joined by Lill Bahadur and Dorje, two chief constables, who with an Indian team had just made the first ski ascent of Trisul 23,500 feet. They had been the first pair to ski down from the summit and I remembered this mountain in Garhwal from an expedition I had been on years earlier.

I had photographed its massive snow-covered flanks from high passes on the way to Joshimath and the source of the Ganges. As Lill Bahadur described their ski descent I also thought of Dr. Tom Longstaff and an evening spent with him at Achiltibui in Scotland. In 1907 Longstaff had been the first man ever to reach the summit of Trisul after a remarkable ascent of 6000 feet in one day. For many years it remained the highest ascent made in the Himalaya. Now it was a privilege, 70 years later to be with the two men to make its first ascent on ski.

A wide climatic depression covered most of northern India during the first ten days that we skied, depositing five or six inches of new snow in the late afternoons and evenings. Because of the weather the Kangra shepherds were unusually late in crossing the high passes to Lahaul and Spiti, and generally they found the conditions to be a trial. Rather selfishly we skiers welcomed the snow, enjoying our skiing on the various slopes and at the Rohtang la. After a good ski at the pass we used to have an afternoon break for a mug of tea at the 'Rohtang View Hotel'. This was a low stone shack roofed with canvas which stood just below the pass. The proprietor came from Lahaul and from a battery of pots, pans and kettles he produced a variety of hot beverages. Other containers held *chang* or *rakshi* of which the Indo-Tibet Border Police consumed little. Hot tea was their favourite drink which often helped to wash down a quickly prepared *chapatti* cooked on the acrid smelling charcoal embers. At frequent intervals the driving snow outside swirled into the 'shack' when the sacking that made for a door was twitched to one side. In might step a lively Lahauli trader, a traditionally dressed Kangra shepherd, or an inadequately clothed Hindu pilgrim. Each time there was plenty of banter and questioning, for our skis proved to be a source of interest and wonder to all who saw us.

Eileen was a constant focus of interest and our friends the police were immensely proud to have her with them. Quickly she used to build up a happy relationship with everyone, would have them helping her in all sorts of ways and was greatly respected. At this time she was skiing strongly and at the end of the day we sometimes made a swift swooping descent of the Rani nala which after three to four miles led us back to the bridge at Marhi. It was broad and steep and we came to know its bumps and turns very well.

Following the day's activities, our evenings at Marhi varied but almost always we paid a visit to the camp of the Border Police. One evening we shared with the skiers of the Mountaineering Institute as well as the police and after liberal quantities of curry, *chang* and *rakshi* there was singing, and also dancing of a kind remarkably Greek in style. As was to be expected the songs were of the mountains, for these were mountain men—songs of Garhwal, Kangra, Punjab, Kashmir, Nepal—and one a song of praise for the skiers of Trisul, Dorje and Lill Bahadur. Ran Singh, the chief ski instructor at the W.H.M.I., made bold by drinking *chang*, sang a strangely evocative song. Again it was music from the hills, this time from his Kangra home. We asked what the song was about and to our surprise found that he made up the words as he went along. It was a lament about the weather and the lack of sun, the early monsoon, the heavy clouds and the cruelty of their persistent appearance.

At the end of the first week of skiing we met Harnam Singh, Principal of the Western Himalayan Mountaineering Institute. The police were joined by Chandra Khanna (Assistant Commissioner) who had been deputy leader of the first ascent of Saser Kangri, 25,300 feet in the Karakoram Himalaya. These two were starting to organise the Kullu Summer Ski Festival to be held one week later. We were asked to help. Having said we would we were immediately taken aback by being asked to choose the venue but with little hesitation we chose the Rani nala, and the Rani it was.

The Kullu Summer Ski Festival

Following so much persistent cloud and snow everyone was pleased that the big day proved sunny and warm. The fresh white snow that had fallen during the previous two weeks contrasted strongly with the green grassy slopes at the bottom of the nala and the deep blue sky above. Much to our surprise over 750 people came from Shimla, Bilaspur, Manali, Kullu, Mandi and from as far away as Delhi to watch the racing. Early in the morning they arrived at Marhi then walked over old snowbeds and across the steep hillside to the Rani. This show of enthusiasm by the Indians for a newly developing sport in their country was impressive, as were the brightly coloured *saris* of purple, yellow, red, blue, orange and emerald green worn by the many graceful Indian ladies who enhanced the scene.

During practice a few days earlier, we realised that the local idea of a Downhill race was a straight 200 yard run down a steep slope and through a tape. Such a course required no technique and with a good pair of skis the heaviest man, even if he couldn't ski very well, providing he stayed upright long enough, was bound to win. On the race day I changed this concept to the correct one and set the downhill course for the seven advanced skiers. It was almost one and a half miles in length and included three large sweeping turns. I also changed the slalom when I found Ran Singh setting seventy-two poles up the slope in a dead straight line. Can you imagine skiing such a vertical course!

Whilst Eileen organised herself as a judge and timekeeper, I set a proper slalom showing Ran Singh how he should start from the top and work downwards. He and the others were puzzled by my varied positioning of the gates which were set to present technical problems and yet provide an essentially pleasing and rhythmical course. To our satisfaction and that of the skiers, the slalom proved exciting and interesting and the problems in technique gave them a thirst for more. Intermediate and advanced skiers vied for places but in the end those we expected to win did so and most of the first, second and third placings were taken by the Indo-Tibet Border Police. Lill Bahadur won the Downhill handsomely and with a cheerful refreshing modesty that was typical of the day. Ran Singh from the W.H.M.I., set the Giant Slalom then proceeded to win the event. I pointed out to him that this was not allowed in racing but who could care when he and everyone there, including those he had beaten were ecstatic with delight at his success. Ang Tharkey, brother-in-law of Tenzing Norgay of Everest, won the slalom and vindicated my confidence in his ability. Prior to our first meeting he had only experienced a fifteen day beginners ski course in Darjeeling. For the two weeks I was his 'Guru' he showed himself to be the most able pupil I had ever taught, picking up new skills with remarkable ease. Against opposition we persuaded the Festival Committee to allow Ang Tharkey to race with the advanced skiers and though he fell in the Downhill, he came third in the Giant Slalom, then skied deceptively smoothly and fast to win the slalom by seconds. Perhaps of them all, his was the best achievement.

Each race, and every competitor, was given a fine ovation by the enthusiastic crowd which in the main sat on a grassy moraine. Not far away we set up our large 'Good Companion' tent with its extended flysheet and not for the first time it proved its versatility, for all afternoon it was used as the tea tent. Inside it, huge multi-jetted kerosene stoves boiled gallons of water which threatened to melt the fabric whilst busy helpers dispensed *chai* and biscuits to all the spectators at the ski festival. Everyone, young and old, thoroughly enjoyed the highly successful and festive day. In the late afternoon General Bakshi of the National Cadet Corp, who had journeyed up from Delhi, presented trophies to the skiers at the foot of the nala. Above us the sun glistened on the snows at the top of the Rohtang and the Hampta passes, whilst small groups of mountain choughs gave sharp clear calls which resounded from the crags. It was as if they too were adding their congratulations to that of the spectators below. The day ended when in the evening over a hundred of us sat around an aromatic campfire of some sandalwood singing songs from the northern hills and listened to several speeches expressing hope and encouragement for the future of skiing in Kullu.

14

Lahaul: An Unplanned Visit

(July 1976)

"Often and often it came back again to mind the
day I passed the horizon ridge to a new country."
–Edward Thomas in *'Over the Hills'*

On each of the days that we skied on the Rohtang la we found good powder and quickly stepped out training pistes where our companions could practice short swings and Welen techniques. Often whilst skiing we watched long trails of ponies, sheep and goats tended by Kangra shepherds struggling endlessly across the snowbound pass. That they were a tough people was abundantly apparent. Squalls of driving snow were frequent and dressed in their traditional skirted costumes, with bare legs and hard leather *chaplis* to cover their feet they remained impervious to the cold. Often the sky was totally overcast and heavy nimbus clouds obscured the 20,000 feet peaks that disappeared into the dark and moisture-laden cloud base at around 15,000 feet.

On one of the days the weather improved a little and for once Eileen and I left the main party. Together we toured right across the Chandra-Beas watershed until we could see into the deep cleft of the Chandra river valley. This time the mountains were clear, stretching as far as the eye could see into Lahaul—west towards Keylong and north towards the area of the Bara Lacha la. To the south-east the Chandra cut deeply into the ranked high masses of the Bara Shigri. The snow was good, travelling conditions excellent and the mountain panorama wild and attractive. There and then we decided that following the Kullu Ski Festival we would discard our skis and backpack "over the horizon ridge to a new country."

Four or five days was as long as we would have in Lahaul but it seemed worthwhile and so a week later we took the Manali bus to Marhi. This was still as far as transport was able to go because of the snow. At the bridge below Marhi we began our walk following the river Beas towards its watershed. The snowbeds had almost disappeared and in their place huge carpets of Himalayan flora, full of colour and refreshing promise, spread over the lower reaches of the pass. Fresh melt-water streams sparkled attractively, the water rippling through layers of blood red primula, golden yellow anemone and freshly burgeoning potentilla. Stone crops, globe flowers, mountain iris, and round-headed *Primula denti-culata* vied with white and mauve flowers to dominate the lush grazing grounds. It was a hot day and our packs laden with tents, stoves, bags, fuel and dehydrated foods seemed especially heavy. Slowly we ascended the Rani nala which seemed strangely quiet and deserted after the life and colour of the ski festival. The stone tea-shack at the top of the pass remained open for business. There we stopped for refreshment with a score of Kangra shepherds who were also on their way to the Chandra valley. It was a good moment to reflect a little on the history of the Rohtang and to be thankful that we could travel into Lahaul.

In 1631 a Jesuit priest, Francisco de Azevedo, crossed the Mana pass from Garhwal into Tibet and followed the route first made by Father Andrade to Leh in Ladakh. On his return journey to India he made the first crossing of the Zanskar and Himalayan ranges into Lahaul. From Lahaul he then made the first crossing of the Rohtang la into Kullu. It had always been an important trade route for the people of Central Asia but until the 19th century few other westerners had visited the area. Only since the early 1950s had it been used extensively by the explorers and mountaineers, and several of our mountaineering friends had been there. Two of my staff at Plas-y-Brenin—Josephine Peacock (nee Scarr) and Barbara Roscoe (nee Spark) had crossed the Rohtang to reach the Bara Shigri peaks from the Chandra valley. Their photographs and accounts of the transformation of the scene as they crossed from Kullu to Lahaul were fascinating and we had always hoped that someday we might go.

When planning our itinerary we had left out Lahaul thinking that permission to go there would not be given. This had been our information since the Indian Army engineers had started to build a military road from Kullu through Lahaul then over the Bara Lacha la into Ladakh. The road was intended to link up in Leh with the road being built from Kashmir. Unknown to Eileen and me, both roads were complete and permission to visit both Ladakh and Lahaul was possible. Now we were going.

Later in the year a bus service would operate between Manali and Keylong in Lahaul but at the time we were there, the pass was still blocked and the country had been cut off from supplies for almost eight months.

Suitably refreshed and rested we soon left the stone shack to continue our journey. Snow was melting fast and several hundred feet below the pass we were walking on open grassy areas interspersed with slopes of greasy bare soil. No clouds broke the even-toned blue of the sky and the crystal clear mountains in the Kulti nala beckoned invitingly. Descent into the Chandra valley to Khoksar seemed long, and we were both glad of a room at the P.W.D. bungalow. Khoksar is a village of wooden houses and shacks of some importance, because traders crossing either way over the Rohtang generally go through it. There is a more solidly built police station and bus booking office but the finest building is the P.W.D. bungalow. Though needing some repair and a lick of paint it is soundly structured and boasts a splendid green lawn on which we were able to sit drinking refreshing tea brought by the *chowkidar*.

It was then we were informed of a bus that ran each day up and down the valley from Khoksar to Keylong. This we found remarkable when we considered the store of fuel supply required to keep the service going but we realised later that this service too had only begun its daily toil a few days earlier.

Without anything definite in mind we had thought of finding some pleasant alp at 12,000 feet or so in the Kulti nala. We could put up our tent and from it walk on the hills above. Now the chance of a journey down the Chandra valley to Keylong proved to be inviting, for by doing so we would see more of Lahaul and still have the opportunity of two or three days of walking. As is so often the way in the Himalaya we had a hair-raising journey along a rugged track, which in places, had recently been destroyed by avalanche. Cuttings through huge fans of old snow, mud, boulders, and shattered remnants of macadam, were frequent and most of the time there seemed but a few inches separating us from the present, and a plunge to eternity thousands of feet below. Although aware of the dangers, sixty-five excited and vociferous human beings squeezed inside the bus at Khoksar. A further thirty or more plus all the luggage perched precariously on the roof! It has often been said that it is better to travel hopefully than never to travel at all—we felt that on this journey the meaning of the word 'hopefully' was abundantly clear. Along the route we made stops at Ropsang, Kharpani, and also at Gondhla bridge. All along the valley we saw typically Central Asian housing—flat-roofed, two-storied and making use of wood as well as mud and stone. Each was freshly coated with a smoke grey wash. They and the lush green fields were remarkably neat and tidy and as usual we could see that the womenfolk laboured long and hard at their daily chores. The Chandra river and swift flowing lateral melt streams provided water for irrigation and already crops of grain, maize, potatoes and other vegetables were well established.

We arrived in Keylong late in the evening and quickly descended to the P.W.D. bungalow in the heart of the small town.

Keylong and Kardhing Gompa

We stayed four days in Keylong. This was unintentional as on the third day we should have departed for a return to Khoksar but the bus had broken down. Throughout a hot and tedious day we waited patiently for its repair, having been promised that at any moment the vehicle would be on the move. Exasperatingly it was not repaired in time and the day was wasted. Our one consolation was that we were promised a seat each for the drive back up the Chandra valley. In no way could the seats have been taken from us. The driver simply unbolted them, took them away and they were only replaced when we were on the bus the next day. But on our arrival in Keylong all this was in the future, and it was to the present that we applied our minds. We had food with us but if possible hoped to augment our supplies with local produce, or perhaps a meal at a local tea stall. Several of these supplied small quantities of curried meats and pulses and at times a wheat *chapatti* or even a small amount of rice. Other shops and trading stalls of varying shapes and sizes lined the one long main street which was a narrow dirt road. Opposite the bungalow, a sign above a doorway proclaimed the building to be the local library. On examination the next day we found there to be a good selection of books, fiction and non-fiction, practically all of them printed in English. Most of the local population passed along this street at some time of the day and already this number was swelled by an influx of Kangra shepherds who from the goat-grazing grounds were coming in to view the town. It was never busy whilst we were there but we knew that later when the passes were free of snow, the buses would bring a multitude of visitors. Traders from Ladakh as well as Kullu would also bring long caravans of pack horses laden with supplies. So far we had seen just one such caravan of half a dozen pack animals struggling across the snow-blocked Rohtang to bring grain and other essential commodities to the town.

Early on our first morning we walked along the narrow street—a patchwork of light and shade. Pigtailed Lahauli women wearing long woollen skirts and small coloured waistcoats carried V-shaped baskets on their way to the fields by the river. Numerous small boys wearing western style shorts and jackets, or pyjamas and sweaters, scuffled their way to the local school and several Buddhist Lamas quietly walked along viewing the shops, wearing their traditional wine-coloured *chubas* or woollen smocks. I felt that this quiet awakening of everyday life, but for a difference in costume and features, was common to many parts of the world and thought of Cypriot women taking similar V-shaped baskets to collect ripening grapes from nearby vineyards, whilst black garbed and bearded Greek Orthodox priests made their way along similar narrow streets.

The Buddhist monks were from the renowned Kardhing gompa, an imposing monastery built on a shelf of the hillside opposite to Keylong. It seemed a good time to go there and perhaps after visiting the monastery to walk up the slopes towards Rangcha, a point of 15,000 feet. From the township we descended along a narrow path which took us by a whitewashed *chorten*, and we then crossed the river by a solid bridge. On the steep ascent towards Kardhing village we carefully traversed by the *Mani* walls on the left hand side in the Buddhist tradition and soon we were at the village 'square'. On this hard mud compound a large weaving loom stretched most of the way across. It was over a foot wide, eighteen inches off the ground and more than thirty feet in length. A group of Lahauli children played in the sun, and a further group, this time men of the village, sat beneath the shade of a tree, drinking *chang* (beer). Immediately we were invited to join them and found it impossible to refuse. Fortunately our hosts were satisfied when each of us downed, with apparent relish, a frothing cup of the thick fermenting gruel. Several times the weaver at the loom became one of the imbibing throng, and we wondered how long it would be before all was chaos. Continuing to walk along the narrow side street we absorbed some of the peaceful atmosphere that emanated from the quiet sun-soaked buildings. Beyond the village a pathway led us along the edge of irrigated fields and up to the *gompa*. Here several large and well-cared for *Mani* walls were a contrast to the eroded and decapitated *chortens*. Having seen the decrepit *chortens* we expected the worst but found the *gompa* buildings to be splendidly clean and like the Lahauli houses, freshly covered with a smoke grey wash. At Kardhing there are many nuns as well as monks, and in the main area of the *gompa* grounds we were met by a good looking nun who seemingly pleased to see us picked several long flower stems, peeled them, and gave them to us to chew. They were astringent and refreshing like the peeled stems of the Himalayan Blue Poppy though they were not Mecanopsis but of the Umbellifera family.

All the nuns and lamas were neatly dressed, clean and very helpful and one of them beckoned us inside to see the living quarters. Wooden butter tea-tubs, silver drinking cups, bamboo *chang* jars, copper pans and brass ladles, plus other parapharnalia typical of Tibetan people cluttered the shelves adjacent to the fireplace, from which arose a smell of *chang* and butter tea mingling with the aroma of herbs and wood smoke.

Later in the afternoon, having descended from the upper slopes of Rangcha, we walked once more along the peaceful alleyways of the monastery and back to Keylong. We were in time to catch the school-children returning home, and in the garden of the P.W.D. bungalow Eileen enjoyed teaching a group of them to sing a song in English "Twinkle, twinkle, little star". During the next couple of days whenever we walked by a group of children we heard the refrain and a tinkle of happy laughter would follow us up the street.

Towards Gangstang

Shushur *gompa* clings to the steep hillside a thousand feet above Keylong. Another five and a half thousand feet higher up a steep glacier protrudes a tongue of ice from between two opposing ridges. The glacier is an extension of the ice slopes and snow ridges of a domed-peak which when seen from Kardhing reminded us strongly of the Allalinhorn in Switzerland. The peak of over 19,000 feet is one of the several Gangstang summits, a mountain massif that rises to 20,500 feet or so at its highest.

The day before our wedding anniversary, as a prior celebration, we decided to ascend as far as possible towards the summit. Though very fit and well-acclimatised, we knew we had no chance of completing the nine thousand foot of ascent but wished to reach the snow and the vicinity of the glacier snout. At 5 a.m. we ate a quick breakfast then began the ascent to Shushur *gompa*. All was quiet at the monastery. The spiralling smoke of a wood fire, vivid blue as it caught the first light of early morning sun was the only evidence of life. Continuing the ascent over a broad and stony hillside we found spreading carpets of flowers, a profusion of colour, sulphur yellows, demure pinks, winking blues and blobs of red peering out of dark leaf green. A series of tall cairns or 'steinmen' built by the semi-nomadic Kangras led to a contouring leat that carried water from the alluvial area below the glacier snout. Redstarts flittered from boulder to boulder and at one stopping point the chilling wind 'fluted' through the interstices of a 'steinman'. In the early afternoon two immense eagles soared majestically above us as we crunched over snowbeds and eventually stopped at a subsidiary and minor point on the glacier moraine at 17,000 feet.

Clouds swirled intriguingly around the pure white pyramid and the glacier tongue just above us. Cold gusts of wind in which there were white wisps of snow threatened heavier snow flurries to come but then the sun emerged and spread its warming rays about us and our craggy perch. Eating sardine sandwiches and drinking coffee we sat for a full hour entranced by the panorama of the Lahaul landscape. Over 7000 feet below us the Chandra-Bhaga rivers had cut a deep valley through the uplifted landscape. Squares and rectangles of green irrigated fields spread out variedly, sometimes in broad swathes but more often in narrow clinging strips on each of the banks of the rivers. Opposite and due south we looked over and beyond the ridge of Rangcha gully to the ice-clad giants of Shikar Beh and Mukar Beh which were wreathed in clouds. Eastwards a massive area of unclimbed, unexplored mountains rose from 18,000 feet to over 21,000 feet.

There was some reluctance to leave and start the descent but eventually we did so, first taking a last look back at the Gangstang pyramid. We knew that to put a tent high up on the mountain would not have been difficult and with a few more days the summit could have been ours. There was no regret. The day had been wonderfully free and the rapid ascent to our 17,000 feet perch a complete surprise. It will be a good mountain to ascend on ski. Perhaps someday we will return.

Anniversary Evening

What was to have been our third and last day in Keylong was the 29th June, our wedding anniversary. During the afternoon we shopped successfully to augment our supplies, and greatest prize of all, from a dusty corner in a trader's tiny store rooted out a tin of pineapple slices. Later we also bought a small bottle of orange gin, the contents of which we allowed to soak into a pile of biscuits. Surrounded by the pineapples, they made a sumptuous dessert following a main meal of dehydrated meat and vegetables —onions, peas and carrots. After the meal we walked to the eastern end of Keylong and there watched the evening light on the snows of the high peaks of Lahaul turn from cream to gold and then to rose. One of the peaks of 20,000 feet we had often noticed during our stay and felt that also to be ideal for an ascent on ski. The attraction was strong, and again both of us wished we had time to put up a high camp and from it reach the summit. What better than to ski back down free as a bird and after a successful day, sit by a tent doorway bathed in a similar rose glow. Just as on the previous afternoon, we promised we would return for a longer period of time and complete some of the things we wished to do. After all, even if we shouldn't achieve all we wished to do, we would still want to try and as I remembered thinking on the bus from Koksar, "It is better to travel hopefully than never to travel at all."

15

Vishnu and the Source of the Ganges

(1952)

Orange-smocked sadhus, and soot-smeared fakirs! Vendors, professional beggars and devout pilgrims! We see all these at the city built on the west bank of the most sacred river in Asia. The city is Varanasi. The river is the Ganges.

Each year several million men, women and children, come to the bank of the river and when the huge golden orb of the sun rises above the trees to the east, the throng of pilgrims descend to the bathing ghats and wash away their sins in the holy waters. How many visitors to Varanasi are aware that the birth of the river begins far to the north amongst the high peaks and glaciers of the Central Himalaya? This is the area known as the Garhwal, bordered in the east by Nepal and bounded by the river Satluj, that drains the mountain areas of Kullu and Lahaul, to the west.

There is a legend that many thousands of years ago, devasting floods poured out of the Central Himalaya rushing with tremendous force down to the plains of India, sweeping away cities, towns and villages and drowning hundreds of thousands of people. The people of the plains then prayed to Lord Vishnu, the Protector, and Vishnu laid himself down to let the water pour out of his mouth, down his body and between his toes. This controlled the flood which formed the great river—the Ganges—'Mother Ganga', that every year takes down life giving soil and water to the Indian plains. If in any year the waters fail, it means famine when thousands, possibly millions, of people die. Such famine you can never forget. Small wonder then, that each year tens of thousands of pilgrims from various parts of India make the journey across the hot and dusty plains, along rough stony pathways and over the upper pine-clad slopes towards the mountains. They are going to Himachal—The Abode of Snow—the source of water and the river of life. They are also making pilgrimage to one of the four most holy shrines in India, the Temple of Vishnu at Badrinath.

The present temple was built over 1200 years ago but it is known that this holy place of Badrinath in the ancient land called Badrikashram was known and revered in the 6th century B.C. It was later because of the influence of Buddhism that the original Badrinath fell into decay. May be militant Buddhists destroyed it or it simply crumbled and decayed through lack of care and the ravages of time. Eventually the new temple was built with its fine facade, a grand entrance and steps, and a small cupola on top of which is a gilt ball and spire. The idol of Shri Narayan was reinstated here having been rescued from the waters at Narakund where it had been thrown down many years before. Until recent times Tibetan monasteries on the other side of the Himalayan divide paid tribute to the temple just as Tibetan lamas had made pilgrimages of obligation many centuries before. This mix of Hinduism and Buddhism clearly relates to the age and sanctity of the shrine—very old and very holy.

When I first went to Badrinath, the village was in a shambles. Half of it buried or destroyed by avalanche, but local workmen were busily rebuilding and repairing what was worthy of repair. Newly arrived pilgrims were descending the time-worn steps of a narrow alleyway to Taptakund, a hot sulphurous spring in which, by permission of Lord Vishnu, resides Agni, the fire god. Immediately below the spring was the swift-moving glacial water of the Alaknanda.

There the pilgrims grasped large metal rings set in the rock then quickly took a cold douche to wash away their sins and afterwards immersed themselves in the hot waters of Taptakund for a cleansing and invigoration of the body and soul. For all who visit Badrinath there is much that is new and strange to take in, the devout pilgrims, the sacred spring, the ash-smeared fakirs and orange-smocked sadhus and of course the temple. Perhaps western visitors, enthralled by the magnificence of the surrounding mountains will feel that it is these that attract the Indians to this remote area of the Himalaya, but this is not so, for the pilgrims know they want to worship at the sacred temple of Vishnu and bathe in the life-giving waters of the river near the source of the Ganges.

Along with the more hardy pilgrims it is worth walking up the valley to the Bhotia village of Mana. Here there are many tiny fields in which grow crops of barley, buckwheat and potatoes. Flocks of buntings, choughs and snow pigeons search busily for food, whilst bright blue Hooker's Iris and ruby-coloured rhododendron blossoms contrast against the brown rock walls that flank the valley. Just above the village there is a deep cut rock cleft filled with rushing foaming water that marks the confluence of the Alaknanda and Saraswati rivers and beyond the confluence, a trail leads north over the 18,000 feet Mana pass into Western Tibet.

It was by this pass that two Jesuit priests made the first crossing of the Himalaya by Europeans.

In the year 1624 Father Antonio de Andrade and Brother Manual Marques, both disguised as pilgrims, followed the route from Hardwar up the Alaknanda gorges to Badrinath. Continuing on beyond Mana the weather deteriorated and altitude sickness became a problem but still they struggled on through a snow storm and in deep snow. Eventually they crossed the pass into Tibet where they set up a Christian mission at the village of Tsaparang.

If at the confluence of the rivers at Mana, Father Andrade had turned to the west instead of continuing to the north, he would have entered the valley of the Satopanth and followed the Alaknanda to its glacier source. This is the way the hardier pilgrims take, walking for several miles over boulder-strewn slopes that lead to a flower covered green meadow beneath the falls of Vasudhara. Here the water plunges spectacularly for 400 feet to the snowbeds and talus slopes beneath, and for the pilgrims these falls are the very start of their holy river—the Ganges. Beginning as a number of small melt-water streams on the high glaciers of the Bangneu, the Vasudhara swoops to the Satopanth valley and there joins the Alaknanda. Eventually the Alaknanda, at its confluence with the Bhagirathi at Devprayag, becomes the Ganges, which flows down to Varanasi and across the plains to finally pour its waters into the Bay of Bengal. Thus the Ganges is one of the major rivers of the world and the Vasudhara its source. It is not surprising these falls have been written of for thousands of years in the Hindu *Puranas* as the place where: "In a thousand ages of the gods, I could not tell thee of the glories of Himachal where Shiva lived, or where the Ganges falls like the slender thread of a lotus blossom from the foot of Vishnu".

On my first visit to Garhwal, I was in this area with three companions and with two of them had the excitement of being the first people to explore an area called the Bangneu. During the exploration, two of us made the first ascent of a mountain we called Avalanche Peak.

Avalanche Peak

"Snow is not a wolf in sheeps clothing—it is a tiger in lambs clothing" so wrote Mathias Zarsky, the great pioneer of skiing. Garhwal in 1952 was a good time to remember his words. Three of us were at about 20,000 feet on the 50° bulge below the west ridge of the peak. At the time, the mountain didn't have a name, we called it Avalanche Peak later. There was a sharp report. The mountain moved and as I drove in my axe, the whole of steep bulge rippled open into wave after wave of blooks and slabs of snow. My descent of the next six hundred feet was rapid and mostly through the air. On the first bounce, I plunged my ice-axe in again up to its hilt but was wrenched from it as if by a giant hand. I lost my mittens and goggles at the second bounce and there was a confused whirling, blinding and flashing of light and snow. At the third contact there was a slowing of all move-ment but still confusion. Immediately movement stopped, I leapt into the air to avoid being buried and landed heavily between two thick slanting blocks of hard wind-slab. That was a bad season in the Central Himalaya. Day after day snow fell without ceasing, to be followed by a short hot sunny spell with only partial consoli-dation before fresh precipitation. Winds from the plates of Tibet used to whip across the high rock ridges blowing the snow onto ice slopes, forming slab, and the slabs were layered one above the other like layers of ice cream ready to slide when something triggered them off. Despite all precautions we had been the trigger.

Fortune was on our side, no one was fatally injured and several days later we got ourselves safely down to base at the Vasudhara. That avalanche was a valuable lesson and a reminder that in moments of great stress fear does not seem to play a part once the action starts.

From the moment of the first volent wobble then being thrown into the air I can remember doing certain things and thinking out the probabilities. I tried to delay my departure by driving in my ice-axe, and felt some relief at realising I was being flung towards a concave hollow to my right and not the steepening convex slopes to my left. Always there was an awareness that I must try to 'swim', keep near the surface, and at all costs stop the snow blocking my air passages. I also knew that the moment all movement stopped I must make every effort to reach the surface and obtain air. When the avalanche did stop, I must have been on the surface possibly because of the swimming action, but I made a prodigious leap, and probably broke all high jump records at 19,000 feet. There had been no time for panic, which wouldn't have helped anyway, but I'm sure my reactions were right because experience, training and thinking had been on the right lines in the past. Years of climbing on snow and ice in the Alps and the Himalaya had helped towards a proper evaluation, and the type of actions to be taken had become ingrained on my mind. Before the attempt on the peak and during the ascent each of us knew the dangers to which we were exposed, accepted them, and decided what we would do in the event of avalanche. Three weeks later, David Byrson and I returned to the Bangneu plateau and from a Camp III at the bergschrund of the mountain successfully climbed Avalanche Peak. Whist we rested at the summit, the clouds sank lower and revealed one mountain after another of the Central Himalaya to us.

Between us and Kamet (25,447 feet) the Arwa glen was filled with mist and to the north above a blanket layer of cloud the unexplored Ganesh Parvat peaks stretched along the Tibetan border. Flakes of hoar frost glistened on the summit rocks, then as the sun's heat strengthened, trickles of water zig-zagged over the surface and ran down to disappear beneath the snow. There we were truly witnessing the birth of the holy Ganges.

A brightly coloured butterfly seemingly blown to that great height by the wind tumbled past us towards Kedarnath and the mountains of the Gangotri, then, rising out of the clouds to the south-east and showing sharply against the intensely blue sky, we could see Changabang, Kalanka, Nanda Ghunti and Bethartoli. Beyond them the peaks of Trisul and Nanda Devi in the inner and outer sanctuaries seemed even more remote and I remember thinking that someday I would return to Garhwal to visit that arca and retrace some of the journeys made by Shipton and Tilman eighteen years earlier.

16

Nanda Devi and Trisul:
Trident of Shiva

(September-October 1981)

"This region is connected with the most ancient traditions of the Indo-Aryan race. The Mahabharata, the Sanskrit Iliad tells that at Bageshwar, in the Kumaon foothills, Shiva was married to Parvati, the "mountain born" daughter of Himachal. She is enshrined in Nanda Devi. Trisul its outlier, is the Trident of Shiva himself."

–Tom Longstaff in *This My Voyage*

The two mountains Nanda Devi East and West are both over 7,000 metres in height. They are guarded by a host of other high peaks which form a great cirque or wall around them. The main approach route is through a wild river cut gorge named Rishi Ganga, which leads first of all to the Trisul gad or 'outer sanctuary' and then finally penetrates the wall to attain the 'inner sanctuary' first reached by Shipton and Tilman in 1934.

When eventually I did return to the Garhwal Himalaya, it was as leader of an expedition which among other things found a second way of penetrating the wall from the Trisul gad to the 'inner sanctuary'. Rather cheekily and because we were a Welsh-based group, we named the route 'Bwlchy Geifr'—the 'Pass of the Goats.'

"Where the wind from Cym Idwal, Cwm Llydaw, Cwm Glas
Comes welcoming over the scree:
Come home mountain friends to your rest on the pass,
Come back mountain climber to me."
                                        —The Gorphwysfa Song

Gorphwysfa means a resting place and Gorphwysfa Peris is the resting place at the head of the rugged glaciated valley of Llanberis in Snowdonia. There at the Gorphwysfa Inn during the early part of the century, Winthrop Young, Mallory and many other mountain men used to meet to share hill days and to pioneer rock climbs on the crags of North Wales. The 'Inn' has now become a Youth Hostel and is also the 'home' of the present day Gorphwysfa Climbing Club.

During an evening when Eileen and I were guests at the annual dinner of the club, several members expressed a quaint desire to ascend Trisul using similar equipment to that used by Dr. Tom Longstaff on his ascent of that mountain in 1907! This laudable ambition was not fulfilled, because the Japanese had already been given permission to climb the mountain. In addition whilst the expedition was being organised, everyone's ideas changed rapidly towards using modern gear such as plastic boots, Jumar clamps, ice-screws, C.B. radios, and a thousand feet of fixed rope! Eileen and I were impressed by this remarkable evidence of flexibility and having been invited to join the Gorphwysfa team felt assured that we were going to the mountains with the right kind of people. A little later I was asked to be the leader of the venture.

Most of the members came from the Oxford area (Jim Murray, a Professor of Zoology came from Charlottesville, Virginia) and were either doctors, solicitors, professors, or senior lecturers of one kind or another. They proved to be a fine bunch of boffins to be with, good companions, splendid mountain people and their youthful enthusiasm (most were aged between 40 and 50, though two were but 24 years old) was very refreshing. During preparations, we met several times in Snowdonia and trained with my staff at the National Centre for Wales, Plas Menai.

We eventually flew from Heathrow early in September. During the flight to Delhi, I reflected on it being thirty years since my last visit to Garhwal, remembering that whilst climbing and exploring north and west of Badrinath, I had been swept down by an avalanche. Though it wasn't realised at the time, I fractured my left femur. It knitted together and self healed so that the fracture was only discovered 17 years later. Eventually this resulted in me having a painful arthritic hip and a shorter left leg. Surgeons gave me a new hip. It was akin to being reborn.

"Yes" I thought "now I have a new and artificial hip, the mountains might take me back in more kindly fashion." They did.

The Moment of Truth

We began the trek into the mountains from the small village of Suraithota and six days later set up the base camp at 15,500 feet in the Trisul gad. All the way I was aware of following the footsteps of many famous mountaineer explorers other than Shipton and Tilman. W.W. Graham who had first had a look into the Rishi Ganga in 1883, then later the well-known Everesters, Bruce, Somervell and Ruttledge, but it was the doyen of them all, Dr. Tom Longstaff, that I thought of the most. His description of the area and of his penetration up the Rishi Ganga related in the book *This My Voyage* is excellent, but it was my memory of poring over the map of the area with him at his cottage near Achilibuie that was freshest in my mind. With Eileen and our two sons I had camped several times on a green stretch of 'machair' below his cottage and we always paid him a visit. Knowing him I am sure he would have appreciated a woman's thoughts of the journey to the Trisul gad and because Eileen wrote a short piece called the 'Moment of Truth' for a W.I. magazine, here they are:

"Well here's the moment of truth" I thought. "From here on you are on your own two feet. The two and a half days hair-raising drive from Delhi to Rishikesh and on to Joshimath was behind us. Following a restless night at Suraithota, my day sack was packed and the trail up to Tolma, our next campsite was before me. As Stella Barczak (one of our two doctors) and I set off together, there was still a lot of activity around the schoolhouse in the village and John Rowlinson (J.R.), our Professor of Chemistry who John had asked to be his deputy leader, was weighing the last of the porter loads. The track led up by fields of millet and buckwheat, through sunny glades of *Deodar* and *Chir* trees with wild orchids and false strawberries underfoot. Then we reached our stopping place for lunch and surprise, this turned out to be Tolma and the end of our walking for the day.

Tents were being pitched whilst Habib Cheta, our Kashmiri cook and Sharma his assistant were preparing a meal. In the evening we were invited to a 'harvest festival' at one of the houses in Tolma. At the religious ceremony or *puja* the family altar had been decorated with fruit and evergreens, and with the many candles burning all around, it was similar to a Christmas crib back home in Britain. We found out that during the festival week, their holy book had to be read from beginning to end and this was the evening of the final reading. It was very much a family ceremony and everyone was there including the little children. At the end of each chapter reading, there was ringing of a bell and a blowing of a conch shell. A twist of blue-grey smoke curled out of a waved pot and a nose tickling smell of incense pervaded the room. One small boy was being allowed to blow the conch shell for his first time but unfortunately when his big moment came, he was so excited, he couldn't raise the 'puff' and no sound came out. His big sister hastily snatched it away, blew a great blast and family honour was saved.

Goats and goatmen were sleeping across the track as in the dark we walked back to camp, a short yet potentially ankle-breaking journey but a memorable end to a very satisfying first day.

The following day's walk proved to be steep and tiring and was made the longer when with Brian Smith, I went down the far side of a ridge instead of along it. Eventually we reached the campsite

—a place ever since referred to as 'dry camp'—because the only nearby source of water had dried up. John went to much trouble unsuccessfully to find a spring of water and then, having sent porters to search in all directions, a sufficient amount was brought back for everybody. All had a cup of tea that evening, plus another one in the morning and a half flask of water for the journey over the Dharansi pass the next day. The night was cold and early on we were all glad to be on our way and over the pass at 14,000 feet. For me, it was the hardest day, with the added hindrance of feeling slightly sick, but Paul Barczak (our other doctor) and Mike Leask chivvied me along. Once over the pass there was a welcome stop for drinks at a stream, then it was downhill all the way to Dibrugheta. On the walk, John had been pleased to find and photograph a variety of flora so late in the year—Edelweiss, Immortelle, Gentian, Mountain Aster and a decaying but recognisable Sausseria. Our sixty or so goats and sheep, each carrying a pack of twenty pounds, were strung out along the path and with the high mountains as a backcloth, they made a fine sight.

When resting below the Dharansi, Jim Murray pointed out a Lammergeir that soared high above the pass and nearby, several furry Mousehares, or Tiakpa as John calls them, were scurrying in and out among the rocks. Just before reaching camp, we had an exciting few moments crossing the rushing river on a single slanting pine log, then there was a welcome brew of tea made for us by a small party of Calcutta mountaineers who were on their way out of the mountains, having been climbing in the sanctuary area.

The narrow path winding along the steep flanks of the mountains high above the Rishi Ganga gorge made our journey to Deodi the next day the most spectacular of the whole walk to base. Nanda Devi, a streamer of cloud blowing from its summit gave us a breath-taking first viewing and the dark cut of the Rishi gorge provided a mysterious lead into the 'Sanctuary of the Goddess'. Before reaching the Deodi campsite, we had to cross a rather rickety and dangerous-looking bridge over the Rishi and Mike Leask who was taking cine, decided it was photographically ideal. Though we had crossed the bridge, he made us go back so that

1. Afghanistan in winter (Chapter 2)

2. Khyber pass (Chapter 2)

3. Nichhang and Amarnath peaks (Chapter 6)

4. Afghanistan peaks above the Tangi-Gharu gorge, 1976 (Chapter 2)

5. Eileen Jackson on Valehead glacier, Thajiwas (Chapter 4)

6. Eileen Jackson at Nichinai. Thajiwas and Kolahoi peaks in the background (Chapter 4)

7. Kolahoi peak, 18,000 feet, Kashmir, 1987 (Chapter 7)

8. Ponyman, Sonamarg, Kashmir (Chapter 4)

9. On ascent of Kolahoi, 1987 (Chapter 7)

10. Leh palace, Leh, Ladakh (Chapter 7)

11. Lamayuru gompa, Ladakh, 1953 (Chapter 11)

12. Rock wall—Shillakang gorge
(Chapter 11)

13. Lingshot below rock walls
(Chapter 11)

14. Ladakh chortens (Chapter 9)

15. Singi peak and Singi la—Zanskar (Chapter 11)

16. Donkeys at 15,000 feet in Zanskar (Chapter 11)

17. Nuzig peaks from Nuzig la at 17,520 feet, Zanskar (Chapter 11)

18. Ladakhis playing polo (Leh stadium), Stok peaks of Zanskar (Chapter 9)

he could film us once more but the first attempt wasn't good enough, and we had to go back over it again and again, in my opinion shortening the odds against us alarmingly!

The campsite at Deodi was a clearing among the trees, a good situation, and at 4 p.m. tea-break, John got all the expedition together to brief us about our various responsibilities when we reached base camp and once we were climbing and camping at high altitudes. The day ended with us and our porters all crowding round a huge campfire where we sang and danced well into the evening.

To reach Bethartoli camp (Longstaff's Juniper Camp of 1907) we took the path up the Rishi Ganga towards Ramani, then turned off towards the Trisul gad. I was feeling fitter now and the whole party except for Mike who had a bad cold, seemed in good form. At the campsite, it was evident that most of the Juniper that had once grown in profusion had been cut down for firewood by goat herders and previous expeditions.

A few Musk Deer scampered away out of sight when we arrived and towards evening we had a few warning flakes of snow. On our last day's walk, Mike and I toiled up and over the gigantic side moraine and as the Devistan peaks loomed nearer and nearer, we knew that base camp could not be far away. Even so, it was quite a surprise when the flagged cairn marking base camp came into view. Within minutes the goats and sheep arrived, followed closely by the porters and quickly the tents were erected. Habib and Sharma arranged their kitchen, got a fire going and before long we were all sitting on the moraine and tucking into a good meal.

Early in the expedition our main meal of the day was chicken. These chickens were carried in crates, and they didn't look very happy. Eventually the poor things disappeared one by one, so we started on mutton, and during the next few weeks we ate our way through three sheep, though what actually happened to the meat on them, I was never quite sure. Mostly, our helpings seemed to be short lengths of bone and gristle with a small collar of meat round the middle. But then, after a tough walk in for six days, perhaps there wasn't much meat on the poor beasts to start with.

Before the end of the expedition, we ran out of fresh meat but we did manage to have an egg for breakfast right up to the last day. *Dal* (boiled lentils), rice and *chapatties* became our staple diet, reinforced with a tin of meat now and again. To some, the meals became rather monotonous but because I hadn't much appetite at altitude, I must admit I wasn't the best judge.

Before leaving Britain, I had been asked to put together about 10 Pounds of food suitable for the higher camps. This I did by buying tubes of cheese, packets of nuts and raisins, packet meals, Cupa soups, orange crystals, Kendal Mint Cake and so on. These items were a great success and in future I would take a lot more and certainly use them on treks. It would be money well spent.

I shall always cherish many happy memories of base camp throughout the expedition, and certainly the splendid companionship we had, plus the many gatherings in the big yellow tent which we christened the 'Club house'. When the weather was bad we had many games of cards there, and long conversations with Ajay Thanka, our liaison officer, about life and times in India. Later we had cheese and coffee 'parties'; made possible by presents from a departing Italian expedition—what a treat to have real coffee—and never again will Parmesan cheese be just something you sprinkle on spaghetti. On a lighter note who could ever forget 'Speedy J.R.'s disreputable sunhat around camp or Jeremy Naish's immaculate tent, or Mike Leask consuming five, or was it six, *chapatties* at breakfast every morning. Then there was Stephen Simpson's affection for goats, as well as his constant letter writing to his wife and children, or Ram Prasad's ever cheerful smile below his tea-towel turban, and Git Singh's run down the moraine to the mess tent with the teapot and his greeting of "Chai Sahib". Finally, there was that last night at base camp when the late sun put a blush on the summit of Devistan and whilst we stood around the campfire, a thoughtful Jim Murray produced an unexpected but magic bottle of 'Virginia Gentleman' whisky for a final toast."

By giving you some of Eileen's thoughts on the expedition, I have jumped ahead of the story which is really about the intention we had of climbing two peaks, Mrigthuni 22,490 feet and

Devistan South 21,810 feet. We didn't in the end climb either of them, but did make the ascent of a third, and also achieved other worthwhile aims. Here is how it all worked out.

Diplomatic Relations

Once base camp was organised we wasted no time but set up a Camp I on the prow of a moraine below Mrigthuni 22,490 feet and Devistan South 21,810 feet. From this camp, Brian and Mike reconnoitered to almost 19,000 feet on the north-west ridge of Devistan and during a two day reconnaissance in misty cold weather, Jim and Stephen worked out a possible route towards a Camp II on the glacier of Mrigthuni. By this time a party of twelve mountaineers, members of an Italian expedition had arrived at Trisul base, and to our dismay they also were to attempt the ascent of the north-west ridge of Devistan South. Some sensible discussion between our two expeditions was immediately essential and along with 'J.R.' and Ajay, I visited the Italian Camp. We finally agreed the following:

1) It was agreed by all that unfortunately the Indian Mountaineering Foundation, through circumstances that could not have been foreseen, had given permission for the two expeditions to attempt the same peak, by the same route, at the same time.

2) All appreciated that the Gorphwysfa Expedition had already established a Camp I that allowed of a two-pronged approach to the two mountains.

   a) to the north-west ridge of Devistan South, and

   b) to Mrigthuni

As our expedition was already on the two mountains, it was not realistic to retreat, however,

3) We agreed on behalf of the rest of the Gorphwysfa team that we would concentrate our efforts on Mrigthuni, allowing the Italians, because they only had permission for the one mountain, a clear run at Devistan.

From thereon, both parties operated amicably and throughout it all our liaison officers did a fine job.

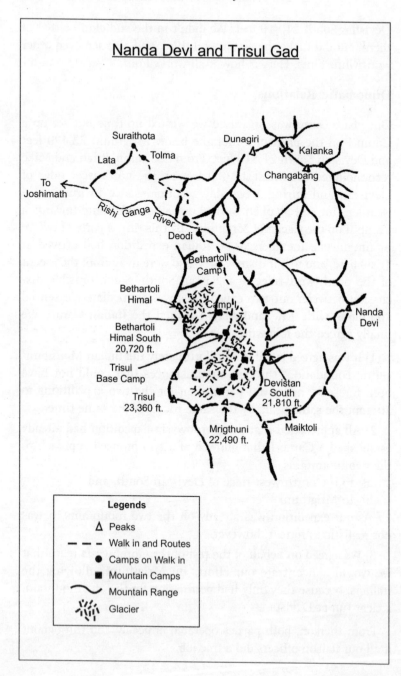

Nanda Devi and Trisul Gad

Attempt on Mrigthuni—High Hopes and Storm

By 20th September, J.R., Stephen and I with the help of Noti and
Govind Singh finally established Camp II at 18,700 feet on
Mrigthuni. Early morning clouds had quickly dispersed so that
soon the whole face of the mountain became clear and east of
Mrigthuni we could see the pass between Devistan South and
Maiktoli summits. I remembered the talks I used to have with
Wilfrid Noyce about Maiktoli when we were in Kashmir together.
In 1943 he had climbed one of the lesser summits and whilst
winding our way through the crevasses on Mrigthuni, I pondered
on the possibility of eventually crossing the pass to see Maiktoli
for myself. Quickly we erected two of our Limpet tents at Camp
II, then returned to join the others. There was no doubt that the
weather was improving and at all our camps the clear, crisp, starry
nights were being followed by days of brilliant clarity that gave
us imposing views of Trisul, the Devistan wall and of Dunagiri
at the end of the valley. Two days later, Brian and Mike with two
high altitude porters set up Camp III at 20,500 feet and mean-
while the rest of us carried supplies to Camp II. Eileen, lips
smeared liberally with 'Labisan' looked like a refugee from a
minstrel show but thoroughly enjoyed her carry to 18,700 feet
and apart from her usual loss of appetite at heights over 15,000
feet was clearly doing well. Around this time the logistics of ascent
were becoming complicated. I had written schedules for use of
tentage and for movements among the team to ensure that by
the 24th of September, three weeks exactly from leaving Heathrow
Airport, I could have some expedition members reaching the
summit. It being the first time to the Himalaya for most, it was
my dearest wish to put all the climbing members on top within
twenty-three days. We all had high hopes and on the 23rd, my
first summit party of 'J.R.', Stephen and Govind Singh were settled
in at Camp III.

"How are you all up there," I asked on the C.B. radio.

"We're fine and the weather is good. The deep snow makes it
heavy going but we will reach the top tomorrow" John's confident
prediction ended with a brief description of the panorama which

took in Changabang, Kalanka, Dunagiri and the nearby massive summits of Nanda Devi.

"Best of luck for tomorrow then. Have a good mountain day".

Switching off, I knew that to reach the summit would be a moment they would never forget. Once again, the night was clear and cold and before turning in to our Meade tent at Camp I, I took an early evening photograph of Trisul. It was one of those iridescent pale gold sunsets and all seemed set for a successful ascent the next day.

During the night, I woke to hear the flapping of canvas and the rustle of snow flakes on the tent fabric. Much new snow had fallen by the dawn and we all knew that at Camp III with the strong wind, the conditions would be much worse and rapidly deteriorating. Our planned early radio contact was unsuccessful and though I made a call each half hour thereafter, there was no reply. The silence seemed ominous and I could imagine the snow packing and piling up dangerously on the slopes above and below Camp III. With no radio contact forthcoming, I felt real concern and considered the following possibilities and alternatives.

1) The summit party was O.K. and on the way down to Camp I but because of conditions and the pressures of the moment were not bothering to make radio contact. This omission would be surprising and most unlike 'J.R.' but nevertheless a decision he could be having to make.

2) The party was down safely to Camp II and staying there but not bothering to make radio contact. This would be so irresponsible I could not believe it to be possible.

3) The party was staying at Camp III. I felt that no one would try to sit out the storm with the small amount of high altitude rations available. If however, they were still at Camp III then it could be that conditions would not allow them to move. If this was so, their plight would be becoming more dangerous every hour. However, this seemed not to be a likely situation because of the lack of radio contact.

4) Finally, I had to consider that the party had left Camp III to descend, without making radio contact and had been involved in some disaster on the route.

I rejected alternative 2 as being unlikely in the extreme, and felt that 3 though possible was much less likely than 4. On the whole I favoured the first alternative but nevertheless knew that by 1 p.m. I must send out a first search party and that because of the possibilities in alternatives 3 and 4 the party must be made up of those who knew the route above Camp II. It had to be Mike and Brian with their two high altitude porters. I watched them leave with trepidation but treated the moment with as much lightheartedness as possible, for I wondered what Stella (J.R's daughter) might be thinking at that time.

I may have seemed callous by showing a lighthearted attitude, but really it was a tense situation and became more so when we saw one lone figure descending towards our rockpoint marker on the glacier. Where were the others? What could have happened to them? Brian moved up quickly to the staggering figure, then there was much gesticulation and Brian shouted to Mike "All is O.K. The others are on their way down." Mike radioed the message back to our waiting group at Camp I and there was massive relief all round. This setback was a bitter blow, but John and Stephen's report of conditions, and the continuing poor weather left me in no doubt that we should immediately return to base camp and there eat better, sleep warmer, save fuel, conserve our meagre high altitude rations, and ride out the storm.

Skis on Trisul and the "Pass of the Goat"

The storms continued for one more week during which time a lot of snow fell in high wind, forming slab avalanches. It was a trying period for everybody but one we didn't waste. We had previously planned to attempt two things in addition to the climbing. The first was to seek out a rumoured goat-herders route to the inner sanctuary of Nanda Devi. Govind Singh had told us on the trek that such a route had been found and used by men from his village. The second was for Eileen and me, along with others who were interested to set up a ski camp on Trisul. First of all we had to obtain permission to ski on the lower slopes, from the Japanese, who were attempting the ascent of the mountain on ski. Like us, they also had been stopped by the storm but already they had set up camps to over 20,000 feet. They gave us the permission and with some excitement Eileen and I remembered ski days we had shared with the Indo-Tibet Border Police in Kullu several years before. Two of our companions at that time were the first to make a ski ascent of Trisul, and loud and long were the songs of praise that had been sung for Dorje and Lill Bahadur.

With the help of Jeremy, John and Brian we placed a ski camp at 18,500 feet on the mountain and two days later, following further falls of snow, we occupied the camp for two days. During these two days Eileen gave Paul and Stella Barczak, our two doctors, their first ski lessons at 18,700 feet. This must be quite a record height for a first ski lesson and beats by several hundred feet the height at which we gave Sirdar Dawa Tenzing his first ski lessons in the Everest area during 1976.

Whilst Eileen was busy teaching, I made a strenuous ascent on ski over virgin convex slopes, to the Japanese Camp at around 19,600 feet. Two of the Japanese team were there, and to my surprise I found that Ajay Thanka, our Indian Liaison Officer, had also cramponed up the lower flanks using the Japanese route. Following the previous days of storm and high winds, we enjoyed the warmth of the sun, the calm, and most of all the clarity of the atmosphere. Changabang, Kalanka and Dunagiri beyond the Trisul gad seemed but a stone's throw away and the twin peaks of the Goddess Nanda rose majestically above the sanctuary wall. At last all seemed right with the world.

The Japanese skiers left for their Camp II and Ajay began the descent back to the ski camp. Reluctant to go down, I followed the Japanese ski trail for some way, reaching a height of 20,000 feet thereby achieving an ambition I had had for many years. It was also a good vantage point for looking at the slopes of Mrigthuni. A disturbing factor was that I could see that numerous slab avalanches had poured down the face of the mountain and over our route of ascent. Slab had also demolished, and apparently buried our tents, which were no longer visible at Camp III. Snow falls in high wind invariably means slab and the decision to pull everybody off the mountain seemed justified.

Finally, I turned away to return to my companions. Descent over the convex slopes was made on long gliding traverses because of areas of breaking crust—the leg-breaking kind—and remembering what had happened in Garhwal thirty years before, I took my time. This ski experience was a particularly satisfying and carefree break, though all too short, and I remember it for reasons other than that it was the coldest camp in which I have ever slept. Stella, Paul and Eileen also skied and in addition provided welcome sustenance and cheer. Mike remained his usual happy and imperturbable self whilst quietly filming our moments on ski, and Ajay Thanka was as always huge and friendly and enjoying being amongst his mountains.

All of us from ski camp returned to base to find that Jeremy and Brian had successfully found the goat route, then ascended to a pass at over 18,000 feet. The pass proved to be a natural break in the sanctuary wall and from it they could see the descent was relatively easy into the inner sanctuary of Nanda Devi. Their's had been a 'tour de force' by making the ascent and return all in one day.

Though it does demonstrate the extreme feasibility of the pass which we named 'Bwlchy Geifr'; (Pass of the Goats) we have to hope it will not be used in the future as an alternative to the more difficult entrance to the 'Sanctuary' via the Rishi Ganga gorge. The sensitive environment could suffer badly from an increase in the number of travellers going there, or from a disastrous influx of goat-herders with their goats.

By now the weather was improving, but perhaps because of the instability caused by the depths of new snow, the hanging glaciers were constantly breaking off and the tumbling ice disintegrating to form powerful airborne powder avalanches. Ice cliffs on Devistan were becoming exceptionally precarious and the Italians decided to abandon their attempts on the north-west ridge and return home. You could almost feel their despair at having to retreat but clearly they appreciated the opportunity we had given them of a clear ascent route on the mountain. Before leaving, they wished us well, generously handed over parcels of Parmesan cheese, packets of roast ground coffee, and a broken, but usable coffee percolator. These things brought a small and welcome change in our diet, luxuries really, but a boost to our morale, a gift from hill people known only fleetingly yet friends we would remember.

Success on Bethartoli Himal South

On one day during the week of storms, Brian, Eileen and I, ascended the slopes rising to the west of base camp. It was snowing, visibility was poor, and there was little to see except at one point we found stone stripes and stone polygons, evidence of permafrost. I photographed them.

"It's good to be moving and not cramped inside a tent," said Eileen.

"Definitely," was Brian's response "and what exposure are you giving those polygons. John?"

"Oh—a hundred and twenty-fifth at F8—and soon we should be stopping for lunch". I was feeling hungry.

Each of us brushed snow off the rocks and sat munching our *chapatties* and egg; the clouds began to break open and for a short spell the weather was clear. Across the valley we could see the sanctuary wall and behind us when the clouds rose higher, a high white peak revealed itself looking promisingly accessible.

Brian was excited, "What do you think it is?"

"I don't know," was my reply "but it looks high. Around 21,000 feet. I should think and wouldn't it be good to have a crack at it?"

Our feeling of despondency because of the weather gave rise to hope and a more buoyant outlook on life. We descended back to camp in much happier mood and a quick examination of maps determined that our peak was most probably Bethartoli Himal South, a mountain 20,720 feet in height.

We decided that having given up our chance of climbing Devistan to the Italian expedition, we would be justified in taking the Bethartoli peak as a replacement. A reconnaissance was needed and whilst Jim and Jeremy made an abortive attempt in thigh deep and heavy snow to reach the site of Camp III on

Mrigthuni, Stephen and J.R. set up a Camp I on Bethartoli at 18,000 feet. Later, from this camp, they made the ascent. First, they traversed a snowdome, crossed a rock ridge, then descended to the Bethartoli glacier.

After the snowdome and the crossing of the ridge the progress across the glacier was slow and laborious for many hours, then the final seven or eight hundred feet was steep and crevassed, providing tiring cramponing for them on blue ice, but it took them to the summit. Success at last!

This the expedition members richly deserved, for all had put in much hard effort throughout the good weather and the bad. Returning from the summit, Stephen and John came right down to base and it was long dark before we saw them. For a time I waited alone some way down in the ablation valley below the camp. Many Mousehares (Ochotona) kept me company, but more exciting, for over thirty minutes, whilst I sat by a glacial erratic, I watched a flock of ten Bharal (Himalayan Blue Sheep), grazing quietly on the sparse grass. Eventually they trotted off from the grazing site, possibly disturbed by the voices and the flashing lights from the summiters coming down the mountain. A memorable day.

Avalanche Peak Again

Later, Brian and Mike made a second attempt to ascend Bethartoli, and early on the same day, Ajay and I left base camp to reach Camp I, then crossed the snowdome and the rock ridge to the glacier. Ahead of us, we watched the two tiny figures of Brian and Mike ascending to the col at 20,000 feet and having reached it, they disappeared from view so we turned away to photograph the surrounding peaks—Dunagiri, Changabang, Nanda Devi East and West and many others. These peaks and those of north-west Garhwal in the region of the Satopanth were breathtakingly crisp and clean following the many days of storm. It is so often the way. Picking out Avalanche Peak from the multitude of mountains, I remembered my vow of thirty years before, and was glad that I had finally attained its promise along with friends from the Gorphwysfa Club.

We turned away from the glacier and on descending the snow-dome found excellent stone polygons and stripes on the broad shoulder of the ridge, again evidence of sporadic permafrost. Small clumps of Wild Rhubarb were beginning to show between the stones, choughs 'chack chacked' overhead and at the head of Trisul gad, the two mountains that had been our original objectives, Devistan South and Mrigthuni stood out boldly and frustratingly clear. Our time in the Trisul gad was at an end but it was no use regretting missing those ascents, and Bethartoli Himal was a splendid alternative prize.

It was later during the walk out to Joshimath that the porter grapevine told us of the many accidents in the Garhwal Himalaya and this was confirmed when in Delhi we reported to the Indian Mountaineering Foundation. During our few weeks' stay in Garhwal, over twenty mountaineers and high altitude porters had lost their lives in the storms and subsequent avalanches—it had been by far the worst disaster year anyone could remember in that region.

From the rock ridge we returned to the lower camp then descended to base, feeling sure that quite deservedly, Mike and Brian would reach the summit but again the fates decided otherwise. Brian, the prize within his grasp became violently ill at around 20,150 feet and later in the afternoon both climbers arrived back at base. Theirs was a fine attempt and it was ironic that sickness had struck at just the wrong time.

Brief Reflection

Our last day at base camp was beautifully clear whilst we packed ready to leave, and Eileen's 'Moment of Truth' reminds me of the sunset on Devistan and of the similar rosy glow produced by drinking a dram of Jim's 'Virginia Gentleman'.

After the others had turned in and it being a clear moonlight night, I walked a little way up the ablation valley. Down below, the glacier gave a creak and a groan and no doubt because of this movement, there was a skittering and crashing of boulders tumbling down the steep moraine. Above me, a soft bleat and rustling of many bodies was a reminder that earlier, a flock of sheep had arrived, each animal to carry a load of 20 or so pounds on the way out to Joshimath. The mountains, gripped in intense cold still showed and I reflected that ours had been but a fleeting moment in their history. Once again, I questioned what it was that drew us to them.

Each person must have his or her own unique reason, each their own difference of appreciation and secret urge. For me, there had always been the attraction of the environment, the pull of the wild and the unknown, as well as the satisfaction of understanding what becomes friendly and familiar. The mountains of south-east Garhwal had been kind to me. It was good to have led a moderately successful team and both Eileen and I had filled our days with worthwhile experiences in the company of splendid companions. Turning back to the tents, I remembered the lines written by Geoffrey Winthrop Young—possibly at the Gorphwysfa Inn at the head of Llanberis.

"I may not grudge the little left undone,
I hold the heights, I keep the dreams I won"

I hoped the rest of the expedition members would feel that 'we' could fittingly be substituted for 'I' in the quotation.

Return and Final Thoughts

We descended the Rishi and returned to Joshimath in mixed weather conditions of sun and snow. At the Dharansi pass, Lammergeir and Mountain Choughs circled hopefully for food and once again the Mousehares scurried amongst the rocks as this time we descended the ridge to Lata Kharak and the mountain village of Lata.

On the way up to Dharansi, we frequently looked back to the peaks of Nanda Devi enclosed within the 'Sanctuary'. It was mountaineers who first gave it that name and when eventually Shipton and Tilman found the way into it, they found it to be an area of lush grazing where wild life lived free from the depredations of man.

Bharal, Musk Deer, Snow Leopard, Goral and other spectacular animals, plus a wide variety of bird life had lived there unmolested for centuries but during the last two decades, expeditions plus goat-herders and poachers have played havoc with the fragile ecosystem. In 1978 all trekking as such was stopped and despite the fact that the area was eventually designated a National Park, the supervision and efforts at conservation did not prove adequate to reverse the trend of environmental despoilation.

Finally in the 1980s the Indian Government closed down all access to the Sanctuary, the Rishi Ganga and the Trisul gad not only to treks but to everyone—expeditions and goat-herders alike. This was for an unspecified period and we have to hope that before the area is reopened, a detailed and carefully worked out plan of supervision and control is established to ensure that conservation of this wilderness area is assured. It would be sad if treks and expeditions were not allowed there again, particularly as the worst offenders are the goat-herders and poachers. But rightly, unless the standards and quality of treks and expeditions improve, it may be decided that man in any numbers should not get there again.

This does not mean that trekking would be finished in Garhwal —far from it. Areas to the north and west are still open. 'Pilgrimage' or *yatra* treks to the Gangotri, Badrinath and Kedarnath are still possible and these are reached via Hardwar and Rishikesh. Other areas such as the Pindari glacier and Rup Kund are even more readily accessible from Karanprayag or via splendid trekking country north of Nainital and Ranikhet. This country takes you right up to the outer rim of those great mountains we climbed and skied on in the 'outer sanctuary' of Nanda Devi.

17

Everest and the Elusive Snowman
(1954)

In November 1994, a report came out of China of a sighting that had been made of three large humanoids in a remote region of the Shennongjia National Forest Park in Hubei Province.

The original report appears to have been made by a group of ten Chinese tourists, all of them engineers and well educated. They described how, whilst driving down a steep mountain road they saw at a distance of 30 yards, three figures, tall, hairy and ape-like in appearance. When the engineers approached the creatures, they fled into the dense forest nearby, demonstrating great speed and strength.

Chinese scientists hailed the sighting as a major discovery and subsequently a number of research teams revisited the area collecting samples of hair and faeces, as well as measuring the size of the footprints. It is said that analysis showed the findings to have come from a long-haired, big-footed herbivorous animal.

An expedition which included some twenty scientists revisited the area of Shennongjia forest in 1995 but their findings were inconclusive.

The report reminded me that I first heard of a sighting of a 'snowman' at first hand over 50 years ago whilst climbing in the

Kashmir Himalaya. Later in 1954, I became a member of a major expedition searching for the creature in the Everest area and subsequently I have returned many times. Having kept up to date with the various stories and sightings of this elusive creature, I feel it is of interest to write of them and to remember also some of the incidents on the big search over forty years ago.

In 1921 when Colonel Howard Bury, leader of the Everest Reconnaissance, along with Mallory and Bullock found footprints on the Lhakpa la, their porters told them that they were the tracks of the Meteh-Kangmi. The name "Abominable Snowman" came into use when a 'Times' journalist, Henry Newman, gave it as the translation of the name Meteh-Kangmi as sent back by Colonel Howard Bury in his account of the expedition's experience on the pass. Meh-Teh is the name used in Sola Khumbu, and Yeh-Teh (Yeti) is the mutation of that name. Newman's colourful translation of Meteh-Kangmi created a lot of interest in the daily press, and this interest was renewed in 1953 following the climbing of Everest. The head lama of Thyangboche gompa gave the expedition an interesting account of a sighting near the monastery. In addition, Ralph Izzard, a journalist with the 'Daily Mail', who had followed the fortunes of the expedition, had met with Tom Stobart, the Everest cinephotographer. Together they discussed the possibility of a search for the 'Abominable Snowman' and subsequently the 'Daily Mail' newspaper launched the expedition of which I was a member.

A Ceremonial Dance and a Symbolic Meh-Teh

Early in the expedition, we were invited to a ceremonial dance at Thyangboche gompa,* so armed with photographic equipment and a tape recorder we ascended the track to the monastery. Once inside the courtyard we noted the gompa bell, an oxygen cylinder from one of the pre-war Everest expeditions. Brought across from

---

*The gompa monastery has been rebuilt following a disasterous fire several years ago. Kapa Kalden who painted the original frescoes in the gompa died many years ago, but his son, who is also an artist has replaced most of the frescoes in recent years.

19. Zanskar peaks from Mulbek gompa, 1983 (Chapter 10)

20. Eileen and Bhagat Singh on Rhotang pass—Kullu/Lahaul (Chapter 13)

21. A shepherd from Kullu Himalaya (Chapter 12)

22. Rataban, Dunagiri and Nanda Devi peaks from summit of Avalanche peak (Chapter 16)

23. Kedarnath and Gaumukh peak from Avalanche peak (Chapter 16)

24. Kamet and Mana peaks above sea of clouds—from Avalanche peak (Chapter 16)

25. Ajay Thanka—Nanda Devi peaks and the Sanctuary wall (Chapter 16)

26. Changabang (Shining Mountain) and Kalanka from Bethartoli (Chapter 16)

27. Guanara peaks from summit of Kang Cho Shar (Chapter 28)

28. Symbolic Yeti mural at Thyangboche gompa (Chapter 17)

29. Sherpa wedding at Khumjung, 1954 (Chapter 18)

30. Thyangboche gompa—trumpets, cymbals, drums (Chapter 17)

31. Ice world, Everest base camp, 1954 (Chapter 17)

32. Thamserku and Kantega from Gaumukhtse, 1976 (Chapter 22)

33. Yeti scalp and hand, Everest, 1954 (Chapter 17)

34. Eileen Jackson on ski at 18,650 feet. Everest, Lhotse and Nuptse from Chola khola (Chapter 21)

the north side of the mountain it now hung suspended from the roof by an open window. From the same window I could see the glaciated basin of Thamserku and above the basin, the steep flanks of the mountain glistened with bare blue ice. The sheer size and savagery of the glacier-eroded landscape held my attention, then the moment of contemplation was shattered by the clashing of many cymbals. Turning at the sound, I saw that several monks led by the head lama had entered the gompa yard. They clashed gongs, beat drums, and blew long silver trumpets, then the monks on the verandah started chanting. From the monastery doorway four figures dressed in brightly-coloured clothing swirled and danced down the stone steps into the sun. Their faces were covered by masks of many colours, grotesque masks, with solid bulging eyes, and foreheads rimmed by a crescent of small grinning skulls. The only way the dancers could see, was through the open nostrils that pointed to the ground. Two long trumpets (Saung Daungs) similar in size to the alpen horns of Switzerland, boomed sonorously, and as the dancers paused, a lama masquerading as Shingje—Lord of the Dead, pirouetted slowly into their midst. His slow revolving speeded up, then all the dancers followed his example. The Saung Daungs boomed louder and more frequently, the silver trumpets (Gyalings) screamed falsetto, and the gompa yard became a whirl of spinning, twisting, stamping figures, with silken robes swirling high and wildly, dazzling our eyes with riotous colour. The ceremonial dancing continued for over an hour, gradually loosing vigour and life. Perhaps it was too hot even at 13,000 feet.

Later we ate lunch inside the main room of the gompa, then slipped away to examine the masks (*gumbu*) of fierce aspect, and the many Buddhas set back in tiny alcoves. All the Buddhas were clothed to keep them warm for it is thought that they possess a life of their own. Carefully the monks undressed them to show them to us, then equally carefully re-clothed them, before replacement in the alcoves. One lama proudly showed us a religious book from one of the many pigeonholes at one side of the room, and demonstrated that each of the leaves were separate, and made of a crude parchment-like paper on which the text had been block printed. The blocks are made of carefully carved wooden boards or sometimes even of chiselled stone. Cloth-bound boards covered the back and front of the book and the whole assemblage was tied together by a length of ribbon. The other walls of the room not covered by books, or by *Thankas* (printed scrolls) were patterned with strange geometrical designs or painted with lively figured frescoes. One of these frescoes created much interest because it depicted a symbolic Meh-Teh being chased by men on horseback. The creature's body was painted blue and had a repulsive green face topped by long green hair. A blue and red tongue protruded from its gaping mouth and snakes writhed about the neck and shoulders. None of us had heard of such a painting before but a few days later, Kapa Kalden, the lama from Kumjung who had painted the fresco, gave us a less symbolic painting of the Meh-Teh, also the Chu-Teh and the Dzu-Teh. From the paintings and by interrogation of the Sherpas, we got a clear impression that the Dzu-Teh is a bear, probably the Himalayan red bear (*Ursos arctus isabellinus*) that kills the Sherpa yak. The Meh-Teh was depicted as a smaller animal. The Chu-Teh was the smallest— seemingly a gibbon-like creature said to live in Tibet. Or is it a langur monkey? All of us I know hoped we might see a Meh-Teh but not for long, if it was anything like the painting on the gompa wall.

Pangboche and a Scalp

Another monastery we were particularly keen to visit was the one in upper Pangboche. This was because of the interesting item of news that hit the headlines after the climbing of Everest in 1953. Several team members had visited Pangboche gompa and seen the 'Yeh-Teh' scalp. This had already been examined by Charles Evans the previous year at which time he had managed to extract a few hairs from the crest. On arriving home in Britain, he sent the hairs along with a few questions to Scotland Yard. Several days later, so the story goes, he received a solemn reply saying, "Sorry, we don't know this man at all!"

Our initial setback was to discover that the gompa monks had carefully wrapped the scalp with cloth, then sealed the ties with wax. Not at any price could they reveal the scalp we were told, but from then on a five rupee note proved sufficient to make them break the seal. A most excellent way of obtaining gompa funds! The same ploy still holds good today, except the price has risen tenfold. The scalp covered with reddish-brown hair, blue tinges at the roots and with a prominent bristly crest running from front to back, resembled nothing I had ever seen before. Small hair pits were clearly visible in the bare areas and Dr. Biswas, the zoologist of our party, examined it closely. He was adamant that there were no signs of stitching or other connections and that the scalp was entire. Dr. Stoner, our anthropologist, ascertained that the scalp had been in the possession of the monastery for some 250 years, and the one strange statement made was that an 'original' could be seen at the Rongbuk monastery on the north side of Everest. This statement plus the thick skin and prominent crest made Tom Stobart and I wonder if the Pangboche scalp was an artifact made possibly from the hide of a wild boar. Altogether three such scalps were found at different monasteries in Khumbu—one of them at Kumjung.

It was the Pangboche scalp that Sir Edmund Hillary, on the payment of a large sum of money, managed to 'borrow' for three months during 1960. In New Zealand, America and Europe many scientists examined the scalp including Dr. Bernard Heuvelmans, the Belgium mammologist, who pronounced that it was made from the skin of a Serow—a chamois type goat that inhabits the Himalaya.

Later, two zoologists named Swan and Parkins from the Californian expedition of 1960 obtained the hide of a Serow, stretched it over a wooden proforma the shape of the 'Yeti' scalps and produced an artifact similar to the scalp we examined at Pangboche. For many, it may seem that the puzzle of the scalps has been solved, but I always remember the statement about the 'original' being at Rongbuk gompa, and think it would be best to see that one, if it still exists, following the destruction of the gompa by the Chinese. Whatever may be decided, we can be sure that the Sherpa did not make the scalps to fool or misguide, for

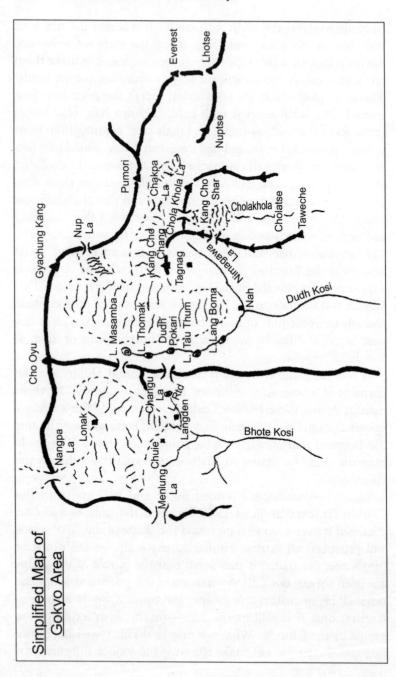

Simplified Map of Gokyo Area

until 1950 no Europeans or Americans had been to Sola Khumbu and we were the first people to seek the 'Snowman' in their country. Why then do the scalps exist at the monasteries? Though having no religious significance they have for a long time been used at ceremonial dances (such as the Mani-Rimdu) at various times of the year. All that can be ascertained is that those who wear the scalps at the dances represent some animal of significance to these people. The age of the scalps suggests the possibility of the animal, whatever it may be, having become extinct, perhaps within living memory. When one is on the spot and faced with a scalp, as well as having knowledge of the numerous stories and sightings by the people of the Himalaya, anyone would be loathe to give a definite opinion either way about the 'Snowman'.

Sightings, Sadhus and Superstitions

Charles Stonor, the anthropologist on the Snowman expedition, met many people in Khumbu who professed to have seen the Meh-Teh either walking on two legs, or bounding away on all four. One old man told him of how, when a child, he had been attacked by a Meh-Teh, and showed Stonor his badly-damaged hand. Mainly the descriptions suggested a shy animal seldom seen at close quarters but which could become extremely ferocious when annoyed. One of our Sherpas named Danu (in earlier years named 'Prometheus' Danu by Tilman because of his penchant for making huge fires) told a story of how a close friend (a cousin?) named Lakpa Tsering had been attacked by a Meh-Teh whilst crossing the Nangpa la. In his efforts to escape he had tripped, been severely mauled, and he had subsequently died of his wounds.

Stories of sightings of the Meh-Teh are not very common but one of the most famous was in 1925 by N.A. Tombazi, a member of the Alpine Club. Tombazi was exploring in the area of the Zemu Gap near Kangchenjunga, and in camp one morning he was called out by porters who shouted that a Meteh-Kangmi was at the side of the glacier. Tombazi described seeing a creature at 300 yards distance, walking upright and stopping occasionally to uproot vegetation among the moraine. The creature showed up dark against the snow and as far as he could make out wore no clothes. He eventually lost sight of it as it moved into the scrub. The footprints he later found at the bushes were similar in shape to those of a man, and some six or seven inches long by four inches wide. Five toe marks were visible and he thought the prints had been made by a biped. My own feelings about this sighting is that he did see a biped, most probably a man—perhaps a fakir or holy man. Such people do frequent remote areas, and once in the Barun valley below Makalu, I remember finding a cave at 14,000 feet in which a naked Sadhu lived. Tombazi's sighting must have been at similar altitude, for there to be scrub and rhodo-dendron bushes by the side of the glacier.

Another sighting was made in 1970 by Don Whillans, whilst on the Annapurna expedition. At 13,000 feet, he photographed a trail of prints and from his tent later in the evening, watched an animal moving along a ridge. In his description, he says the animal resembled an ape or ape-like creature bounding along on all fours. Examination of the photograph taken by Whillans, shows the animal to have been moving in deep snow and my own feelings are that it was quadruped such as a snow leopard, a Tibetan snow wolf or more probably a mountain deer. There was also Tom Stobart's strange experience on the moraine at the base of Pumori and Kala Patthar.

Early one morning he sat watching for game beneath a boulder-studded ridge. He let his eyes travel along the ridge, stop for a moment at a reddish-brown boulder, then move on before he brought them back to the same spot. He was surprised to realise that the boulder had disappeared and when later he told the story, he assured everyone there was no doubt in his mind that he himself had never changed position. Examining the area he found no prints among the boulders and on the little evidence, he refused to claim that he had seen either a Meh-Teh or a red bear. Nothing more was seen in that area, and the question of what he saw was never solved.

Lord Hunt in his book *Ascent of Everest* tells of a meeting with the head lama of Thyangboche. This elderly gentleman told him of a visit by a Meh-Teh to the gompa grounds. Sometimes it moved on its hind legs and sometimes on all fours, eventually ambling off into the bush, after horns and conch shells had been blown to frighten it away. Everest team members had been fascinated by this story but clearly the success of the expedition was not affected by the telling of it. I say this because in an interview many years later, Lord Hunt pointed out that Sherpas are superstitious about the Meh-Teh and associate a sighting with impending disaster. His personal Sherpa and great friend, Pasang Dawa Lama told him of the deaths of two people following a sighting. The two were members of a German party in the region of the Zemu Gap near Kangchenjunga in north-east Nepal. With Eileen I remember similar superstitious feelings being evident following a sighting of some creature. We were guests in Changup's house in Khumjung and he along with Dawa Tenzing and Lakpa Thondup were talking with Urkien, Changup's daughter, who had just come down from the village of Langden in the Bhote Kosi (Urkien now runs the 'Snowland Hotel' at Periche which is on the main track for trekkers going to Everest base camp). She was telling them that the people living in Langden were very disturbed and frightened that they had seen a strange creature that could only be a Meh-Teh. Our hosts obviously thought the same, talked rather furtively in whispers and were very subdued. More recently, Reinhold Messner told of meeting a Meh-Teh at a range of twenty yards. The meeting was in 1986 but it certainly didn't end in disaster because towards the end of that year he came by our trek camp in Chukhung on his way to attempting an ascent of Lhotse Shar! Perhaps the most intriguing sighting in recent times is that by Tony Wooldridge. This was in the Garhwal Himalaya in a valley north of Joshimath. After following footprints, he came to an area of unstable snow where recently there had been an avalanche. On the far side of a snow-slide was a bush and beside it he tells of seeing a shape that was a dark hairy creature, perhaps two metres in height, and standing erect on two legs. A photograph he took at the time was from quite a long distance and an enlargement does seem to show an anthropoid type shape. Apparently Wooldridge could also see footprints leading out of the avalanche. It is unfortunate that he was not able to get nearer to the 'object' on the other side of the avalanche, to make a more positive identification of both the 'object' and the 'footprints'.

Two Professors pronounced differently on evidence produced by Wooldridge, one favouring the concept that it was most probably a Himalayan langur monkey but adding a proviso that there was a marginal possibility of it being a large-bodied primate as yet undocumented by zoologists. The second Professor, a noted anatomist and anthropologist concluded that the 'creature' in the photograph was an hominid allowing of a remote possibility that the figure was a 'Sadhu' (a Hindu holyman) caught in the avalanche. I have never seen langur monkeys above 10,000 feet for they live in areas of the bamboo, nevertheless, this primate is often put forward as being the answer to the riddle of the 'snowman' and if a langur is not suggested, then a sighting is said to be a wandering ascetic.

When we look for other clues it is perhaps the footprints that are of greatest interest. I saw my first ones on my way to the Everest base camp.

Everest and Footprints—Gorakhshep and Mouse-hares

From Pangboche we walked up the Imja khola until we branched off to the villages of Pheriche and Phalong Karpo. We camped there at the junction of the Khumbu and Chola khola valleys on the huge lateral moraine left behind by the retreating Everest glaciers. My companions were Biswas, a zoologist and 'Stan' Jeeves, a photographer. Early the next morning, we ascended to Lobuje yak-hut which had been the rest campsite for the Swiss and the British Everest teams in 1952 and 1953. Wilfrid Noyce, and Alfred Gregory had written to me from this yak-hut the previous year whilst on their way to the icefall, and I looked for evidence of their expedition, finding just one packet of orange crystals in a crack in the wall. Fresh snow had fallen earlier in the day and all around us we found the footprints of fox, Tibetan mouse-hare, snow leopard and the Himalayan snow-cock, a bird about the size of a pheasant. Quickly we erected a Meade tent, dumped our packs inside the yak-hut and then Stan and I continued to journey up the ablation valley again finding spoor, this time the prints of mountain deer and of wolf. Near the wolf prints we found other larger prints, some ten inches long and six inches wide. They seemed old, the outline softened by wind and sun. Possibly they had become enlarged because of this, but certainly they were the prints of some large animal and the tracks much larger than any of the others we had seen. We followed them for some eighty yards to the lateral moraine of Khumbu glacier where they disappeared among the stones and rubble. Two prints were particularly clear, toe marks were visible and there was a deeper depression at the heel. Later, on return to Lobuje, I wrote in my diary as follows:

"I think certain prints are not of cat, canine or deer family but from knowledge gained of animal life in Kashmir and Ladakh would say the prints are of a bear or some similar large animal".

It snowed for the next two days but on the third day, we set out for Gorakhshep and the Everest icefall.

Our progress seemed ungainly as we slid down slopes, hopped frenziedly over moraine and stumbled in the deep snow. Pumori and Nuptse on opposite sides of the valley, flanked the Khumbu basin and beyond these two rugged sentinels rose the ice-clad walls of Lingtren, Khumbutse, Changtse and the Lho la. These were the days before trekking groups and large expeditions to climb Everest, so we were alone in a strange world of frozen lakes, blue-green ice pinnacles and just the sigh of wind providing strange music to fit the mood of this cold land in the winter of the Himalaya.

The further along the valley we went the more puzzled we became at not seeing the Everest icefall. Where could it be? Did it really exist? We found the top of a biscuit tin, next a piece of cloth and then a button and it seemed as if we were following a paper chase that would lead us to the Base and eventually the icefall. Many hundreds of people have been to the icefall since that time and I have returned there with my wife Eileen on many occasions but I am sure that everybody has his or her vivid memory of the moment that they first see it. This is what I wrote of my first sighting and the memory is still just as strong as it was then. "A great tumble of ice blocks below the Lho la indicated the entrance to the Western Cwm and at last I was satisfied of its reality. Silly I know, but then even though you know it is there, you come upon it with such suddenness at the very last moment of believing in its existence.

It must be seen to be realised, this remote part of the earth, a strange place for a man to seek. It seems almost timeless for the never-ceasing erosive forces of the elements have changed the rocks but slowly. Yet how many minds turn upon it—this lonely spot visited by relatively few human beings; how often must vivid mind pictures conjure up the rough and tumble of ice at the foot of Everest? I was glad to be there. I knew that as long as I remained a sentient being, it was a memory I would treasure."

On leaving the icefall to return to Lobuje, we passed by the 1952 Swiss Base campsite at the lake bed of Gorakhshep. Some of the shelter-walls they had built for tents were still standing and small clumps of grasses grew between the stones. To our surprise several Tiakpa or Tibetan Mouse-hares were scuttering between the stones, and we finally caught one.* They are bonny furry creatures about the size of a guinea pig but perhaps quicker and more dainty in movement. Later we were to find more mouse-hares, some of them at well over 18,000 feet and throughout our stay in Khumbu, it was pleasing to discover that an abundance of mammals lived at high altitudes during the Himalayan winter. People often ask me if there is life at such heights, and this is clearly true. At varying heights from 16,000 to 18,006 feet, we were aware of fox, mink, weasel, mountain deer, wolf, snow leopard and mountain hare. Large birds such as snow cock, bar-headed geese and brahminy duck (Ruddy Shelduck) are also seen. The Sherpa takes his yak to graze at heights between 16,000 and 18,000 feet during the monsoon period, an annual transhumance, that is an important part of the Sherpas economy.

What is quite clear is that at those heights, there is a supply of vegetable fodder sufficient for animals even as large as a yak, and also that carnivores find a sufficiency of food among such animals as the deer, mountain hares, goat and the tiakpa. Several

---

*My Sherpa Ang Dawa caught the Tiakpa (Ochotona) and because it was a new species, it was named 'Ochotona angdawai' by Dr. Biswamoy Biswas.

times, we found large lumps of faeces and carefully disintegrated the material. In amongst the matrix were partly digested seeds of grasses, berries and the bones of many small mammals. Once we were able to reconstruct the skeleton of a mouse-hare, concluding that like the bear, the animal that voided the faeces, was an omnivore, but we remembered too that the 'snowman' was always said to be omnivorous.

After we had first been to the icefall and then caught the Tibetan Mouse-hare at Gorakhshep we eventually arrived back at Lobuje in the dark. It was very cold but by morning, snow was falling heavily. Any hopes of investigating the footprints we had found the previous day were at an end, and yet it is such spoor that have often been a reason for great excitement and a matter for conjecture.

More Footprints and Riddle Remains

Six of us had just ascended an old glacier moraine in the Chola khola. My Sherpa, Ang Dawa, was pointing excitedly to the ground and shouting 'Meh-Teh, Meh-Teh'. With care we all stepped forward to avoid disturbing the large footprints in the snow. They were close together and very large, but they were only close in one particular area. There we found the spoor of snow cock and realised that the animal making the large prints had been stalking the bird which must have got away. There were no feathers around and no signs of blood. Carefully we examined the prints and photographed them too. Three toe marks were visible but the rest of the front part of the foot was indistinct. Always there was a deeper depression at one side of the heel than the other—the same side as the toe marks. Measuring them for length and breadth we found them to be eleven inches by six inches. The snow was crisp and the tracks were crisp too, with no sign of wind change or sun melt round the edges, leading us to the conclusion that they had been made during the previous twenty-four hours. Certainly they were much larger than any bear prints I had ever seen in Kashmir and different in form to the prints of the cantankerous Himalayan black bear we had captured down at base camp near Thyangboche.

They did remind me of the prints photographed by Shipton and Ward on the Menlung la. The size and the shape were similar and the only thing missing was the big round toe of Shipton's photograph. At the time of our discovery of the footprints in the Chola khola, other expedition members were following footprints in an adjacent valley—the Upper Dudh Kosi. Ralph Izzard, a journalist with the *Daily Mail*, along with a big game hunter, Gerald Russell, had found tracks and followed them for over two days. Comparing notes later, we realised they were a little smaller than the ones we had seen, nine inches by five inches, and with a stride length of two feet three inches. They too had the same appearance as those photographed on the Menlung la with the exception of the round big toe. Izzard and Russell followed the prints up to 17,000 feet.

Similar prints were found by Rene Dittert, and Andre Roch in 1952 whilst they were with the Swiss Everest expedition. Again the tracks were found at high altitude, but were described as having a big toe separate to four other toes. Stride length was two feet four inches. Photographs of the prints found by the Swiss resemble the photographs of the prints we saw in the Chola Khola and I feel that in each case they were made by the same kind of animal. Dr. Wyss Dunant, leader of the Swiss Expedition thought the prints on the Swiss photographs had been made "by a bear or a relation of the bear". Comparing the photographs of the Chola khola prints with those of Shipton's on the Menlung la, I find a large degree of similarity except for the constant enigma of the large and very round big toe. It is as if a Sherpa had inadvertently dropped a prismatic compass, or a coffee container lid, for the toe shape is so perfectly round and the edges are so distinctly sharp. It would be interesting to see more than the one Menlung la print that is shown in all the illustrations, for this might lead to a valuable assessment of the 'big toe' enigma.

One suggestion that has been made by Professor John Napier in his book *Big Foot* is that the footprint is a double, that is, that two tracks of some animal have been superimposed. Professor Lawrence Swan suggested that the double track could be that of a snow leopard, but Napier, rightly in my opinion doubts that the relatively small pugmarks of the snow leopard could be responsible for producing such a large 'Yeti' print. I discussed the question of the 'snowman' prints with Swan in 1987 whilst in California and realised then that he was far from won over by his own suggestion. Having seen, and photographed the pugmarks of snow leopard myself, I really don't see that they could be responsible for producing the Shipton 'Footprint'. In every respect, other than the 'big toe', the Shipton photograph is like the photographs of the prints we found in the Chola khola.

There is no doubt that many large 'prints' attributed to 'snowman' have been made in very strange ways. Once in Kashmir, Wilfrid Noyce and I followed large prints across a glacier, becoming more and more puzzled as the indentations came closer together. Finally, we saw the solution to the puzzle—a boulder had tumbled down the steep mountain side and bounced across the glacier. The wind and the sun had finalised the shaping, enlarging the marks and softening the edges.

Another set of prints we found in the Chola valley were made in an odd way. Bill Edgar and I followed a set of prints that had been softened and spread out by melting. Later we found similar but newer tracks, and I took a photograph. It was whilst taking the picture that I realised how they were made. Below the glacier moraine where we found the prints there was a lot of tough grass —nardus. Some animal on the move during a heavy snowfall had, in placing its feet, bent the grass over. This had been quickly buried in the snowfall before its elasticity had time to spring the grass upright again. A trace of the original print was visible and round the print, an area of weakness had been created. As the grass re-erected itself, it had pushed up an oval pattern of snow around the original print. In some places the grass had pushed its way through altogether, the sun melting the snow quickly and leaving a clear patch of ground around it. The effect of this was to give the appearance of a large toeless creature walking in the snow. This is a variation of the "elephant effect" described by Eric Shipton, Norman Hardie, and others. Any one who skis or travels in the mountains will have noticed that on occasions, when the surface of snow is frozen, a much larger section than that of the foot, falls inwards leaving a large saucer-like outline. Eventually, sun melt and wind effects produce a large hole or "elephant print". In his book *In Highest Nepal* Hardie, who was our Deputy Leader on the 1955 ascent of Kangchenjunga described such saucer-shaped depressions in the snow. "Their size was about that of a small elephant but I was not deceived by that aspect, well aware that when new snow falls on a deep footprint, a large circle round it collapses with the melting snow making a mark far bigger than the original foot". He concluded that the original prints had been made by a yak.

A number of people have concluded that this collapse of melting snow round an original print of a smaller animal is the answer to the riddle of the snowman tracks. Wolf, snow leopard, deer, goat, langur monkey, yak and other large mammals have all been proposed as the answer at various times. There are many ways in which large prints are made in the snow and I have described a few of them above.

I also feel that there are some large prints made by an animal which as yet have not been conclusively identified. Some of these for example are the large track photographs taken by Wyss Dunant near Everest, those taken by Lester Davies in the Kulti nala in Lahaul, and the Eric Shipton prints on the Menlung la, as well as those I photographed in the Chola khola. All are similar in appearance, size and stride length. The differences vary the most in interpretation.

After all of the above, it would seem unfair not to attempt to give some opinion of what I think may be a possible answer to the riddle of the 'snowman'. I have for years suggested the possibility that it is the Tibetan blue bear, though with some trepidation, for no less an authority than George Schaller does not even mention the animal in his book *Stones of Silence*. It is however mentioned by some writers, and in the book *The Himalaya*, edited by John Lall, the writer Ramjitsinh has this to say:

"The bear family is represented in the Himalaya by the brown and the Himalayan black bear. A third member, the Tibetan blue bear is so rare that practically nothing is known about it". He goes on to say that one was reported across the border in Tibet when he was camping on the Bhutan-Tibetan border in 1965.

Though the pelts of this animal have been known for a hundred and fifty years, there has never been a Tibetan blue bear in captivity. Pelts were first brought out of Sechuan in Northern China early in the last century, and since that time a number of game hunters have brought back pelts from the Himalaya, but not the animal.

Why should I think the answer might be the blue bear? Sherpas and other people of the Himalaya are very observant of their environment and its natural history, and this became increasingly clear to me when after the ascent of Kangchenjunga, Sirdar Dawa Tenzing, and Sherpa Changup came to Britain with us. At that time I was teaching in Redcar and they were both tremendously impressed by the sea and sandy shore. Shellfish, crabs, sea-anemones, jellyfish and a whole host of sea birds created their interest. Each time, I had to give them the name of each creature, which Dawa then wrote down in Sanskrit in his little book. Similarly, observations were made when they joined me with a school party in the Lake District. Because of their knowledge and keen observation of flora and fauna in the Himalayan environment, I feel that it must be a very rare animal indeed, and perhaps of unusual colouring, to which the Sherpa give the name, 'Meteh Kangmi', or 'Meh-Teh'—a 'frightening or startling animal of the snow'.

The Dzu-Teh or red bear is sufficiently well known to them to be ruled out, and any suggestion that the Meh-Teh is a langur monkey is received with incredulity by the Sherpa. I have never seen a langur monkey above a height of ten, or at the most, eleven thousand feet, and feel sure that is as high as they have ever been seen, though there is an account of a sighting of these animals at a height of 13,000 feet near the Kolahoi glacier in Kashmir. I have been often to Kolahoi, but have certainly never seen langurs there, and feel that it was a case of mistaken identity! It seems to me that the blue bear (*Ursos arctos pruinosus*) is rare enough, and unusual enough in colouring, to startle and surprise any inhabitant of the Himalaya seeing one for their first time. In a similar sort of way the white rhinoceros had a frightening, or startling impact on the inhabitants of Central Africa, and eventually the white rhino took on a religious significance in their minds. Is there any special reason that the symbolic Meh-Teh of Thyangboche gompa is painted blue? Is this another possible clue that the answer is a blue bear? Or is the colour just a product of Kapa Kalden's mind?

Certainly there are still many questions to be answered, and one of the strangest is the odd fact that on the old maps, the mountains of the Everest, Nuptse, Lhotse and Makalu massif are named the Mahalangur Himal—the mountains of the big apes!

A last thought. There are two passes at the head of the Chola khola and one of them the Nimagawa la* is where on the Yeti expedition we set up a climbing camp to ascend Kang Cho Shar— the "east snowsided peak". During our first evening at the pass I left my companions in their tents and sat down to enjoy the last moments of dusk. Sharp cracks and musical creaks emanated from the glacier to be followed by infinite stillness and silence. The Nimagawa and the huge valley of the Dudh Kosi was but a dim and hazy rift between me and the mountains on the far side. Somewhere there I thought, there must be many different animals on the move—hunting and hiding. Some of them might be the creatures that left large footprints in the Chola khola, and I found no difficulty imagining them in that rugged environment, seeking food and shelter. If they were, I felt sorry for them, for this could be their last retreat, and as with the cave bears of Europe during the ice age, the last phase of their existence. Quietly I stood up to return to the tents, and as if in agreement with my thoughts, there came a soft sigh on the wind out of the silence.

---

*This is also variously named Chola South, Chugima la or simply Chola la.

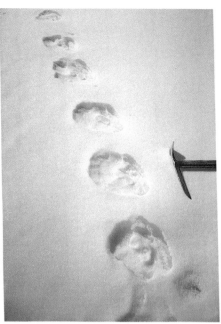

35. Sherpa house with prayer flags
(Chapter 19)

36. Yeti or Meh-Teh footprints,
Chola Khola (Chapter 17)

37. Thamserku and Kantega from Thyangboche (Chapter 18)

38. Chola glacier search—Khumbu (Chapter 17)

39. Ice pinnacles—1953 Everest base (Chapter 20)

40. Ama Dablam with rhododendrons above Imja khola (Chapter 19)

41. Pass of the Wolf (Chapter 22)

42. Ngojumba glacier, Gokyo lake and trekkers, 1986 (Chapter 22)

43. Sunrise from Milke Danda. From L to r: Chamlang, Everest, Pethangtse and Makalu (Chapter 24)

44. Sir Edmund Hillary and Brian Wilkins on Makalu glacier (Chapter 24)

45. Traders and yak caravan—crossing Rhaka la (Chapter 24)

46. Bridge at Dobhan (Chapter 24)

47. Camp in the Yalung valley (Chapter 25)

48. Sunset on Kangchenjunga (Chapter 26)

49. Ice climbing—Kangchenjunga (Chapter 26)

50. Limbu house and Kangchenjunga peaks (Chapter 25)

51. Sunset on Rathong, Yalung valley (Chapter 25)

52. Headman of Walung Chung Khola, 1954 (Chapter 24)

18

Return to the Land of Sherpas

(1954-1998) Many Journeys

"When will we go to the Himalaya again? I only know that we all want to go back to see the Sherpas and all our friends once more, to wander through the flower-filled valleys and climb to the heights of rock and snow", so wrote Josephine Scarr (now Dr. Josephine Peacock) at the end of her book *Four Miles High*. 'Jo' had been a member of my staff at the Snowdonia National Recreation Centre, Plas-y-Brenin, and along with Barbara Roscoe (nee Sparks) had spent several months in the Nepal Himalaya, following a drive overland from Britain in 1962. Before the two of them left the centre at Capel Curig I gave them a warning that having once been to the Himalaya, they would not be satisfied until they returned, and that a return would need to include a visit to the Sherpa.

When I first went to the Everest region and the land of the Sherpas, I walked in from Banepa, an old Newar town outside the Kathmandu valley, and followed the same route eastwards that had been taken by Hunt's Everest team nine months earlier. It is a journey still worth taking, and one I described in the book *More Than Mountains*.

At the present time the trek is shortened because a seven hour drive by car or bus can be taken to Jiri which cuts out a fine section that includes the Chyabas ridge and a first introduction to Buddhist country at Risingo gompa. The trail from Jiri continues to cross the grain of the country and from the ridges provides magnificent views of the high Himalaya to the north. Eventually on reaching the valley of the Dudh Kosi the trail also turns northwards leading towards Namche Bazaar, the main village or small township of Sola Khumbu. An alternative to making this longer walk into the Everest region is to fly from Kathmandu to Lukla airstrip—a flight of 40 minutes that puts you down at 9000 feet (2800 m) on a high shelf above the Dudh Kosi river. The airstrip was first built by Sir Edmund Hillary in 1965 and eventually enlarged by the Royal Nepal Airline (R.N.A.C.) in 1977. Though by the 1990s many small hotels have been built and the village of Lukla is much enlarged there is no way in which the landing strip can be further extended. Plans are afoot to relocate a landing area nearby. With Eileen I used Lukla airstrip after we had driven to Kathmandu and left our caravanette in Mike Cheney's garden for six weeks. It was Mike who drove us to the airport so that we could take a flight that had been brought forward by a day. Knowing that because of it we would not be met at Lukla by our old friend Sirdar Dawa Tenzing as arranged, he introduced us to a twenty-four year old Sherpa.

"This is Lakpa Thondup. He is returning home to Khumjung from Pokhra. He might be able to help you".

We looked at a slim, serious young man of medium height who seemed rather shy.

"Will you come with us as far as Thyangboche," I asked.

"Yes, I will," he agreed.

He then told us he would arrange porters as soon as we arrived in Lukla. This he did, both quickly and efficiently once we put down, and whilst he allocated loads of food, tentage, clothing and other gear to a variety of porters we had time to look around. It is always a fulfilling moment when you return to a country and its people where at sometime you have spent some of the most exciting and memorable days of your life. This time mine was spiced with the desire to see Eileen's reaction to it all. We were invited by a local Sherpa to have tea with him in his newly-built house. New wooden window-frames were still being inserted and a smell of fresh shavings mingled with the odour of yak and yak butter. There was a nose tingling smell of fermenting *chang* and a pervading aroma of juniper wood smoke. Nima, for that was the Sherpa's name, brought hot steaming mugs of tea. Yak milk gave it the rancid aroma and bland flavour of butter tea and golden globules of fat glistened on the surface. This Sherpa home of nostalgic smells, smoky atmosphere and sincere hospitality was just as I remembered and I smiled at Eileen over my mug. She smiled back, then winked and I knew as I suppose I had always known, that Sola Khumbu was going to be an important part of Eileen's life, just as for many years, it had been a part of mine.

Soon we left Lukla and took the descending track to Chauri Kharka, then on to the hamlet of Phakdingma. Children, carrying schoolbooks and satchels, were returning home from school and greeted us with a cheerful 'Namaste' as they passed by, then, near to Phakdingma, Lakpa turned to us saying,

"You might know my father. He often went on expeditions with Dawa Tenzing. He was with him on Kangchenjunga".

"What is his name? I asked.

"Changup," he said softly.

Eileen and I looked at each other in astonishment. Following the successful Kangchenjunga expedition in 1955, Sirdar Dawa Tenzing and Sherpa Changup stayed with us at our home in Redcar in North Yorkshire. Later I took a school walking party to the Lake District and Changup along with Dawa had gone with me. At Newlands hostel near Keswick, Changup had seemed a little homesick, sometimes taking out of his pocket a photograph of his wife and two-year old son taken at the village of Khumjung. Wistfully he would say,

"Ah, *hamara* Khumjung, *hamara* Karmi, *hamara* Lakpa" (my Khumjung, my Karmi, my Lakpa).

Amazingly, this young man was the two-year old son, now acting as our sirdar! Fortune had smiled on us, and Changup's son stayed with us for the next six weeks.

We have seen him often since that first time, and he is now

married with children of his own. (From 1986 he and his wife Sonam have kept a sleeping lodge and tea house at Teshinga, a place we visit whenever we pass that way. In 1998 on a trek we made on the 45th anniversary year of the Everest Ascent. We met them with their tall charming daughter Pasang now aged twenty-four).

"Where is your father now, Lakpa?" Eileen questioned.

"He's working in Pokhra, but will return home before the monsoon".

"Good, we might see him then," I interposed, "and if so, we must meet him with your mother in Khumjung". Eventually, we did.

With remarkable suddenness it began to rain which changed to wet snow, and we camped by a rock-shelter one hour beyond Phakdingma. The varied coloured rhododendrons, white, lilac, pink and ruby surrounded our campsite and way up above us a brilliantly white and fluted spire changed to gold as it caught the last light of the day.

Leaving the camp early in the morning, we followed a broad track leading to the confluence of the two rivers, Imja Drangpa, and Nangpa Tsangpo. Here the gorge narrows and we began the ascent to Namche. Soon we lost sight of our porters as we rose higher up the twisting turning trail. From above us a metallic ringing of bells attracted our attention, and as the sound increased in volume we saw the shaggy heads of yak and dzumjok bobbing above the scrub as they came down the track. Wild mountain iris, purple and speckled with white, added colour to the greys and greens of soil and vegetation whilst clusters of mauve florets of *Primula denticulata* attracted our eyes away from feet making a steady rhythmical progression up the steep and narrow path. It was warm work, but the sort of day when the mind tunes in to sight and sound and the heart sings with gladness at being a small part of the whole. A thousand feet or more above the gorge we stopped for a breather at an obvious halting place where there was ease for the traveller provided by a low seat of stones—a *chautara* —a bench of stones on which porters rest their loads. Here Eileen had her first view of Everest. Beyond the foreground scrub and pine, a number of interlocking spurs led our eyes onto the pointed summit of Taweche and the long ice ridge leading to it.

"Look to the right Eileen," I called, and pointed to the long wall of Lhotse and Nuptse. There above and behind the wall we could see the final thousand feet or so of Everest—a fan of powder snow blowing from its summit crest.

For years now an enterprising Sherpa from Namche has had a wooden shack at this halting place and there sells tea, beer and cola as well as hot soup, *chapatties* and *dalbhat*.

On we walked to Namche Bazaar which is laid out in an old glacial mountain bowl and its sturdy white-washed houses form a tiered crescent on the steeply curving sides. When we arrived all seemed quiet in the high hills and soon by far the greatest noise and bustle came from a trekking group of the Deutscher Alpen Verein. As the years have gone by, there is no doubt that trek groups and expeditions have made a big impact on the village, for many new hotels have been built and different colour washes are more commonly in use. But Namche retains much of its original character. Low stone walls continue to separate the houses and the many small fields are still used for growing potatoes. At the times the trekkers arrive, these fields are brown and bare prior to the planting of seed potatoes, and so they have a more lucrative crop, the many colourful tents of the trek groups on their way to the base camp of Everest. As always when we see those tents we hope the people using them take time to meet the Sherpa, to get to know them, and learn something of their history, character and culture.

Sherpa

Shar-east, Pa-people, the name means 'people of the east'. This is eastern Tibet, for they are Tibetans who several centuries ago migrated across the watershed of the Great Himalaya and settled on the south side of the mountains. A number of Tibetan groups have done this and their settlements are to be found in Garhwal and along the length of Nepal. Many such groups are called Bhotia which means 'Man from Tibet' and most of them are from the central and western areas of that country. Bhotias, like the Thakalis and the Sherpa speak the Tibetan language. Just as a Scotsman comes from one particular part of Britain, so does a Sherpa come from one part of the Himalaya—this is Sola Khumbu. They live on the flanks of the highest mountains of the world and within that mountain fastness have developed their own way of life and become a very independent people. Probably they first came to the notice of the outside world after Colonel Howard Bury, leader of the first expedition to Everest in 1921 took them as high altitude porters. They proved to be such strong mountaineers, so adaptable and loyal, that they have continued to be the best known of all Himalayan peoples.

Since that time, expeditions throughout the Himalaya and Karakoram have relied on their Sherpas, without whom many ascents would not have been successful. Often they are not given the credit which they have earned and richly deserve.

Phu Dorje, with whom I shared five exciting months of travel and exploration during a search for the Yeti (abominable snowman) was the epitome of all Sherpas. He was tough, loyal and intelligent, had a grand sense of fun and was always a fine companion. He became one of the world's great climbers and was certainly one of the most remarkable men I have ever known. Over three decades ago in 1969, he lost his life in the Everest icefall, but he is still remembered in many ways. Those who visit the Himalayan Mountaineering Institute in Darjeeling will find his photograph on the wall and beneath it a tribute written to his memory. Not only do the Indian mountaineers revere his memory but the Nepalese too, for they opened a Nepalese mountain training school in his name and now Nepalese youth and budding mountaineers benefit from Phu Dorje's experiences. This school can be visited by all who trek the Annapurna circuit for it nestles in a lightly-wooded valley below the peaks of Annapurna III and Gangapurna. Not so very far away the Buddhist gompa of Braga look down on the Marsyandi river and the area around the school. Dorje, a religious man would have been delighted with the choice of site. I wrote the following little piece about Phu Dorje after we had been together during the Snowman expedition in 1954 and it perhaps gives the best insight into his character and that of the Sherpa people in general.

"In the simple, unspoiled Phu Dorje were embodied most of the things I liked about the Himalayan peoples. He had simple charm, showed strength and devotion, had great ability, and the same cheerful disposition and faithfulness shown by so many other people I had known in different parts of the Himalaya. He lived with his wife and his parents in a simple home in Khumjung. No hair-cutting for him! This burly, jocular Sherpa who twice carried loads to the South Col of Everest in 1953 liked his hair plaited into pigtails and decorated at the ends with vivid coloured tassels of red, green and gold. On the mountain he wore climbing-boots and carried an ice-axe, but down in the valleys preferred his yak-soled boots, a short stick and the rough woollen Tibetan *chuba*. Though all his life he had lived in Sola Khumbu, the expeditions coming to Everest and Cho Oyu had given him an insight into other men's lives, brightened the days of the pre- and post-monsoon, and created an excitement in life that he would long remember."

"These things had not given him the desire to go to live in Darjeeling and already now the Snowman expedition was nearing its end, he was looking forward to the day when he could drive his yaks up the Dudh Kosi to Gokyo, beside the Dudh Pokhari. There it would be quiet and along with other young Sherpas and Sherpanis from the village, he would live for a few months the simple life of a mountain shepherd or yak-man. Almost everyday he would see the plume blowing from the top of Everest. Perhaps prior to 1953 he briefly dismissed the mountain as an abode of lamas and of gods, but I wonder what it means to him now. I cannot believe that his climb to the South Col had no meaning for him at all—I think he will remember with pleasure his many weeks on the mountain with the British expedition and think back with pride to the part which he played in the great adventure".

He lived for fifteen years after I wrote the above, during which time he went to the South Col of Everest eight more times. On four occasions he carried loads and climbed to the top camp at 27,700 feet and in 1965 reached the summit of the mountain with the Indian expedition. Between these expeditions he continued to tend his yak at the hamlet of Gokyo. He was a rare breed, a truly remarkable man.

You will find that most of the Sherpas with whom you travel and trek are of the same calibre, so always value their strength, experience and companionship and do take time to visit a Sherpa village.

19

A Sherpa Village and Hospitality

(1954 to 1998, many journeys)

Some of the best fields and finest crops of vegetables grown in Sola Khumbu are to be found at the village of Pangboche. This village is situated on the steep hillside above the Imja Khola. Down towards the river the ground is less steep, the fields larger and separated from each other by dry stone walls some three to four feet high. This part of the village through which the main trek path winds its way on to the Everest base camp, is known as lower Pangboche. Upper Pangboche being higher is where the contours steepen and the fields become narrow and elongated. The walls, in the nature of containing walls rise to seven or eight feet in height, their tops only a little higher than the succeeding fields above. Here, as elsewhere in Sola Khumbu prior to the rains, you find people busily sifting the soil, planting seeds and generally preparing for the coming of the monsoon at the end of the month. Sometimes a yak or a dzumjok is harnessed to a plough, but mostly it is the men and women working in small groups who turn the soil using mattocks and hoes.

Freshly hoed and ploughed, the fields look dry and dusty, short of humus and manure. This is one of the problems that needs to be tackled strenuously in Khumbu. Because wood is scarce, the dried yak-dung is used for heating and cooking and little of it is put back into the ground as manure. Hillary, with much help from the Canadians has for some years instigated a re-afforestation programme, but wood is not the answer to the fuel question nor does he intend it to be. More use of kerosene for heating and cooking would be the sensible approach with eventually some further development of hydro-electricity schemes so that yak-dung can be put to use as manure for increasing crop production.

Developments of this kind are discussed at village councils and in we have often had enlightening evenings listening to Sherpas discussing Khumbu politics. Originally the government 'panchayat' system consisting of electing councils of five at local and regional level were an important political progression in Khumbu. From the village councils or 'panchayat', candidates were put forward at election time for membership of the regional council. This most important panchayat representing Khumbu was then involved in negotiations with the Nepalese Government. At the beginning of the 1990s, the 'panchayat' system was dissolved throughout Nepal and political fractions of various persuasions put themselves forward for election. Those elected in Sola Khumbu still hold regular meetings and discussions that will have an important bearing on the development in a rapidly changing society.

Certainly a larger share in the proceeds from trekking and expeditions is always a burning topic, as is future development in the Sagarmatha National Park (National Park of the Everest area). As we have come to know more of the younger Sherpas and Sherpanis such as Lakpa Thondup and Nima Nurbu Lama and many others, so we have appreciated the excellent work done by Hillary's schools. Much of the development and eventual prosperity of Sola Khumbu lies in the hands of such young men and women who are showing that they wish to stay and help to work out the future of their country.

Ama Dablam is the mountain that towers above Pangboche and the rushing whitewater river named the Imja Khola is the torrent that carves a deep 'V' below the village. The blossoms of the ruby rhododendron (*Rhododendron aboreum*) contrast with the white of the snow in the early morning, when there is a crispness to the air, a clarity to the atmosphere and the day is sparkling with light. On such mornings, children splash and play in the stream and Sherpanis collect water in large casks called the '*som*'. It is a happy domestic scene and the more pleasing when Sherpanis are dressed in traditional style, which is not as common a sight nowadays as one would wish.

Each Sherpani wears a long sleeveless pinafore type dress and a shorter handwoven overskirt of many colours with horizontal stripes at the front, vertical stripes at the back. A small *choli* or waistcoat is worn over a long sleeved blouse, which is usually of brilliant jewel colours. In each ear many wear a copper *Na-long* inset with semi-precious turquoise stones. Necklaces of silver, turquoise and coral are usually draped around their necks and often a crowning glory is a Tibetan style hat, its curving brim lined with Siberian mink and the rest of it embroidered with threads of red, silver and gold. Boots soled with yak-hide are the old style footwear and these have calf length uppers made of a mixture of goat wool and yak hair. Before collecting water in the '*som*' the Sherpanis often wash their raven black hair and dry it in the sun, then grease it with butter and plait it into pigtails. Unfortunately, the butter does go rancid rather quickly and as often been said, you can tell the whereabouts of a well-buttered Sherpani all too easily.

As the chattering water-carriers return to their homes, they pass by lines of mani walls (prayer walls) built up of stones on which is carved the mani mantra *Om Mani Padme Hum* and if the prayer is intoned the *Hum* is strongly emphasised by a fierce expellation of the breath. The walls are put there by the local population who at a particular time of the year make a special ritual of walking round them, sometimes adding further stones or leaving little piles of quartz pebbles. These pocked out stones and piles of quartz pebbles are a similar custom to those followed 5000 years ago by neolithic farmers in Europe and in the same way demonstrates the people's devotion to their religion. Further evidence of this is to be found in the many small square buildings placed over the streams, each strongly built and roofed with rough-cut slaty stones. Wood-framed openings reveal large prayer drums (religious water wheels) spinning in a clockwise direction. Each drum is filled with a roll of mani prayers printed on paper so that as the drum turns the *mantra* makes an unceasing round throughout the year. These little prayer buildings are as well constructed as a Sherpa house.

A Sherpa Home

Most Sherpa homes are two-storied but a few in the past were of three storeys, and practically all dwellings in the *yersa*—the upland summer settlement are single storey dwellings. Each house is constructed sturdily of wood and stone and a mixture of clay, glacial sand, and yak-dung is used for mortar. The external walls are often white-washed. In the last decade an increasing number of three-storied houses (mostly used as hotels or lodges) have been built in Namche Bazaar. These have either been colour washed, or, the fine stonework has been left bare for all to see, which is much more satisfactory. Each time we trek to Sola Khumbu we visit a Sherpa home, taking our friends with us. The welcome and the hospitality never fails to gladden the day. The interior layout of a Sherpa house is very traditional and our first stay with Dawa Tenzing at Diboche was typical both of design and hospitality.

At the time of our first visit, Dawa's youngest daughter Angmou was still living with him. Later she married the brother of the head lama of Thyangboche and is now called Ang Neesha. With her husband, she now runs a most excellent lodge and restaurant, the 'Tashi Delek', opposite the gompa. Trekkers stop there for food and refreshment, for it is a steep, hot walk from Phunki bridge to Thyangboche but when we stayed at Dawas's house in 1976, no such restaurant existed and we walked on to Diboche.

Once inside the house, we sat talking, and at the same time watched Angmou prepare a meal. It was also an opportunity to look around the room. The two-storied house was not large, but built in traditional style with a cattle byre, plus wood and tool store at ground level. From the interior of the byre a wooden stairway led to three upper rooms. There was a latrine in which a deep layer of dried moss and rhododendron leaves always ensured a lack of odour and a feeling of cleanliness. A second small room, in which the owner of the house usually sleeps, was now being used for guests and storage, so already our rucksacks had been placed there. The third and largest room was the kitchen which is the living quarters and sleeping area combined.

Wooden panelling, wooden cupboards and wooden shelving predominated and on the shelves brass and copper bowls, some used as water containers, caught the flickering light from the fire. Dawa's fireplace at that time broke with tradition because having been to Britain he had seen the value of a chimney and his wide chimney flue opened to the sky. Many Sherpa homes now have chimneys or open flues but at that time Dawa's house was the least smoky of any we visited in Sola Khumbu. By the doorway a butter tea-tub held a special position above the kitchen work-table and below the shelving several large round containers proclaimed their origin from a Swiss Himalayan expedition. Some of these held Dawa's spare clothing, whilst others contained rice or other grain. A musical tinkle attracted our attention to a corner by one of the three windows. Dawa had just given a clockwise twist to a large prayer drum attached to which was a metal arm that clanged a bell on each full rotation. His carefully wrapped prayer book sat on a shelf by the drum and beneath it hung an illuminated scroll. This had been presented to Dawa by Ned Kelly on behalf of the British Broadcasting Company as a token of their thanks for his help in making a documentary programme 'Sherpas of Everest'. A presentation clock ticked quietly on the opposite wall and by it hung a picture of the 'Memsahibs Expedition' to Kanjiroba Himal. The shelf by the clock held a conglomeration of interesting objects including a hand prayer-wheel, a Tibetan butter lamp, Dawa's battered felt hat and a couple of soot blackened kettles. By them hung a picture of the King of Nepal. A chased silver teacup with ornate lid and silver stand held pride of place and from it Dawa always drank his *chang*, the local beer. I like rooms that are filled with possessions that are a part of everyday life and also of a person's memories. This was such a room.

Dawa was a very religious man and so later we were to discover a fourth room. This was the small square private chapel containing sacred scrolls, tiny brass butter lamps and an altar with a statue of Buddha. The *la-khang* (prayer room) is an important part of all Sherpa homes, and in the houses of the more wealthy it can be richly painted, hung with scrolls (*thankas*) and containing many Buddhas. Usually a smell of aromatic azalea leaves smouldering in an incense bowl pervades the air, and this was so in Dawa's home for as I have said, he was a very religious man. But a second more appetising aroma quickly took all our interest for the walk from Phunki had made us very hungry.

Potato Cakes in Khumbu

Whilst Angmou was cooking, she showed pleasure whenever Eileen asked about a special dish. Throughout our stay at Diboche, these were many and consisted of variations of cheese, rice, meat, lentils and a large collection of herbs picked from the hillside. For this first meal, Angmou was making potato cakes. It was good to see them being made and at times exciting too! Diboche is at 13,000 feet and the atmospheric pressure much lower than at sea level. Water boils at about 88° Celsius and tea doesn't brew. Potatoes don't cook either, but Sherpas don't mind.

For many years they have had their own form of pressure cooker and this is how it works. First of all, Angmou poured about one inch of water into her biggest metal pot or *dekchi*. This was then filled with washed but unpeeled potatoes. Standing above the fire in every Sherpa house there is a metal trestle, and on this trestle, Angmou placed the pot of potatoes. On top of the pot she placed a metal lid and on the top of the lid she put the heaviest stone she could lift. Now she had assembled a formidable contraption. Then, and always, we felt it was like playing Russian roulette, sitting round a blazing fire listening to the water boiling in a *dekchi* (pot) and the innards rumbling. Our imagination boggled at what must be happening inside as the pressure of steam built up with no apparent safety valve. At each ominous rumble we edged nearer the door of the house certain that at any moment the room would become a holocaust of flying pot, lid, and steaming potatoes. At the moment our courage seemed about to fail, the *'dekchi'* lid and its stone capping lifted and emitted a jet of steam. The primitive safety valve worked, and with the lid removed we could each dip in a hand to remove a perfectly cooked potato. Taking out the rest of the potatoes, Angmou then rubbed them on a ribbed stone that resembled the old fashioned washday scrubbing boards. With the potatoes well mashed she added herbs and other delicacies, then shaped the mash into flat cakes like small pancakes. With a smear of *ghee* (clarified butter) and a quick turn or two on hot charcoal embers there were our cakes, hot, tasty and thoroughly cooked at 13,000 feet.

Tsampa made from roast ground barley grain in still an important food in Khumbu but an increasing variety of vegetables are now being grown in the village fields. These are turnips, peas, cabbages, lettuce, huge white radishes, spinach and onions but it is the potato that is the main crop and staple diet of the people. In addition to making potato cakes, (*gurr*) they eat large quantities of boiled potatoes taken with salt and ground red peppers. For travel or prolonged winter storage, they cut potatoes into strips and dry them in the sun.

Sometimes instead of using rice or barley, they ferment the potatoes for making their beer (*chang*) which is then distilled to produce a potent spirit called *rakshi*. As regards flavour and aroma, the nearest western equivalent I know to this distillation of *chang* is the *grappa* of Italy which possesses the same yeasty aroma of newly-baked bread. During our stay in Dawa's house we were able to watch Angmou prepare some *chang* and then able to see her distil some *rakshi* too.

'Rakshi'—A Sherpa Drink

Having ensured that the utensils for distillation were scrupulously clean, Angmou poured the *chang* of a thin porridge-like consistency into a bottom pan; a large brass bowl which was then placed on a fire of slowly burning yak-dung. On the top of this base she fitted a strangely-shaped vessel that we named the 'mine'. Many holes were cut in its smoothly rounded bottom which sat closely to the rim of the brass bowl. Inside the 'mine' which had a high rim, was slotted a smooth and highly polished hollow copper cone, inverted and filled with cold water. The joints between the 'mine' and the brass bowl, and the copper cone with the 'mine' were carefully sealed with a concoction of *'tsampa'* and water so that the whole formed one complete still. Though Angmou was most careful to regulate the head of the fire, Eileen and I found it difficult to decide which was the most dangerous device—the primitive Sherpa pressure cooker or this equally explosive-looking still.

Gradually the fermented grain or rice was heated to the right temperature so that alcohol plus a small amount of water vapour rose through the holes of the 'mine' to impinge on the cool base of the copper cone. There the vapour condensed, ran down to the point of the cone and dripped into the pan placed in the bottom of the 'mine'. The cooling water in the copper cone rose rapidly in temperature at this time and had to be changed at frequent intervals. Rather than waste the heated water, Angmou generally did the week's washing whenever she made *'rakshi'*. Five times the cone was filled with cold water and allowed to heat up before the still was removed from the fire and the clear distillate revealed. It proved to be a particularly potent brew and whilst it was still warm, Eileen and Dawa consumed large quantities which they regretted the next day!

53. Baruntse peak from Ambu Lapcha at 19,250 feet (Chapter 24)

54. Everest massif from Gaumukhtse, 1988 (Chapter 22)

55. Crossing the Ambu Lapcha, 1954 (Chapter 24)

56. Tibetan traders and yaks, Rakha la (Chapter 24)

57. Pandim and chortens and trek group at Dzongri (Chapter 27)

58. Tenzing in the Onglakthang valley, 1982 (Chapter 27)

59. Snow pyramid and rock spire—two peaks climbed by
Brown, Hardie, Cheeta, Jaj (?) in 1955 (Chapter 27)

60. Kangchenjunga peaks from Kabru ridge (Chapter 27)

61. Kwangde peaks from Namche campsite, Yeti Expedition, 1954 (Chapter 17)

62. Tibetan traders—Nangpa la journey, 1954 (Chapter 29)

63. Tibetan traders—men, women and children with Izzard (Chapter 24)

64. Tibetans at Nangpa la over 19,000 feet looking into Tibet (Chapter 29)

65. Annapurna II and the Jacksons, 1996

20

Om Mani Padme Hum
and Soldiers on Everest

(April-May 1976)

A dignified Dawa Tenzing met us on the track below Thyang-boche holding a *chang* (beer) jar in his arms. *Chang* made from fermented rice or barley is a basic commodity of every Sherpa household. The thick brew, porridge-like in consistency is filtered and strained and the resulting milky liquid is quite refreshing, though the taste must be acquired. Dawas's *chang* had been in the sun all day, so that on taking the lid off the jar, it fizzed, and its curd-like contents bubbled forth with vigour and permeated the heavy air of the afternoon with the heady smell of a brewery. Fortunately not all the *chang* escaped and the remainder was downed quickly between questions, exclamations, and gestures of welcome and friendship. A few hours earlier we had stopped at Phungitenga, a small hamlet near the confluence of the Dudh Kosi and the Imja Khola. Two refreshment houses stand there side by side. One of them, the 'New Sherpa Tea House', was owned at the time by Lakpa Thondup's sister—Ang Urkien. A pretty young Sherpani holding a baby in her arms, helped Ang Urkien to make our tea, then Lakpa proudly presented her to us as his 'girlfriend'.* Such pre-marital offspring are not unusual, for being semi-nomadic, the Sherpa men travel far and wide and there can be a long delay between betrothal and marriage. Sherpa morality is different to most other peoples though we have found a similar freedom towards sexual matters among the Toda in the Nilgiri Hills of South India and both groups of people practice polyandry. Sherpa and Toda males spend a lot of time in high grazing pastures, though only the Sherpa goes away for long trading and trekking journeys or on mountaineering expeditions. Perhaps in both instances the frequent absence of a 'husband' is one reason for the polyandry, for in this way the continuation of the race is ensured by having at least one male in the home at any one time. That men, but not women, are found to be less fertile at altitude must be another factor in natures equation.

Tragedy in Khumbu

Having linked up with Dawa, we could now organise our *bando-bast* for the next few weeks. Dawa and Lakpa would stay with us and a third Sherpa to join our 'permanent' entourage, Ang Norbu, would arrive from Pangboche the next day. He turned out to be the Ang Norbu who had carried with Charles Evans and Neil Mather to Camp VI on Kangchenjunga in 1955. Sadly, I found that now he hadn't any fingers—just stumps. He had lost them in a storm on Annapurna in 1971, but he was fortunate. Eight of his Sherpa companions had died on that Japanese expedition. We were to discover that during the previous decade, over seventy Sherpas had lost their lives on expeditions, and for Khumbu with its population of less than 2500 people, this was a staggering total. It was as if there had been a war or a pestilence in the land.

Later, Lakpa explained that out of his class of eighteen scholars at the Khumjung school only he and one other were left alive.

---

*Lakpa did eventually marry his 'girlfriend', Sonam. Ang Urkien, Lakpa's sister now lives at Pheriche and runs the 'Snowland Hotel'. They both revisit their old home in Khumjung, though their father (Changup) and mother died several years ago.

Sadly, this death toll has continued during the last two decades and it is not good. It is true that many mountaineers abhor the situation and in many ways make efforts to remedy the problem. However, there are still some modern expeditions that should think long and seriously about what they are doing. Some of the reasons for the dreadful toll can be quickly ascertained and practical moves made to remedy the situation.

A Link with Makalu and Darjeeling

On arrival at Dawa's house in Dingboche, his daughter made us welcome, providing us with a huge bowl of boiled *aloo* (potatoes) which we rapidly consumed after adding tasty pinches of salt and ground red peppers. The meal was helped down by taking generous swigs of Dawa's *rakshi* and we slept well.

In the morning we were able to make an early start having put together all our loads the previous night. We were joined by a cheerful and powerful porter called Pasang Temba plus a young yak-boy who drove three yak and once we were loaded up and away, we must have looked a picturesque sight as we crossed the bridge over the Imja Khola.

Pheriche and Phalong Karpo are the last of the Sherpa villages on the way to Everest base camp and we made quick time arriving early in the afternoon. This was so despite a stop at a refreshment house in Pangboche kept by another of Dawa's daughters, where naturally we were regaled with *chang* and once again plied with mounds of *aloo*. Pheriche had grown in size since my first visit over twenty years earlier. Now tea-houses provided refreshment and accommodation for trekkers and a sign by a large new building proclaimed it to be the Mountain Rescue Post. There was also a helicopter pad, and because Pheriche is situated on the flat outwash plain far below the Khumbu glacier, it is an ideal place for such a landing zone. We had another fine surprise later in the day. Phu Cheeta, who had been my personal Sherpa on the Kang-chenjunga climb, arrived dressed in traditional Sherpa costume. It turned out they were Phu Cheeta's yak we were using and it pleased us a lot to find that he was now quite well off. He had saved his money, bought wisely and now owned 21 yak. I had first met him with Hillary's party at the foot of Makalu when I made the journey from Everest to reach Kangchenjunga and the following year he was with me on that mountain. Later in Darjeeling, he met Eileen and our son John who was then just three years of age. He often looked after John at that time, so naturally enquired about him. His pleasure was a delight to see when we showed him a recent photograph of John, and he felt our meeting called for a celebration. Rather ominously, several large containers of liquid were produced.

A Touch of Spring and Lobuje

Calamity! Phu Cheeta's *chang* had been too plentiful and too potent and all of us wakened the next morning with crashing headaches. Celebrations apart, we had spent a lively evening discussing Sherpa problems, reminiscing about previous journeys, arguing about the 'Yeti' or discussing the expedition on Everest that we hoped to visit during the next few days. Fortunately the morning was clear, warm and sunny—a touch of spring—as we crossed the alluvial flat to Phalong Karpo and entered the Chola Khola.

Our plan was to set up tents in each of several valleys and from them, place ski camps on high glaciers. Our base in the Chola khola we placed several hundred feet above the yak *karka* of Dzonghla and after paying off Pasang Temba and the little yak-boy, we packed ready to leave for the Everest base camp the next day. This we did and having crossed a low col at 17,000 feet we were back in the main Khumbu valley and staying the night at Lobuje—the site of a yak-dwelling which for years had been a rest campsite for Everest expeditions. Originally Lobuje was a grazing pasture during the Sherpa summer transhumance, then later used as an expedition rest camp, but now it is a halting place for treks to Gorakhshep and Kala Patthar or to the present day site of the base camp for Everest.

On arrival we found the main stone structure had been given the name of 'Tibetan Hotel' and the once quiet oasis in the ablation valley of the Khumbu glacier boasted a busy cosmopolitan population.

An American, a Swede and a young man from Manchester were the first people we met; all of them feeling the cold and the altitude. Sixteen thousand feet during a cold snowy period is no place to be if you are poorly equipped and we felt they would probably not go much further. The didn't, and early the next morning moved off back down the valley to warmer altitudes.

Back in Britain during the winter we had met members of the British-Nepal Army Everest Expedition at the Peny Gwryd Hotel in North Wales and knew that they would be on the mountain at the same time that we were climbing and skiing in the area. From Darjeeling I had already sent a card to Tony Streather with whom I had been on the mountains in Greece, Greenland and on Kangchenjunga and told him that we would be up to Everest to inspect his base camp sometime in April. Tony was the leader of the team made up mostly of members of Army Mountaineering Association, and if they successfully climbed the mountain it would be the first mountaineering club to do so. Both Eileen and I felt a thrill of expectation as we walked along the ablation valley to Gorakhshep. Because there was little change, I was soon able to find the shelter stones built by the Swiss where with Ang Dawa, I had caught the new species of Tibetan mouse-hare whilst on the Snowman Expedition. (It was pleasing that this place was much the same as in the past, but little were we to know that ten years later we would be there when microlight gliders were landing at Gorakhshep and at least two stone resthouses provided accommodation and food for trekkers.) Soon we began the tedious journey over the moraine-covered glacier. A lot of new snow had fallen during the night so that the mid-day sun reflected back from it, burning our skin, as well as creating a general feeling of lassitude.

No tents were visible when we walked by the fluted ice seracs where in 1953 the Hunt Expedition set up its base and we began to wonder where the Army camp might be. *Dekko Sahib* called Dawa Tenzing and pointed across the chaotic jumble of ice which disgorged from the icefall of the Western Cwm. On the far side, we could see a number of orange tents and many tiny figures standing near the opening of a large green cook-house. This had been Bonnington's cook-house site during the south-west face ascent and was now sensibly taken over by the soldiers. This base camp position well along the true right flank of the icefall and its height at 17,700 feet, reduces by a considerable amount the distance to be travelled on each day's carry to Camp One. Not only does it save time and energy but the safety factor is thereby increased for everybody. Our welcome could not have been better and I felt exhilarated to be back at the icefall again after so many years; the more so because Eileen was clearly tremendously happy to be there too. She was acclimatising without trouble and would, I thought, do well when later we would be skiing at up to 19,000 feet.

Sherpas brought us hot mugs of tea, Dawa handed over his container of *chang* and we sat outside the mess tent chatting with friends—old and new. Brian Martindale and Roy Frances from the Joint Services Mountain Training Centre at Towyn came over and made it a 'Snowdonia' reunion party. This increased in size as we were joined by Ronnie Faux of 'The Times', whom I had often met in Wales during gatherings of foreign mountaineers at Plas-y-Brenin in the 1960s. Tony Streather was still at Camp II and John Peacock, who was running Base, joined us as soon as his chores were finished. In no time at all he and I were busily discussing the Ski Mountaineering Committee of the British Ski Federation of which John was Chairman, and expressing hopes for the good of future developments.

Perhaps our news, small talk and Eileen's general cheeriness was a lifting influence. I like to think it was, for just a few days earlier we had heard of the tragic death of one of the team members, Captain Terry Thompson. Apparently he had stepped into a crevasse at Camp II and though rescuers had got to him quickly, he had subsequently died. At any time a tragedy of this kind is a terrible experience but on a major climb on the highest mountains in the world where companionships and friendships are even more close than normal, it is cause for depression that is difficult to shake off. That this fine group of mountaineers did so and carried out a successful climb says much for their team-work and strength of character.

Yellow-billed choughs made the hills ring with their chatter whilst we put up our Good Companion tent, then blew up our air beds in preparation for the night. Later, the last rays of the sun disappeared behind the peaks and the fierce cold struck quickly, gripping and binding, so that the rattle of tumbling rock debris ceased from all points around. There were no clouds and the stars were incredibly clear. Those stars, the crackling cold of night time, and the towering silent giants above us attracted as do all lonely places, creating a strange indescribable sense of wonder—a longing to know more about such remote corners of the world and the whole broad sweep of the Universe.

"Om Mani Padme Hum"

On the afternoon of out second day at Everest base, the radio link through to the Western Cwm enabled us to talk with Tony Streather. Eileen was in good form throwing radio procedure to the wind, and saying some amusing and light-hearted things that no doubt reached all camps on the mountain. *Lung Ta* (prayer flags) fluttered bravely at the 'Sherpa shrine' and whilst we spoke we looked beyond them and through the icefall seracs as if to create an even stronger link or bond with those yet higher. By now the sun was shining strongly, warming the sleeping bags put out to air, and again as on the previous day, several of us sat chatting of many things irrelevant to climbing the mountain but relaxing and refreshing to those who had recently returned from the icefall. Sherpas were laughing and chattering over by the cook tent, they too relaxing after a safe and successful carry. Earlier in the day, I had surprised Brian Martindale and Philip Horniblow, the doctor, by joining them for breakfast before their icefall journey. I would have liked to be with them, but that was impossible, yet I had to get up and see them off and a lump came to my throat when once again, as in previous years, heard the Sherpas chanting their *Om Mani Padmes* as they went on their way.

Later in the morning, Douggie Keelan could see how much I

would like to meet a returning party so we took cold lemon drinks to 'Crampon Point' where we met Brian and Philip on return from their carry. After a short stop and a chat we took photographs some of which nowadays provide good material for talks on glaciation in mountains.

On the afternoon of the third day, we began the journey back to our own camp in the Chola khola and though invited to stay as long as we liked, felt it was important that we return, to begin our ski experiences with the Sherpas. We were well-pleased with our journey and stay at Everest Base knowing that good progress was being made up the Lhotse Face. Everyone was in good heart and we felt there was every chance the expedition would be a success. They were a grand Everest team, climbing for the right reasons and we wished them well.

21

Sherpas on Ski
(1976)

S-s-h-h the soft sibilant sound of running skis and a swish-h-h of snow spraying sideways on a smooth turn as white glistening crystals and flat glinting naphthalene-like plates of snow lose their pure smooth virginity in the early morning. A crisp cold wind freezes tissues, chills the cheekbones, nips the ear-lobes and eyes water as air whips at the lids and loose surrounding skin. The heart beats strongly as blood courses through the body feeding oxygen to muscles and tendons now working smoothly, absorbing shocks, turning tips, releasing heels and biting edges. Nerve endings at feet ankles, knees and eyes transit messages to the brain at high speed, then back again to produce the perfect co-ordination of mind and muscle that is the essence of efficient downhill skiing in mountains. The slope steepens, sharpened metal crunches and bites into hard ice—a rock protrudes, edges release and a swift side slip avoids the danger as the skier speeds on at thirty to forty miles per hour. At last the angle eases, there is a chance to look up and see the hills, as legs, still working smoothly continue to transmit their important messages to skis and brain.

This is how skiing is anywhere and it was skiing also for Eileen and me on the virgin snows of the Chola khola glacier.

With Sirdar Dawa Tenzing, Lakpa Thondup and Ang Norbu we had set up our camp at approximately 18,000 feet on the glacier. From that camp for the next few days we extended the experience of our Sherpas on ski, but our first full day was the best. We were up and away early, reaching the Nimagawa la just after dawn. The sun soon warmed us but at first the snow was crisp and when Eileen and I had our first run, we experienced those thrilling nuances of skiing that I have tried to describe. At the pass, we looked down into the Nimagawa and across to mountains dividing the Ngojumba or upper Dudh Kosi from the Bhote Kosi. In the clear morning air, Kariolung, Numbur and other peaks of the Rolwaling seemed but a stone's throw away and over in the north-west Gaurishankar and Menlungtse dominated among the serration of peaks etching the azure blue sky at the Tibetan border. Condensation snow crystals sparkled and glistened on the surface of the glacier around us as spreading webs of light dispersed by ice and snow on the high ridges expanded into our domain. Above and beyond the ridges and peaks that flanked the northern side of the valley plumes of ice particles curtained southwards from the summits of Everest, Nuptse and Lhotse. Amongst those majestic timeless hills it was not just the keen cold morning air that took our breath away.

Sherpas learn quickly from visual example which is essential teaching practice for skiing. Some verbal instructions, minimal and to the point were needed and this we managed with a mixture of basic English and a few words of Tibetan—the Sherpa language. Yawa (meaning right) Yumba (meaning left) were in constant use and a source of amusement to Eileen as she watched me make turn after turn over the snow, closely followed by Lakpa or Norbu. As our figures dwindled in size and went almost out of sight across the glacier, the sounds of yawa-yumba-yawa-yumba, constant as a metronome, floated back to her. Soon the snow softened, slowing the skis a little which was good for Lakpa and Norbu. For several hours they skied, making rapid progress with basic swings and wide stance basic parallels. Soon, with real assurance they skied away for a mile or more across the glacier until almost out of sight. This was also the day that our old friend Dawa Tenzing, proud that Sherpas were learning to ski came up to watch—but not for long. Eventually, he couldn't resist the temptation and asked if he could have a try, and he did! He sat down unintentionally a few times but persevered for an hour or more and was then content to let Lakpa use the skis again. Good old Dawa. We had to take off our hats to a man who at 74 years of age had just taken his first ski lesson at almost 18,500 feet. He was well satisfied with his efforts and was content not to try again either in the Chola Khola or later in the Ngojumba. Always he would say "I want the young Sherpas to learn to ski," and it was clear that he was looking ahead to the future of his people.

Lakpa Thondup, with his strong social conscience developed whilst a scholar at Hillary's Khumjung school often enthused saying "This is a good thing for Sherpa society. I must show our children how to ski when the snow comes to Khumjung in November". With his words in mind we hoped we could leave skis and sticks with Lakpa when we left Sola Khumbu, and this we did.

On a chill grey day in November 1998, we were walking from Khumjung to Thame when we met Lakpa who was going to a council meeting in Thamu. I asked him if he kept on skiing and we were delighted when he told us that a group of Norwegian trekkers had invited him to their homeland. His final comment was "Oh yes, they were very surprised how well I could ski".

22

The Pass of the Wolf
(1954)

The first visitors to Sola Khumbu, Houston and Tilman in 1950 were followed by the members of the Everest Reconnaissance of 1951 led by Eric Shipton. Several exploratory journeys were made and on one of them Murray, Bourdillon, Ward and Riddiford, traversed westwards from the Khumbu valley along a tributary glacier that led them to the upper basin of the Dudh Kosi and the Ngojumba glacier. The head of the glacier was rimmed by two mighty peaks, Gyachung Kang (25,910 feet) and Cho Oyu (26,750 feet). Later they decended the glacier and the valley to reach Namche Bazaar. In 1952 Shipton led another expedition, this time to Cho Oyu and after a reconnaissance on the mountain, other exploratory journeys were made. This time, Gregory, Bourdillon and Collidge, then later Hillary and Lowe, crossed eastwards from the Bhote Kosi over an unnamed pass which led to the head of the Ngojumba glacier. Two years later, I crossed to the upper basin of the Dudh Kosi from the Khumbu valley by ascending the Chola khola and crossing the Nimagawa la. With Bill Edgar and Ralph Izzard, I then ascended Ngojumba glacier and traversed westwards over the same unnamed pass to reach the Bhote Kosi and the Nangpa la. In the early 50s this was heady and exhilarating travel and on returning from the Namgpa la, I left Edgar and Izzard determined to explore for a high rock gap, that previously with my companions I had discovered above Gokyo lake. At the time, we had trailed the spoor of two Tibetan wolves which had led us to the rock gap and so we called it the Changu la—the Pass of the Wolf.

With three Sherpas, I stayed overnight in the Bhote Kosi at a small yak village called Langden and with them did cross the rock gap. I won't say we found the gap or pass because once again it was the spoor of a Tibetan grey wolf that led me there.

Later I was assured by my Sherpa companions and the local inhabitants of the valley that this pass from the Bhote Kosi to the Dudh Kosi was hitherto unknown to them. However, the pass has been used frequently ever since and Japanese trekkers and guidebook writers have renamed it the 'Renjo pass' after a lake and yak *karka* near to Langden. I still prefer our original name— Changu la—The Pass of the Wolf. It is far more romantic and much more fitting when I remember our experience when making the first crossing.

Having spent the night before in the yak-hut at Langden, we were wakened in the early morning when a huge creamy-coloured wolf attacked a yak in a nearby field. The local yak-man was hopping up and down and shouting furiously when I joined him. We frightened it away by throwing stones which it didn't like, so it moved off in the direction of Renjo (I knew this as Henjo at the time) and I decided we should follow its trail. It was soon clear that the wolf was heading towards the pass we hoped to cross and its prints became easier to follow after we traversed a remote little corrie above which a steep glacier or ice tongue led up to the rock ridge. To our surprise the spoor of the wolf led straight up the glacier and it was here we parted company with the yak-man. He had come with us so far hoping to find the lair of the wolves, for the people of Langden thought the she-wolf was about to have cubs. Perhaps he felt that it was getting dangerous for the ice was certainly steep and I see the modern guidebook writers stress the steepness saying that after an ascent from the Gokyo side "you must descend the steep incline from the pass with great caution—and when there is heavy snowfall, it is desirable to fix ropes". In fact since we made the first crossing, the route is much easier. In a short period of time, the steep glacier tongue, like the one that used to be on the west side of the Nimagawa la has completely melted away.

Leaving the yak-man, we followed the spoor up the glacier tongue towards a cirque of peaks. Swirling grey mist filtered between several large rock teeth and these I named the 'Changu So' the teeth of the wolf. Once we were through the gap of the rock teeth, we had completed the first crossing of the Changu la. Still we followed the wolf prints, at times glissading as we descended the glacier which led us to the Dudh Pokari (milk lake) and the summer village of Gokyo.

There was a strong aromatic aroma of crushed azalea leaves filling the air when we reached the stepping stones that cross the ablation stream flowing into the lake. Here a number of geese and duck bobbed lazily amongst the ripples created at the inlet.

Many trek groups now go to the area around Gokyo and in the last few years it has been good to see that as yet the increase in visitors hasn't disturbed the water life. There are just as many duck and geese as when I made that first crossing of the Changu la and also more than three decades ago when in the 1970s Eileen and I went there in the pre-monsoon season. At that time we had crossed over the Ngojumba glacier from Tagnag then walked up the ablation valley to the hamlet.

Spring at Gokyo

Our early arrival at Gokyo underlined the value of an early start and we were able to use the rest of the day to settle in and explore the locality. The lake at Gokyo named Dudh Pokhari seemed even greener than I remembered and to my delight, just as twenty-two years earlier, a bar-headed goose and several Ruddy Shellduck foraged near the inlet. A cluster of small black and white waterfowl skittered like water beetles away from the shore and made towards fans of rock talus that spread a grey mantle beneath the rock bar of the Changu glacier. A white band of ice marked the lip of the glacier which was mostly hidden, whilst above the band, the three rock teeth, the *Changu So*, marked the watershed between the Dudh Kosi and the Bhote Kosi. We were startled by a cleaving of the air when scores of snow pigeons in tight formation swooped low over the yak field behind us. Now that it was early May there were the signs that the spring sun was warming the land even at 16,000 feet and throughout the day we were visited by perky wagtails, cheeky sparrows, cocky chaffinch, squabbling snow cock and the majestic, though for the birds, disturbing presence of an eagle.

A solitary Ruddy Shellduck set up a loud excited calling—a trilling k-k-k-k and a chuck-a-wa that echoed back from the steep rock buttresses across the lake. Swiftly, a newcomer, a second Ruddy Shellduck came winging in from the high moraine of the Ngojumba. It was as if he or she was being scolded for being an erring mate—"Where have you been? What took you so long?" There is an Indian legend that the souls of erring lovers are imprisoned within the birds, and that the lovers, as a form of punishment, must remain within sight and hearing of each other but separated by water. These two Shellduck were not having any of that! When we left Gokyo the pair made a fine picture together, their bright orange and gold plumage with black and white wing markings contrasting with the cold green glacial water of the lake.

Gaumukh-tse—'Peak of the Cow's Mouth'

Above Gokyo hamlet there is a bulky grass covered mountain that has two summits linked by a rock ridge.

It was covered in deep snow and the rock ridge was corniced, when I first went up it with Ralph Izzard and Bill Edgar. It was Ralph's first ascent of a mountain, so unimaginatively we named it 'Ralph's Peak'. Since then various travel book writers have given it names such as Gokyo Kang, Gokyo Ri and even Gokyo peak. It was Phu Dorje who told me its proper name—Gaumukh-tse which translated means the 'Peak of the Cow's Mouth.' Later Sirdar Dawa Tenzing confirmed this when we went up the mountain with Eileen from our camp at Gokyo. The name bears relationship to it being in the valley of the Dudh Kosi (milk river) and it rising above the Dudh Pokhari (milk lake).

The ascent gives a splendidly scenic walk, entailing two hours of steady plodding over grassy slopes that lead to the first rocky summit. Here is one of the most stupendous mountain panoramas anywhere and certainly the finest view of Everest in the whole of Sola Khumbu.

Down below, the Dudh Pokari is an opaque blue-green and along its shore dots of red, blue and orange mark out the position of tents in the many small yak fields of Gokyo. A thin blue stream from the outlet of the lake meanders through the vegetated ablation valley to lake Tan Thum and beyond it to the south, the ice ribbed walls and rocky flanks of Thamserku and Kantega rear up dramatically to 23,000 feet.

All round, one peak after another, add grandeur and majesty to the scene—Kariolung, Menlungtse, Cho Oyu, Gyachung Kang, then Everest, Lhotse, Nuptse, Makalu, and a host of other mountains, many unnamed, and some still unclimbed. Moving further along towards the second and higher summit, the ridge steepens becoming more craggy so that at frequent halting places, you can stop and sun yourself, letting time go by without a care in the world. Now you tune into the environment mentally as well as physically and always across the way, the huge dark pyramidal shape of Everest dominates the scene.

For all who go there such moments will endure.

That time of our journey to Gokyo lake and Gaumukh-tse was when we also taught our Sherpas to ski. Eleven years later, we were reminded of the skiing and the wolves that live in the mountains of Sola Khumbu. We were prevented from visiting the lake and Gokyo hamlet (Yersa) once again because of the birth of a 'child.'

23

The Wolf-Hunters of Pangboche
(1987)

At the end of April 1987, Eileen and I returned to Galapagos Islands with a party of friends. We saw immediately that everywhere the islands were greener and much more heavily vegetated than previously. The temperatures were higher than normal and the humidity exceptionally high. Clearly it was an El Nino year.

El Nino—The Child

What is El Nino? The spanish name means The Child and the child is born when the warm water normally retained within the great bowl of the Bay of Panama is swept out by winds into the Pacific Ocean. For the Galapagos Islands, this creates a dramatic imbalance in the environment. The cool waters of the Humboldt Current are replaced by the warm waters of El Nino and the abundant fish life leaves the area. Colonies of sea birds disappear. Sea lions and fur seals die of starvation. Iguanos, painted locusts and a variety of other insects, plus the birds that prey on them, flourish. For us this made for a very interesting stay among those enchanted islands. Even so, as we left them, we knew that globally,

El Nino was an 'ill wind' that caused dangerous swings in the weather cycles throughout the world. I wondered how soon we would see or hear of some of the problems it would cause.

October—Nepal—the Same Year

Early on the evening of October 17th Eileen and I stood on a small promontory at the hamlet of Dole in the upper Dudh Kosi. We watched with awe whilst high clouds lit by the last rays of the sun, sped from the west across the sky at high speed. In everyway, they moved as clouds do, when projected on a screen by time lapse photography and I felt a strange foreboding.

At Nerebu the next evening and throughout the following thirty-two hours, snow fell in huge quantities enveloping tents, snapping tent poles, destroying visibility and generally creating havoc for trek groups throughout the area. Our party of fifteen battened down inside the sturdy mess tent but not before rescuing four German trekkers who, following the death of one of their porters had stupidly abandoned their Sirdar, his staff and all their equipment except sleeping bags. They would have assuredly perished but for us discovering them wandering about aimlessly in deep snow below our campsite.

Later we were to discover that at the same period of time in the rest of the world, much greater disasters were unfolding. In Bangladesh a typhoon from the Bay of Bengal created havoc and enormous loss of life. Back home in Britain, millions of trees and much property was destroyed by the winds of hurricane force. Australia suffered from draught followed by raging bush fires that destroyed wild life and whole townships. Once again famine spread across huge areas of Africa when the water holes dried up, whilst America was swept by storms and floods. At Edmonton in Alberta there was a destructive tornado where none had been known before and unusually the same snow-bearing clouds that we saw at Dole swept across the Himalayan divide into Tibet where hundreds of Tibetans perished in the snow. El Nino had been busy.

Footprints

For two days following the snowstorm in the upper Dudh Kosi, the atmosphere was brilliantly crisp and clear. There was not a breath of wind. All sound was deadened by the deep covering of snow but the sun shone warm and life giving. Apart from our own movements, other life forms having temporarily holed up in the storm began to stir. Soon we saw the footprints of mouse-hare, serow, and musk deer, then there was much excitement when Ken Hall and Neil Heaton were sure they had come across the prints of a snow leopard. I was not sure and because of my previous experiences in the Dudh Kosi I was inclined to think they were the tracks of a wolf. The wolves of Khumbu are the large creamy coloured Tibetan wolves that cross over from the plateau where they are able to live on hare, marmot, gazelle and antelope but in Khumbu find easier pickings among the Sherpa lifestock. I thought of the time years earlier when with Eileen, I was with Lakpa Thondup, Ang Norbu and Dawa Tenzing on ski. We were across the other side of the Ngojumba glacier from Nerebu and up at the Nimagawa la. We too had found the tracks of wolf on the glacier and the story of what happened to us during the following few days is worth telling.

Nepali Sharpshooters and Buddhist Sensitivities

We noticed the wolf prints early in the day whilst skiing with our Sherpas on the Chola glacier, but by the afternoon, had decided to strike camp and return to Dawa's home in the Imja Khola. Whilst we were descending the glacier, two Sherpas hurried down towards us. Dawa knew them both for they had carried on several expeditions to Everest.

Down in the valley of the Nimagawa, not far from their village of Taknak, they had been surprised to see our figures at the pass. Both had been searching for tracks of a wolf and decided to ascend to the Chola glacier to see if we had seen anything of the animal. We could imagine how puzzled and excited they must have been to find both our ski tracks and also those of the wolf. Having caught up with us they then wanted to descend with us to Dzonghla and go on to Pheriche where they hoped to locate a Nepali rifleman who could shoot the wolf, once they found its lair. To our surprise, later that evening, they returned to our Dzonghla camp bringing with them an ill-clad, shivering Nepali complete with rifle. All three were given hot food and drinks but we felt sorry for the Nepali rifleman, when most reluctantly he left with them to find a cave to sleep in higher up the valley.

Eileen asked why the Sherpas didn't use a rifle themselves and I pointed out that being Buddhists they wouldn't want to kill an animal, even one that was a menace to the community and that they wished to see dead. However, they would be perfectly happy if someone else killed the wolf—hence the Nepali. Before leaving they told us that all the prints we had seen had been made by a wolf that had killed a yak at Pheriche. It was a lame wolf, and very clever because it never killed livestock in the same valley in which it had its lair. We knew that the killing of a yak would be a real calamity amongst a Sherpa community for these mountain cattle are highly prized. The wealthier climbing and trekking Sherpas who stay in Khumbu buy them whenever possible to build up herds for later years.

Our friend Phu Cheeta already owned twenty-one yak and Ang Norbu was the proud possessor of eighteen yak plus two dzum or dzo. A dzum or dzo is a fertile female, good for milk production, that is obtained by cross breeding a yak with a Nepali or Indian cow. The males which are infertile are called dzubjok or dzopkio. They are strong, work well and are often used for ploughing or carrying loads. Yak meat is a scarce commodity, for though Sherpas enjoy eating it, none of these animals are grown for their meat. A yak will only be eaten when it dies. Usually it is buffalo or a cow that is killed to provide meat for trekkers at Sherpa eating houses or 'hotels'.

We took our time on the journey from Dzonghla to a campsite below Pheriche the next day, stopping for a couple of hours for a long lunch in the sun at a sandy 'beach' by the mouth of the Chola lake. Later at Periche, situated on the alluvial flats below the terminal moraine of the Khumbu glacier, we wondered how the trackers were faring in the Chola khola, for this was the village where the yak had recently been killed.

Early the next morning, we arrived back at Dawa's house in Dingboche having enjoyed the photography of freshly blooming primula and the many varieties of coloured rhododendrons. Angmou (Dawa's daughter) made us welcome with a huge bowl of *aloo* (potatoes) which we rapidly consumed along with tasty mounds of salt and swigs of *rakshi*. Would we ever hear more about the wolf was a question constantly on our minds.

Pangboche Gompa and the Yeti Scalp

On the following day, Dawa's young cow bellowed in the byre waking us all to a mellow dawn, and the early morning sunshine quickly melted a light covering of snow. A line of snorting yak, throat bells clanging, steam rising from their shaggy flanks, plodded slowly behind a yak-boy on the trail to Pangboche. We were also going there for Ang Norbu had invited us to visit his home which was close to the gompa and where we hoped to see the 'snowman scalp'.

Departing early, we left Angmou humming a Sherpani tune whilst she tidied round the fire. The day was particularly clear and we enjoyed seeing the broad high wedge of Ama Dablam, an ice festooned chisel of a mountain that towered above us. Possibly Dawa was feeling penitent having drunk too much '*rakshi*' the night before. He stopped frequently to read out the mani mantra carved on the rocks and each time he gave the ending of the mantra a particularly powerful *Hum*!

Crossing the bridge over the Imja Khola we began the steep ascent of the track that eventually led us to Pangboche village and the gompa.

Many prayer flags or *torcho* whipped and cracked in the breeze outside the entrance to the gompa, each wave and crack marking the equivalent of saying the many prayers printed on the fabric. Within the gompa we looked forward to seeing the Yeti (snowman) scalp. The one that Tom Stobart and I felt might have been made from the skin of a wild pig, when we carefully examined it during the search for the 'Snowman'.

Dawa located the lama with the key who then brought out the scalp for us to photograph. To my surprise, I discovered that since that time, a 'Yeti' hand had also been added to the exhibit. I believe the general opinion now is that the hand is human. The scalp was the same one we had first examined but seemed to have less of the bristly hair. Either visitors were extracting hairs surreptitiously or the Yeti was going bald! It was good to examine the scalp again but I was surprised that we only needed to pay 10 rupees to see it. I had always felt the charge was an excellent way of obtaining gompa funds but thought the cost might have inflated more. (Now in the new millennium I'm told it has been stolen by a visitor to the gompa).

The head lama had been at special meditation when we arrived but hurried round to see us before we left. For an extra 20 rupees he offered to arrange for us to hear the blowing of the silver trumpets called the *Gyaling*, and even the great booming horns, the *Saung Daungs*, similar in appearance to the alpen horns of Switzerland but we declined his offer having already heard them many times.

Leaving the gompa we wound our way along the narrow pathways to Ang Norbu's house, meeting his wife and children at the door and soon having been regaled with typical Sherpa hospitality, felt not only well-fed but slightly inebriated from the large quantities of *chang* consumed. Norbu was a bundle of nervous energy, never sitting down, hovering over our plates and *chang* cups, anxious to be the perfect host, pleased that we liked his spacious home and its breathtaking view of Ama Dablam. Dawa too, seemed ill at ease and before long we knew the reason why. He wanted us to visit Annie's house—Annie being his second daughter.

Annie's House and the Wolf-Hunters

The late morning sun glanced down from many hanging ice-walls across the valley as we trudged unsteadily through the fields, over high protecting walls and into the tiny outside yard of Annie's home. Sprays of bamboo lashed to the wooden eaves sported gaily fluttering prayer flags of many colours—blue, red, orange, yellow, green, fresh clean white and dirty grey. In the courtyard were six men talking loudly and excitedly and all at once. A motley crew. All went quiet as we entered. Swaying gently, they looked towards us and six pairs of eyes stared a little vacantly at our party. One pair I noticed in particular, bright and shining mischievous eyes they were, that reminded me of someone. The face was familiar too and then I realised who it was. Twenty-two years had gone by but I still had many memories of Nima Tenzing and of the journey I once made with him from Everest to Kangchenjunga. One in particular was of crossing the Rakha la to the Naktang chu in Tibet. There had been a lot of snow and obscuring clouds on the pass but after an hour of descent there was a quite sudden transformation. Sunlight and cloud shadows enhanced the beauty of the rolling pastel coloured landscape and close by, red sprays of azalea blossom sparkled with drops of water that also dripped from its dark green leaves.

'Tibet side' shouted Nima Tenzing and I could still see him clearly in my mind's eye, his face one huge smile and his eyes, as always, bright and shining.

In the courtyard I took one step forward crying enthusiastically, "Nima Tenzing", and his face took on a puzzled look.

Everest, Kangchenjunga jaiga—Tibet side malum? I continued, and another look, this time of incredulity plus dawning comprehension appeared on his face. He smiled as of old, flung his arms around me crying,

Malum Jackson Sahib, Bahut achha rasta, malum Everest— Kangchenjunga jaiga. His Urdu was crude and basic as mine but obviously he still remembered the journey of twenty-two years before. His shoulders squared and he stood another inch higher, his companions too stood a little straighter yet swayed in rhythm as if controlled by puppet strings. All blinked dazedly, then like Nima beamed with pleasure, faces wreathed in alcoholic smiles.

Dawa was displeased. Nima was some distant relative of whom he didn't approve. This sudden notoriety for Nima and his heightened standing in the immediate company galled Dawa. To smooth matters over I suggested we go inside and offered *chang* all round. Nima shook his head, put off by Dawa's obvious distaste and explained that unfortunately they were a wolf hunting party. He was the leader, he explained and reluctantly at real cost to his innermost desires, they must go immediately to Pheriche. The wolf (no doubt the same one whose prints we had seen in the Chola khola) had already killed two yak he said and implied that the safety of all Sherpa animals in the valley was laid squarely on his shoulders. Thus, full of duty and recognising the importance of his mission he proudly refused the offer of *chang* and departed.

"I must see him again," I said to Eileen as we lowered our heads and went through the doorway into Annie's house. There despite all our protests we again received typical Sherpa hospitality so that soon the table was a clutter of *chang* kettles, cups, jars and plates laden with *gurr* and tasty *chapatties* made with *tsampa*. Annie had been forewarned!

Five minutes went by when in trooped the six wolf-hunters apologising for their rudeness. Not one of them, Nima said, could think why they had been so rude as to refuse our offer of *chang* and they sat down forthwith to make amends. More jugs of foaming *chang* were brought and the determined hunters rapidly becoming more merry and inebriated, continued to down the contents.

Nima then told us that five of them came from Pangboche but the sixth man was a friend of theirs from Namche Bazar. Rambling a little, he went on to try and explain something of his relationship to Dawa and throughout his narrative his eyes twinkled mischievously. His friends became more voluble and boisterous and to my amusement, so did Eileen and Dawa. Almost an hour went by when at a word from Nima the wolf-hunters stood up noisily, bowed ceremoniously, shook hands with us, and swaying alarmingly, trooped out once again to catch the wolf of Pheriche. At least that is what we thought. It wasn't long though before three of them returned, sat down and looking owlishly across at us began to quaff more *chang*. Ten minutes later, the friend from Namche made a big effort and as he went outside mumbled to Dawa that he would catch up with Nima and the others.

Ang Norbu then arrived at Annie's house hoping to return with us to Dingboche. Quickly he took in the situation and grinned at me, particularly relishing the merry mood of Eileen and Dawa. Leaving Annie to cope with the remaining 'hunters' we stepped outside and carefully picked our way along the narrow stony pathway.

Soon we heard the sound of voices, jocular but slurred and turning a corner found Nima Tenzing with his two companions, talking and arguing volubly yet with good humour. They were oblivious to the rest of the world and quite obviously not bound for Pheriche. Of the friend from Namche Bazaar there was no sign.

Our own little party went along quite happily with Norbu and I almost helpless with laughter at times as Eileen and Dawa, arms linked together, danced along the track singing the well known refrain

"We ain't got a barrel of money, maybe we're ragged and funny but we're rolling along, singing this song, side by side".

Round the chortens, down the steps, through the archways, past the prayer wheels, and along the mani walls they danced and sang their merry way. It was an hilarious journey home.

Finally at the long 'mani' wall near Dawa's house, we found the friend from Namche. Laid out with his back against the mani wall, he was sleeping in the sun, mouth open wide and snoring loudly. As with the rest of the hunters, all thoughts of the wolf had gone. Not surprisingly, before we left Sola Khumbu, we were told that the lame she-wolf was still alive and running free.

A Final Word (1987)

That meeting with Nima Tenzing and the wolf-hunters had happened over a decade earlier, and the 'wolf' tracks we had found following the snowstorm reminded me of the story. But what had happened to the she-wolf I wondered? Probably she had died after all this time, as had Dawa Tenzing, but I thought perhaps the tracks were made by one of her progeny and I feared for the sheep and yak of Pheriche.

We retraced our steps to Khumjung two days after the storm and seeing the tracks. There Eileen and I were overjoyed to meet

Lakpa Thondup again. Then to our astonishment and great delight at the hamlet of Pheriche, we met Ang Norbu with his son Ang Sombu. Most amazingly after we returned from a visit to the Everest base camp and the ascent of Kalar Pattar, we were trudging through the snow in upper Pangboche when we found Nima Tenzing.

He was a trekking Sirdar now, having been on many journeys and expeditions. In 1979, three years after he 'led' the wolf-hunters, he was assistant Sirdar with Doug Scott, Joe Tasker and Peter Boardman on their Kangchenjunga ascent. There he had made such an impression that Peter Boardman wrote to me asking for more information about this exceptional Sherpa. He had found him to be a good companion, strong, faithful and diligent and like all Sherpas of the old school deeply religious. In Pangboche, Neil Heaton gave him a copy of the *Climber and Hill Walker* in which an article had been written about Nima Tenzing by the son of Eric Hoskings, the bird photographer.

Later at the 'Tashi Delek Hotel' in Thyangboche run by Ang Neesha (Angmou, Dawa's daughter at Dingboche) I left a few photographs taken of him when he was a 'wolf hunter', and several others that I had taken of him thirty-three years earlier on our journey to Kangchenjunga.

We met him again in Sola Khumbu after 1987, and then much later on the Milke Danda ridge in north-east Nepal. Each time it was a pleasure to meet an old and faithful friend who was still diligent, strong and religious and who, despite the passing years, still had the same bright and shining mischievous eyes.

24

Everest to Kangchenjunga:
Thoughts about a Long Walk
(1954 and 1990)

"Wherever the nearer range dropped, fresh peaks and
horns shot up over its unknown and untrodden passes.
Below the bright belt of new-fallen snow on which I
stood, the great spurs of the mountains were spread
out range beyond range."
–Douglas Freshfield in *'Round Kangchenjunga'* 1905

With a group of friends, Eileen and I were walking along the
Milke Danda ridge in north-east Nepal. It was 1990, the
35th anniversary year of the first ascent of Kangchenjunga and
our destination was the upper Yalung valley below the south-west
face of the mountain. Early in the morning at our campsite near
Gupha Pokari, we had marvelled at the sheer majesty of a blush
sunrise on Makalu, Chamlang and the Kangshung face of Everest.
Now, further along the ridge, our breath was taken away, not by
the altitude, but by a new panorama when we rounded a bend of
the track near Gurja Gaon. A wall of mighty ice ramparts guarded
the head of the Tamur valley ahead of us. These were the towering

flanks of Jannu and the huge massif of Kangchenjunga, attended by a host of princely peaks, Koktang, Rathong, Kabru Dome, Talung and Pandim. It was then the quote from Freshfield's book sprang to mind.

A Chance Meeting

The track descended through small fields growing crops of millet, buckwheat, maize, potatoes, and the air was heavy laden with the scent of Frangipani. Steeply, we diverted into a rocky gully where the path was narrow. Coming up towards us were two trekkers and a Sherpa and we stepped to one side to let them pass. With a shock of surprise, and at the same moment, the Sherpa and I recognised each other.

"Its Nima Tenzing," I exclaimed, and a feeling of great joy rose up within me.

"Yes, Jackson Sahib it is" and the toothy grin splitting Nimas's face told me he felt the same.

During recent years we had met several times in Sola Khumbu where he had become a famous trekking Sirdar. However, I am sure that Eileen, like me, was remembering an occasion in earlier years when he was the proud leader of the wolf-hunters of Pangboche.

"Where are you going?" I asked.

"I'm taking my party to the Makalu base camp in the Barun. They are friends of Doug Scott".

Mention of Makalu then set me thinking of a journey he and I made with other Sherpas even earlier in time. A long walk that began at the foot of Everest, led us by Makalu base camp, took us through to Tibet, on to the base of Kangchenjunga and finally ended in Darjeeling.

Our two groups were going in opposite directions and each with a long day ahead of us, so we couldn't linger long. Even so, there was time for photographs and time for Nima to meet Charlotte McKinnon, the daughter of Tom who had been with Nima and me on the ascent of Kangchenjunga in 1955. It proved a happy meeting for everybody and whilst continuing the descent to

Nesum, I was able to tell Charlotte more of that earlier climb. But it was the mention of Makalu and memories of the long walk that kept impinging on my mind.

Usually when we travel, we are aware that others have gone before us and often the pleasure of the journey is enhanced because of the knowledge and added interest we have gained from their experiences. There is however something very special about making a journey that no one has made before. Everest to Kangchenjunga was such a journey.

A Cold Swim and the Journey Begins

Before leaving the Sola Khumbu, I had one of my more 'dicey' experiences when trying to swim a rope across the icy raging torrent of the Dudh Kosi. At the time, the Phunki bridge below Thyangboche had been swept away and the river was in ferocious mood. Somehow we had to place a rope from bank to bank above the river and though people were sceptical, I felt sure I could swim a rope over. My thinking was that with a powerful dive and rapid free-style swim, I could reach a boulder two-thirds of the way across, climb on to it, then plunge to the far side.

"How about making a belay," I said to Stanley Jeeves, "Then with us both linked by the rope, nothing can go wrong".

Stan agreed. From the start things didn't go to plan. Instead of taking a powerful dive, I had to push off from a slimy boulder. With arms tearing at the water and legs beating rapidly, I did reach the rock but it was rounded and undercut. Ice cold fingers searched for a hold, but the water-worn boulder was smooth as marble. Quickly, the powerful current tore my grasping hands from their flimsy grip and straight away I was whipped into mid-stream.

There was no time for fear, just time to roll on my back and look at Stan on whom now I felt my life depended. Letting my body go slack, I took in a deep breath and caught a glimpse of wild white water crashing powerfully over rocks. In moments, I was over the falls into a deep cold world of green water consisting of millions of beautiful bright and shining bubbles streaming past me to a glimmer of light above. By now there was no feeling in my body and as strongly as possible, I lunged upwards, following the bubbles to the surface.

At the very last moment, the rope jerked at my waist and stopped me plunging over the next foaming cataract. There was time to notice Ralph Izzard throwing out a lasso which miraculously I caught. This slim life-line swung me round beyond a large boulder and into a calmer eddy. Momentary relief disappeared when the Sherpas, who by now were sure I was going to die, pulled hard on the rope linking me with Stan. Immediately it swept me back into mid-stream then hauled me backwards beneath the pounding waterfall. Unable to breathe and weakening rapidly, I heaved frantically on the lasso rope, cleared my head above the water and shouted "Stop pulling, stop pulling". Though he couldn't hear, Ralph understood and stopped the Sherpas in their efforts and the current swept me round to the calmer eddy once again. The river was still deep and the strong surge was pulling me down but by clinging to the lasso, I was able to gulp in lungs full of life-giving air. Unceremoniously, I was then dragged out of the river to the top of a smooth rock where I lay gasping like a stranded fish. My right shin was bleeding from a deep gash but I was too frozen to feel anything. To be alive was a terrific relief and I managed to smile.

Sherpas were crying, for like the shaken expedition members they thought they had been watching the last moments of my life. It was the following morning when I realised just how fortunate I had been. Stiff and sore after the battering amongst the rocks, I could barely move. Both legs were discoloured yellow and blue from hip to ankle and the whole of my back was also severely bruised

Clearly, just one of those bangs on my head and the story would have had a different ending. I was reminded of the episode several decades later, when at Thyangboche gompa I found parts of a broken kayak. It was a remnant from one of the most exciting outdoor films I have ever seen called 'Canoeing Down Everest'. A nonsensical name for such a fine and exhilarating adventure. Canoes were split and smashed in the raging waters of the Dudh Kosi, and even in life jackets, the canoeists risked life and limb throughout their tremendous journey.

At the time of my swim, Tom Stobart filmed practically the whole episode but missed out the landing and being a dedicated cine photographer, asked me to do that bit again—which I did! For several years afterwards, at least once a year, the film was shown on television but I never managed to see it. Friends used to tell me that they had seen the film when I 'fell' into the Dudh Kosi—and because I didn't "fall' in but, went in of my own volition, my replies were always unprintable.

It was shortly after my swim that I collected my Sherpas together including Nima Tenzing and began the journey from Everest to Kangchenjunga. Curtis, the Foreign News Editor of the *Daily Mail*, had given the go ahead for me to seek out Hillary's New Zealand expedition on Makalu. For some reason there was a rumour in Khumbu that Ed Hillary had died of malaria, and it was hoped I might discover the truth of the matter. I was then to carry on and find my way linking up with the reconnaissance team on the south-west face of Kangchenjunga. Maybe they had seen signs of the 'Yeti'. Many years earlier it was in that region where Hunt (Lord John) had found large footprints at 19,000 feet near the Zemu gap.

Nima and I along with others of our team said our farewells to the rest of the 'Snowman' expedition at the village of Tola then off we went to Chukhung in the Imja Khola. From thereon the journey took almost twenty days.

Whilst with the anniversary group we continued to trek along the Milke Danda, passing through Nesum and then on to Dobhan, I continued to think of Nima Tenzing and my other companions and my mind went quickly through the bare bones of the journey that we had made in 1954.

The Bare Bones

From the Imja Khola, we crossed the Ambu Lapcha to the Hongu and then traversed the west and east cols of the Barun Saddle at 20,000 feet. In the Barun valley it was a superb relief to see Ed Hillary striding up the glacier with a huge pack on his back and clearly very much alive. Without more ado I took a photograph and sent the film back to Ralph Izzard by a couple of Sherpas. The picture was eventually circulated to papers around the world and the revenue paid for most of the expedition. In addition to Hillary's party I also met some of the Californian expedition members who were attempting Makalu from the long east ridge. Dick Houston and Fritz Lippman made me very welcome and later Al Steck arrived back from the mountain. It was another twenty-three years before I met Al Steck again and showed him my 'Snowman' pictures at his home in Berkely, California.

From the Barun, we crossed over to the Arun valley and reached the Arun river after a descent of seven thousand feet. Crossing the swaying bamboo bridge, the Sherpas and I then travelled to Chepua and eventually Goyem. We had to cross the Lumbasamba Himal to the Tamur river and Walung Chung if we were to reach the Yalung glacier and Kangchenjunga before June. To do this we crossed the Rakha la 17,800 feet then descended to the Naktang Chu in Tibet. There we found sunnier and drier conditions as we travelled through Tibet for three days eventually crossing back into Nepal over the Tipta la. From the Tipta la the descent of the Tamur valley took us to Walung Chung village which the famous botanist and traveller Sir Joseph Hooker first visited in the 1840s. It would appear that over a hundred years later, I was the second European to visit that large Bhotia village. This makes you realise just how remote the area was until recent times. But then one has to remember that it wasn't until 1950 that the first people from the west (Britain and America) visited Sola Khumbu and the south side of Everest!

It was actually nineteen and a half days after leaving the Everest base that we arrived in the Yalung valley at the base of Kangchen-junga. There we met the reconnaissance team, John Kempe, Gilmour Lewis, Jack Tucker and for me the greatest thrill of all, my brother Ron.* Having climbed together in Britain and the Alps over many years it was a tremendous experience to share days

---

*Two members, Don Mathews and Trevor Braham had already left for Darjeeling.

with Ron in that rugged part of the Himalaya. There has never been any doubt in my mind that meeting was the richest memory of the walk, but there are other memories too. Most are happy and pleasing though one or two are tinged with sadness. The Ambu Lapcha was one.

Ambu Lapcha

The Ambu Lapcha is a pass over 19,000 feet in height at the top of the Imja khola. It varies in difficulty. Sometimes it is icy, requiring much cramponing, step cutting and careful belaying. At other times, following a fall of snow, it can become relatively easy. It had been so the first time I crossed it whilst making a climber's appreciation of the difficulties of ascending Ama Dablam. At the time the *Daily Mail* thought that a team led by Hillary was going to attempt the climb. Before putting pen to paper I looked at the mountain from the summit of Pokalde, then crossed the Ambu Lapcha and visited the Mingbo la. Two of us then climbed a glacier peak near the Mera pass. Many years after, I was pleased that the route I thought the most feasible was the one by which Ama Dablam was first climbed. But a great sadness was that the great ice ridge I condemned in the appraisal, written for Ralph Izzard, was the ridge on which later, two climbing friends lost their lives. A similar sad memory was linked to the Ambu Lapcha.

Annullu, a younger brother of Sirdar Dawa Tenzing had been with Tom McKinnon and me on the carry to establish Camp V on Kangchenjunga. He had also been the Sherpa who with Wilfrid Noyce, had first reached the South Col of Everest in 1953. Later he was involved in many fine climbs on Makalu, Pumori and other mountains. Years afterwards, whilst leading a couple of German trekkers on the Ambu Lapcha, there was a slip and all three of them were killed.

On a more cheerful note I thought of Nima Tenzing's great friend Ang Nyima. Whilst crossing the pass an our way to Kangchenjunga, the route had been made more difficult because of debris at the bottom of the couloir. It was ice all the way to the top, having been swept clean by avalanche. Ang Nyima had been a tower of strength, helping me to safeguard several of the party who were heavily laden with *'lakri'* (wood). This was for Hillary's expedition if, or when, they camped at Hongu lake.

Ang Nyima was a young and bold Sherpa from Darjeeling and he was looking forward to returning home. He and two other Sherpas shared a tent with me for most of the journey and because he smoked incessantly, I banished him from the tent on many occasions. It was particularly amusing watching him 'train' and lord it over his simple unspoiled brethren from the 'wilds' of Khumbu. One of the many chores he taught them was to bring his tea to the tent each morning. The previous year he had carried to the top camp on Everest during the first ascent, and then in later years he went to the summit of Annapurna II. He was also a most reliable and stalwart Sherpa with Wilfrid Noyce and David Cox on Macchapucchare. All this was long after our crossing of the Ambu Lapcha, where I first began to notice him change from being a loner to a fine member of a team.

Eventually he served with the 10th Gurkha Rifles in Borneo and Malaya where he rose to the rank of Sergeant. Perhaps the camaraderie engendered throughout the walk to Kangchenjunga was a help to him in his future life.

Once across the pass, we left Sola Khumbu behind and after traversing the west and east cols of the Barun Saddle at 20,000 feet deceded the Barun glacier to the base camp of the Californian Himalayan Expedition. Later in the day we camped at the New Zealand base where we stayed for two days with Doc 'Mike' Ball and Jim McFarlane who was badly frost bitten. After we left the New Zealand camp to descend the Barun khola, we met two Sirdars, Dawa Tenzing (with us on Kangchenjunga the following year) and also Ang Tharkay who had been with Shipton and Tilman on many exploratory expeditions. With them was an American biologist Dr. Lawrie Swan who was also investigating the mystery of the 'Snowman'. He and I had a good chat and exchange of experiences before we went our different ways.

Little did I think at the time that we would meet again but not until 33 years later. This was in San Francisco during 1987 when I was lecturing with a set of slides that illustrated the very journey on which we met. An astonishing coincidence.

The next seven days were full of incident taking us through exciting country. Quite rugged and remote it seemed at the time. For three days we saw no other people, then at a squalid bamboo village named Mankim we met many charming and friendly locals. Being the first white man they had ever seen, I was a great curiosity. At Mankim we were able to buy fresh food, barley flour (*tsampa*), potatoes, onions, eggs and much to Ang Nyima's liking, bamboo jars filled with foaming *chang*. It was not long before he and some of the others were smiling happily and I am sure if they had known it, would have sung with fervour the chant:

"I have no pain dear Mother, now
But oh, I am so dry,
Connect me to a brewery,
And leave me there to die."

From Mankim our route took us across the river Arun and through the villages of Chepua, Chyamtang and Goyem, then finally having traversed the Lumbasamba Himal, we crossed the Rakha la into a new country—Tibet.

The terrain through which we travelled to get there was not only remote but many years later became an important area for the study of basic plant species—particularly barley. Dr. 'Len' Beer who frequently used to visit me at my home in Capel Curig, eventually led a botanical expedition from the School of Plant Biology at the University College of North Wales, Bangor. This took him and the rest of the expedition right into the Lumbasamba Himal and I was able to provide useful information, as well as photographs, prior to them going.

Now in the 1990s, trekking organisations take groups to the Barun via the Arun valley and Shipton la (Sedua pass) which is what Nima Tenzing was going to do with his party when we met him on the Milke Danda ridge.

But that will be the journey to make if ever the border is opened. Through the Lumbasamba Himal, over the Rakha la, down to the Naktang chu and to the village of Kudo in Tibet. Like me, I was sure that Nima Tenzing would never forget the moment we first saw that country and felt pleased that I had written about his reactions many years earlier.

Tibet Side!

During our walk, we left the village of Goyem in very damp and dreary conditions. Early on we found the specimens of large Himalayan blue poppy—*Meconopsis grandis*—their hairy leaves covered in rain drops, sparkling in the feeble yellow light of the early morning sun. Rain turned to sleet and as we climbed higher, the slopes became barren, covered with mushy snow and slimy moss. It was drear. Then we heard the snorting of yak, and the tinkling of yak bells and out of the swirling mist appeared a Tibetan yak-man. This was a watering place named Jalong and the elderly Tibetan supplied us with creamy yak milk for which I paid him well. He was quite alone and living in a canvas-covered bothy, the roof of which was sagging beneath the weight of wet snow. Most of the time, this would be the only life he would know, a lonely and harsh existence, yet he appeared content, was very hospitable, and obviously delighted at our meeting. It is so often the way amongst people living a simple life, almost entirely devoid of material possessions. They are constantly in touch with nature, indeed they are a part of it, and having sufficient to live on, seem quite happy to share with others any excess that they have.

We left him sitting by a tiny fire of yak-dung, and within moments of leaving his bothy, all we could see was a drift of blue smoke, then all was gone; enveloped in the mist.

Higher up towards the pass the wind increased, blowing powder snow horizontally onto our chests where it formed a thick crust protecting and insulating us from the elements. Then finally, we wound our way through a group of rock gendarmes and could see a fluttering of flags, a *Lung-Ta*, that marked the top of the Rakha la. We were still in the clouds but I felt there was a growing excitement among the Sherpas and a sense of anticipation. What was to happen I wondered? Within an hour I knew, for the transformation from the cold and fierceness of the day was astounding. There was no snow or rain. The sun shone brightly.

Below us a smooth grass-covered valley stretched ahead, flanked by a host of rolling green hills. The lovely pastel colouring of the Tibetan landscape was a dramatic contrast to the harsh snow and wind-riven environment we had just left behind. It was quite enchanting.

"Tibet side!" shouted Nima Tenzing. He was leaping excitedly and his face was split open by one huge cheery smile. It was probably the most exciting day of his life.

(At our meeting on the Milke Danda ridge many thoughts flashed quickly through my mind. In 1954 he had helped to haul me out of the Dudh Kosi after my swim. We had also ascended the Everest icefall together, and made the journey to the Nangpa la. He had been with me on carries to camps on Kangchenjunga in 1955 and of course in 1976 he had been the leader of those hilarious wolf-hunters of Pangboche. In 1986 it had been good to meet him again at Pangboche and then at Phakdingma in 1987. In 1988 we shared the same campsite but with different people, for then he was the Sirdar with a party of American trekkers.

But on the Milke Danda, I realised that the most enduring and satisfying memory I had of Nima was that moment when, below the Rakha la, he saw for his first time, the original homeland of his people—Tibet.)

Ibis Bills (*Ibidorhynchus struthersii*)

Dr. Biswamoy Biswas was the Curator of the Mammal Section of the Calcutta Museum when he was invited to join the 'Daily Mail' Yeti Expedition. We always called him 'Bis' for short. During the expedition he did identify and name several new species and sub-species of mammal but mainly he concentrated on collecting, or observing, as many types of birds as possible. There was one species in particular in which he was interested. These were the *ibis* bills. For a long time the whereabouts of the nesting sites of these snipe-like birds had been sought. He said they were expected to be found somewhere high and remote in the Himalaya, perhaps on the alluvial flats below the terminal moraines in old glaciated valley. On the walk in from Kathmandu to our base camp in Sola

Khumbu we did see several on the wing and possibly migrating. They were somewhat larger than a redshank and mainly grey with a black forehead and face. The bill was quite long and decurved, that is, turned downwards towards the tip which enables them to forage for food beneath small pebbles in stony streams and sandy river. 'Bis' constantly reminded me to look out for their nesting sites whenever I moved off to meet groups of team members in the higher valleys. I did hope I would find them in the upper Dudh Kosi, perhaps near Macherma or in the Bhote Kosi during our journey to the Nangpa la. It was not to be.

Once 'Bis' knew I was going to make the journey from Khumbu to Kangchenjunga, he became quite excited and reminded me again to look out for the *ibis* bills. I shall always be glad he did.

Once we were down below the Rakha la, we descended to the upper reaches of the river Arun, here given the Tibetan name of Naktang Chu. Clumps of red azalea were a blaze of fire down by the river and less than a mile away, we could see the flat-roofed village of Kudo. We camped nearby and the following morning moved off early because now we were in Tibet I had no desire to meet up with any Chinese soldiery. I felt sure we were in far too remote an area, and in any case, I hoped my ragged clothing and sun-burnt skin would disguise me if we did. I had a massive beard and my Sherpas said I looked like a Sadhu anyway! We arrived at a yak-hide tent and having been hailed by the inhabitant, a handsome Tibetan woman, the Sherpas quickly disappeared inside for refreshing yak milk and *tsampa*.

The sun shone warmly and outside the tent a rippling fresh water stream flowed swiftly towards the village. Beside the stream a clump of blue poppies swayed in the gentle breeze and golden-haired yak grazed contentedly nearby. High peaks tipped with snow and ice rimmed the valley to the south, a fine backdrop to the flattened and marshy valley floor beneath. I was reminded of Mini marg, east of the Zoji la in Ladakh and of the alluvial flats below the glacier near Phalong Karpo and Pheriche in Khumbu.

Suddenly a pair of *ibis* bills rose up from the meandering river bed. Their penetrating flute-like calls resounded throughout the valley and I wondered excitedly if at last I had found one of the breeding grounds of these shy birds. Throughout the rest of a long day, first along the Naktang chu then up a side valley we continued to see them rising from nesting sites among the marshes by the river. Our altitude was around twelve to thirteen thousand feet. Between the village of Kudo and a small dwelling site named Tashir-haka many hours further along the valley, the terrain seemed to fit in well with the description of the breeding grounds that 'Bis' had given me. I felt elated.

(Back in India weeks later, I left behind a write up of my findings, giving 'Bis' a description of the area and the nesting site. Though I never met 'Bis' again, I did on several occasions read of journeys that he made with that doyen of Indian ornithologists— Salim Ali. Did they also visit the Naktang chu? I never found out.)

Tipta la—An Important Trade Route

The track along the Naktang Chu and out over the Tipta la back into Nepal was broad. This was because at the time it was the most important trade route between the two countries across the Umbakh Himal. Even though the Chinese had already invaded Tibet and the trade routes were closing, the Tipta la being such a remote area, was still open. Throughout the day large herds of yak, and nak (female yak) were moving up and down the valley. Mostly they were carrying loads of cigarettes, paper, kerosene, felt hats and grain from Nepal or in the opposite direction were taking yak-dans (panniers) filled with salt or borax. We noticed the yak-men separated the herd of yak from each herd of nak by at least a mile. A wise precaution.

Stops were fairly frequent, for once the yak were below the stony and icy pass they found the grazing among the marshes much to their liking. The yak-men too used such opportunities to light a fire of yak-dung and make a brew from brick tea, salt, and yak butter. Perhaps they were also giving thanks after a successful crossing of the high pass, a custom I had come across in other parts of the Himalaya over twelve hundred miles away in Kashmir. I noticed too, that on occasion the yak-men cut down the long stems of the large blue poppies which in appearance resembled sticks of rhubarb. The stems were peeled and the stalks then eaten. I found them to be almost tasteless, slightly astringent and quite refreshing. Perhaps they are medicinal and I have since discovered that the roots possess narcotic properties.

Because Nima Tenzing had blood poisoning from a leech bite, I was giving him Aureomycin and at one stop, a yak-man gave me a pan of hot water with which to bathe Nima's arm.

Once again there was a profusion of blue poppies and it reminded me of the first time I ever saw them. They were not the large *Meconopsis grandis* of Tibet but the smaller *Meconopsis aculeata* to be found over in the west and central Himalaya. The blue colouring of the petals can vary greatly and I noted that the flowers of the *grandis* were generally a deeper, richer blue than those of the *acaulis*. The stalks too were longer and these *Meconopsis* certainly deserved their name. They were truly imposing and majestic plants. Blue poppies and azaleas, yak and nak, ibis bills and nesting sites, snow-tipped mountains and softly rolling hills: I really felt it to be a privilege to be part of the environment of Tibet side! Though I had met but few of the Tibetans, all were charming and hospitable. It was a good preparation for the next few days among the Bhotias.

Shortly after bathing Nima's arm, we set up camp on the Tibetan side of the Tipta la. We were soon to leave the drier Tibet for a much wetter Nepal but because we were already so near the Himalayan watershed, the weather deteriorated rapidly. Swirling spindrift filtered through every crack in the tents. It was a very cold night.

The Bhotias

We wakened to find it a bleak white world and wasting no time crossed the pass to enter the Tamur valley. Rain fell in torrents throughout the day. Crossing the Tamur river by an exciting and rather dilapidated bamboo bridge, we then sloshed our way down to the village of Walung Chung where we stayed the night. Walung Chung village was well described by Sir Joseph Hooker in his *Himalayan Journals* and though his visit took place in 1848, I found in 1954 that very little had changed. It was still playing an important role with caravans of yak carrying trade goods to and fro between Nepal and Tibet. The inhabitants of Walung Chung are Bhotias. They are people I have written about before, but there's a little more worth the telling.

The name arises from Bhote, the old name for Tibet. These are Tibetan people who at some time in the past have crossed the mountain range and settled on the south side of the Himalaya. It is clear then that the Sherpas of the Everest region must be Bhotias for they too originate from eastern Tibet, and migrated to Sola Khumbu some three hundred and fifty years ago. Nima Tenzing and the others were quite affronted when I suggested this to them. When we were in the upper reaches of the Arun at Mankim, Chepua, Goyem and other villages, it was clear to me that they did not consider it strange that they could converse with the Lhomi Bhotias. Yes, they sometimes had problems with dialect, but basically the language was the same. At Walung Chung they again had no difficulty in conversing with the Bhotias, and I was able to point out that the form of dress was very much the same as with the Sherpas of Sola Khumbu. In particular, the Bhotia women dressed almost exactly like the two Sherpanis in our party. Like the Sherpanis, they wore the 'pangden', the wool skirt, with coloured horizontal stripes at the front and vertical stripes at the back. The same kind of long-sleeved cross over blouse was worn over a small *choli* or waistcoat. Jewellery was also very much the same with much use made of turquoise, coral and silver. Probably because they were wealthy traders in Walung Chung, the womenfolk wore more necklaces made up of silver rupees or possibly it was because they came into frequent contact with the Limbu people lower down the Tamur valley. I had met Bhotias in other parts of the Himalaya and in particular, remembered the inhabitants of Mana in the Alaknanda of Garwhal. In every way they were like the Sherpas or the Bhotias that I found in Nepal.

Nima Tenzing, Ang Nyima and Mingma had not been at all pleased when I again pointed the similarity of dress, language, physique and features to that of the Sherpas. But I felt sure that at the time of our meeting on the Milke Danda, Nima Tenzing would have roared with laughter if I had reminded him of the episode. Over the years he, and other Sherpas, have travelled far and wide, not only throughout the Himalaya, but often throughout the world. They have now no problems in accepting their similar origins to those of the Bhotias of the Himalaya.

When we all arrived at Walung Chung in 1954, we were invited to the house of the *Gova*, the village headman. There I was introduced to *tomba* a pleasant liquid drunk out of bamboo jars. Fermented millet seeds were placed in the jar and hot water then poured on the grain. After a few minutes, the liquid could then be sucked through a hollow bamboo stick fitted through a hole in the lid of the jar. I found the flavour to be similar to cider and there was no doubt the contents were very alcoholic. When I caught Ang Nyima glancing coyly at sherpani Karmi whilst he drank his *tomba* I contemplated the possible consequences of "sipping cider through a straw".*

Being Bhotias the whole population of Walung were Buddhists. Prayer wheels lined the many mani walls that led towards a large and well-decorated gompa that dominated the village. Apart from its size, it was also readily distinguished by the large *torcho* standing outside the building and the many lines of gaily coloured prayer flags hung across the entrance. We found most of the streets were cobbled, and on each side, in addition to dwelling houses, large wooden storehouses had been built for storing grain and other trade goods. Though short, it was certainly a very interesting stay with the Bhotias of Walung Chung who, as we found with people throughout the journey, were most friendly and tremendously hospitable.

Before leaving the next morning Nima Tenzing foraged for provisions eventually buying eggs and *tsampa*. We then went on our way down the Tamur before turning east and crossed the Nango la to reach another Bhotia village, that of Ghunsa in the Ghunsa khola.

Within another thirty-six hours I reached the Yalung valley and

---

*'tomba' is the name in common use today, but in 1854 Hooker used the name 'murwa'.

was finally camped with my brother Ron and other members of the Kangchenjunga Reconnaissance Expedition.

(It was just over a year later that a party of us made the first ascent of the mountain on 25th May 1955 and another thirty-five years on, when in 1990 I met Nima Tenzing on the Milke Danda. I knew that Walung Chung was greatly changed from the time of our first visit. In the 1960s an earthquake caused a large landslide that destroyed much of the village so that the number of inhabited houses was reduced to a third.

All trade between Nepal and Tibet across the Tipta la had ceased because of the Chinese occupation and many of the wealthier families of Walung Chung had left to live in such places as Kathmandu and Darjeeling. I did wonder if, now that the area of north-east Nepal was open to trekking, whether like Ghunsa, Walung Chung was also receiving more visitors. If so, like Ghunsa, there would be a little more finance for the inhabitants. It would have been good to have talked longer with Nima, and have asked him if he had revisited that Bhotia village. There wasn't the time, and it wasn't to be.

When at Dobhan, I finally turned into my tent that evening, I did still think the meeting with my brother in the Yalung was the highlight of the long walk, but I also knew the deep rich seam running throughout it all was the memory of the cheerful and sincere companionship of my Sherpa friends, and in particular of Nima Tenzing.)

25

Kangchenjunga:
The Five Treasures of the Great Snow
(1955, 1976, 1990 and 2002)

This massive mountain with its descriptive Tibetan name, Kangchendsonga (Kang—snow, chen—big, dso—treasures, nga—five) usually written as Kangchenjunga, meaning 'The Five Treasures of the Great Snow' has a long history prior to 1955 of attempts by British, Swiss, German and International expeditions.

The Journey

In the year of 1955 a team of mountaineers from Britain (with one member from New Zealand) went to the south-west face of Kangchenjunga and made the first and second ascents of the main summit at 28,208 feet. I was a member of that expedition. Until the 1970s few expeditions returned to the area of the Kangchenjunga massif though in 1965 an unsuccessful attempt was made by Yugoslavian mountaineers on the lowest summit named Kangbachen, 25,925 feet. Then in 1974 a Japanese expedition ascended to the west summit of Kangchenjunga now known as Yalung Kang 27,668 feet and a group of Polish mountaineers successfully climbed Kangbachen. These ascents sparked off renewed interest in the mountain massif and Yalung Kang was again climbed, this time by an Austro-German expedition, in 1975. In October of that year I had a group of Polish mountaineers re-visit the National Mountain Centre of which I was the Director, and I showed them slides of Kangchenjunga stressing to them that the Central (27,874 feet) and South (27,855 feet) summits were still unclimbed. I like to think that this was the time they were imbued with the idea of making the ascent of the two remaining summits for they finally did so in 1978. With them on the ascent were members of a Spanish expedition that had abandoned an attempt on Yalung Kang. Twenty-two years after 1955 a third ascent of Kangchenjunga main summit was made by an Indian expedition lead by Colonel Kumar. The climb was made by the east ridge which was a new route.

In 1979, two years later, a third British ascent was made to the main summit, this time via the north-west from the Kangchenjunga glacier—another new route. The three British climbers who reached the top, Joe Tasker, Doug Scott, and Peter Boardman, did so without using additional oxygen.

It was twenty-one years after the first ascent of Kangchenjunga

when my wife, Eileen, and I re-visited Darjeeling and stayed at the Himalayan Mountaineering Institute. As I looked out of the bedroom window on our first morning there I thought not only of Kangchenjunga and the climb in 1955 but also of my journey from Everest to Kangchenjunga in 1954. Climatic conditions were similar to when I had looked out from the Rungneet Tea Estate in 1954, a moment of which I had written: "despite clouds massing huge between us and the mountain we occasionally caught a glimpse of the glistening white giant with its five pointed summits thrusting boldly up and high towards the Central Asian sun".

I remembered too that the following year in 1955 when I returned with the expedition we took ten days to journey out to the mountain. In the Yalung valley we set up an acclimatisation camp at a deserted yak village named Ramser and the following is my memory of how we made the journey to reach it.

Butter Tea and Tsampa

For our departure from Darjeeling on the first morning we were up by dawn helping Tony Streather and Dawa Tenzing who were busily organising loads in military fashion. Climbers, Sherpas, porters, all descended on the laid out gear, removing it from the lawn at Rungneet and loading it on lorries. There was a bustle of excitement, calling and shouting and hurried explanations in Urdu. There were a few last minute details such as collecting wax, needles, a cake from Jill Henderson, final photographs and then our six lorry loads departed from the tea estate in grand style.

The journey to Mane Bhungjung had the traditional puncture on route, plus the inevitable police delay which was quickly cleared up by a telephone call. Once we were on foot, it was tremendously refreshing to be back once again in the foothills of the Himalaya knowing we were on our way to some of the highest mountains. Our first day's walk provided a pleasing re-acquaintance with the interesting local people who were part Indian and part Limbus. Butter tea was available at Tonglu and the Sherpas, Tashi and Phu Cheeta frequently offered us *chang* and *rakshi* to drink. The most refreshing beverage was tea made without milk but mixed with a liberal amount of added *tsampa*. *Tsampa* is a barley flour, roasted and stone-ground into a rough mealy consistency and the golden juicy grains are slightly sweet with a flavour that is unique—a flavour produced of the wind, the rain, the warm golden sun and the rich good earth.

Though still early in the year, there was much life stirring along the ridges and trackways and we noted scarlet minivets, tree creepers, tortoise-shell butterflies, a weasel at Khalipokri and already the flowers of yellow magnolia, pink rhododendron, and mauve primula were beginning to show. The 'old man's beard' or Usnea was particularly prolific, glistening with drops of dew that twinkled and sparkled as they caught the rays of the early morning sun.

Storm Music

Each day, at the same time, we had a lightning storm followed by hail and snow. From late afternoon until late in the evening, lightning streaked hard, sharp and jagged across the sky or on occasions, lilac sheeting lit up the sombre looking ridges. Thunder rolled and reverberated from peak to peak, reminiscent of the roll of the base tympany in a Berlioz symphony. Huge quantities of large hailstones covered the ground to a depth of many inches and as they fell they beat and rattled on the taut canvas as if buckets of peas were being thrown on the resthouse roof.

To Chyangthapu

This was a day of contrasts. The morning was cold, misty, dank and uninspiring at Phalut. Our porters who had been carrying bare-footed in the snow quickly decided that delay was of little use and the camp was soon a hustle and bustle of the ragged bare-footed figures shouting, gesticulating and roping up their loads. Exhaled breath condensed and slowly spiralled away from each figure silhouetted against the thin mist that was refracting the light from a wan morning sun, and a steady drip, drip of melting snow from the resthouse eaves, served to accentuate the slow stirring to life of the day.

Later we camped at Chyangthapu and for some time sat beneath the *pipal* tree, sheltered from the hot sun whilst porters relaxed thankfully amongst the bamboo and wild fig trees. The descent from the ridge and over the shingle flats of a dried up river bed, a tributary of the Inwa Khola, was a thirsty and dusty experience so that a delightful bathe in the crystal clear water of the rock pool outside the village was doubly welcome.

Grain Pounders, Carrying Frames and Pigtails

We had another majestic mountain storm in the evening at Chyangthapu and the following morning was cool and fresh after the rain as the Hindu inhabitants of the village watched us depart. Each day as we continued the journey we were getting to know our Sherpas better. My own Sherpa was called Phu Cheeta, a man I had met the previous year with Hillary's expedition at the foot of Makalu. I remembered that then he had worn the traditional single pigtail common to the Sherpa male but having been to Darjeeling, he had cut it off. It is only 1949 since the first European people visited Sherpa country, Sola Khumbu, but already by these manifestations of westernisation such as lopping of the pigtail, they shed centuries of tradition. But the man doesn't change for all that and Phu Cheeta was still the same willing and cheerful character, I had met at the New Zealand base camp in the Barun khola. Another of our Sherpas was Lobsang whom I had met on the Nangpa la. There I had seen him carrying an old dying Tibetan woman across the glacier at 19,050 feet and into her homeland of Tibet. Lobsang's carry had been with the old lady perched on top of his load, but in south-east Nepal, people are often carried in a frame or 'back' chair just as the older or less active pilgrims are carried to the source of the Ganges in Garhwal. They too are Hindus like the people we met in the villages on route to Kangchenjunga and it must be that this is a very old traditional method of carrying brought to Nepal during the migration of Hindu people from the plains.

The method of pounding grain was much more sophisticated than in Ladakh or Garhwal or even in other parts of Nepal for instead of using the hand-lifted pounding pole, they had a foot treadle to raise a heavy wooden pounder that pounded the grain in a specially hollowed out stone or quern. It used the simple lever principle very effectively and must have been much less tiring.

Terracing and Fire Lighting

Once again, we got away early between 5 a.m. and 6 a.m. and some three hours later we had breakfast at Mahele. Early starts made sure that we got many miles of walking in during the cool of the day and later it gave us time to stop and meet the local people as well as write letters and get to know each other better.

Joe Brown, Neil Mather and the others who had not been out to the Himalaya before found the country doubly fascinating and the way of life of the people a constant interest, if at times a little bewildering.

Hill slopes were terraced to help prevent erosion during the monsoon rains and this terracing also increased the area of land on which to grow crops. Each tiny field was carefully hoed and later would grow its crop of barley, wheat or maize according to the seed sown. Narrow winding tracks enabled us to descend the steep terraced spurs to the rivers thousands of feet below which we crossed by fragile wire and plank bridges. Houses had thatched roofs and solid eaves with superbly thatched gable ends. Verandahs were a common feature and the walls either a pleasing terra cotta or white-washed, reminded me of those I had seen in the Chyabas-Risingo area on the route to Everest in 1954.

At a low pass, Joe, John Clegg, George Band and I stopped to talk with a group of itinerant traders and had an amusing time practising fire lighting. Never before had I realised that one of the small skinning knives kept in the sheath of a *kukri* could also be used in the same way as a Tibetan *chakma*. A *chakma* is a small yak-hide purse usually studded with brass decorations and with a base made of medium soft iron. Inside the *chakma* they keep kindling and quartz or better still flint if it can be found. The kindling and stone are held between thumb and fore-finger then struck with a long glancing blow by the iron base or striker and this produces a shower of sparks so that quickly the kindling begins to smoulder. In the same way the blunt iron back of the small *kukri* knife is used to strike stone and kindling. It sounds simple but Joe tried for a long time without result, whereupon one of the traders lit a kindling at the first blow. With practice and a lot of tuition all four of us eventually managed to make a light.

A Reminder of Burma

Because of a heavy deluge of rain after we had left the traders at the pass, the previous day, we camped a little earlier and about half an hour's journey from the village of Khebang. Our tents were erected on newly-hoed terraces by permission of the owner who turned out to be a cheerful little Hindu. Nearby, several gulmohar trees (the golden trees) were in flower and looking beyond the rich golden-red blossoms, our view plunged downwards many thousands of feet to the river then across to the steep partly terraced slopes on the far side. Certainly, it was most impressive this gorge country of north-east Nepal and where there were no terraces, the natural vegetation was prolific and jungle-type dark green. Occasionally ochre-coloured slashes of landslips broke up the overall powerful green of this subtropical landscape at 7000 feet and it strongly reminded me of the ridges and valleys of Burma. Perhaps it was also a reminder for our leader Charles Evans for in conversation he and I realised that we were both in Burma at the same time during the war. Whilst he was the doctor at Tiddim in the Chin Hills it was quite possible that I had air-dropped supplies to him.

Khebang—A Song and a Smoke

We had quite a large reception committee waiting for us as we walked into Khebang in the early morning. Local beauties sprinkled water on our heads as we walked beneath bowers of rhododendrons and garlands of flowers were festooned around our shoulders. What an incredibly friendly people they were. The president of the school at Khebang was also the headman at Yamphodin, the last of the villages we would go through to reach the Yalung valley, and he and the Schoolmaster Lakshmi Prasad led us to the schoolhouse where the children sang songs to us in falsetto voices, high and shrill. It was a laugh, when after about twenty minutes of this, Joe and I nipped outside and round the corner for a quiet smoke and found one or two scholars also playing truant. They too were having a quiet smoke using an enormous bamboo pipe with a perfect 'cadgers' bowl that must have held about a pound of tobacco. This was the only school I had ever seen in Nepal at the time and the enterprising villagers paid out all the money themselves. Initially, only boys were being allowed to go to the school where they had lessons in Nepali, English, Arithmetic, History and Geography.

After the visit to the school, we had breakfast in the village square surrounded by a throng of men, women and children, most of whom had walked through the night from other villages to see us strangers on the way to Kangchenjunga. John Clegg, the doctor, was kept very busy attending to those that were suffering from injuries or sickness and through Dawa Tenzing acting as interpreter, he answered hundreds of questions. "Where are you going?" "Will you find gold when you get there?" "What is the sickness that makes my baby so thin?" "Why must you leave so soon?" "When will you return?" We left with their blessing—"May the gods be with you". At the village of Tamphodin, we pitched our tents by the river bank where, on arrival we had already seen the paradise fly-catchers, plumbeous redstarts and the Indian robin. Soon an Indian laughing thrush added its cheerful call to the general noises of a busy camp which was placed in a much wilder mountain setting than hitherto. Banana trees provided fruit and also part shade for the mud-walled, thatched-roofed houses, which were two-storied and often had a verandah on which the womenfolk threshed out barley and wheat grain. Occasionally chickens scurried out of the doorways of the houses and no doubt would later be fed on the corn from some of the hundreds of maize cobs stored beneath the eaves. Yamphodin was the last village on the way to the valley of the Yalung and was possibly situated at the highest permanently inhabitable height. If so, they were an industrious people for in addition to crops of bananas, maize and barley, they were cultivating potato and a variety of other vegetables.

Changes in Vegetation and a Lament

We were two days crossing the mountains that rise to 12,000 feet above Yamphodin. Our first day was a short one so that we could camp low down to give the porters a warm night's sleep. The second day was a long one and led us over the high ridge to the Simbua khola. The vegetation changed in an interesting way for by keeping low on the first day it was still subtropical and we saw much 'Flame of the Forest'.

On the second day, we reached a more temperate zone, ascending through lichen-draped woodland, passing by the yellow magnolia, scarlet rhododendrons and trod on the dew wet, mauve primula which lay under foot. Eventually we came out onto a grassy saddle from which we had clear views of Kang Peak, Sharphu, majestic Jannu, and other mountains above Ghunsa. Our descent from the ridge took a peaceful couple of hours through a silent forest of Himalayan spruce and blue pine, soft cushioning pine needles lay under foot and a rich smell of resin permeated the air. As we reached the Simbua Khola, the river that drains the snows of Kangchenjunga, it began to rain and we had a busy time guiding loaded porters over the rushing glacial torrent by the 'bridge' which was a slippery lichen-covered tree trunk. Once across and on the true right bank of the river, we built huge fires, dried out and settled for the night. Even when most were sleeping one disconsolate coolie still lamented:

"The Sahibs are warm and have feasted like Rajahs over there and here am I, cold and alone. There is no *baksheesh* for me".

On the tenth day out from Darjeeling, we arrived at Ramser just above Tseram where there is a tumbled down monastery. Ramser, at 12,000 feet was to be our acclimatisation camp, and because there were many broken down walls surrounding several fine fields, we used the walls as part shelter for out tents.

Thondup, our cook, quickly built himself a cookhouse, Sherpas gathered *lakri*, we sorted out equipment, paid off the porters, then met the yak and the yakmen of Tseram.

It was the next evening that for me really completed this part of the expedition. The weather had temporarily cleared and the date was the 24th of March, Tony Streather's birthday and mine. After a tasty meal followed by rum and a cake made by Thondup, we sat by the camp-fire of juniper wood. Sparks and blue smoke spiralled lazily above the ruddy dancing flames and lit up the faces of our laughing, chattering and singing Sherpas. They and our Sherpanis broke into the soft shoe shuffle of a 'zing a zing' dance and looking beyond them, I could see peaks with glaciers of intense cold and a covering of eternal snows high above the dark valley. The expedition seemed well founded and ready to seek out the "Five Treasures".

26

"Five Treasures":
To the Summit or Nearly!

(1955, 1976, 1990 and 2002)

Accounts of climbs entail ascending from a base camp to yet higher camps up the mountain. The telling can become quite monotonous yet there is little else one can do. Having written of a long walk I made from Everest to Kangchenjunga and also given a description of a trek to the "Five Treasures" I feel I should give a short personal account of the ascent of the mountain.

Our leader, a Welshman, was Charles Evans (later Sir Charles Evans) and the deputy leader Norman Hardie came from New Zealand. The oldest member was Tom Mckinnon, a tough Scotsman and the youngest Joe Brown was a plumber from Manchester. George Band, a graduate from Cambridge University had been the youngest member of the successful Everest Expedition in 1953, whilst Tony Streather, an army officer had summitted Tirich Mir with the Norwegians in 1950. Neil Mather, another Lancastrian was an old friend whom I had first met whilst climbing gritstone crags on the Bronte Moors. John Clegg was the doctor who had good memory from a store of student songs and stories he could produce at any dull moment to cheer us all. Throughout the six months of the expedition he was never known to repeat himself which was a remarkable performance. It could be said that his general cheerful attitude each day was a far greater tonic than were his pills or medicines, but I remember one time he was in dismay when he found that the Sherpas had found his 4 Pounds tin of Gees Linctus Cough Pastilles—they thought them an excellent sweet and scoffed the lot inside twenty-four hours. John resorted to making a cough mixture which seemed to contain a lot of ether, made us 'burp' and tasted foul. We told him so. However, in the end it did John's heart good when he gave a dose to little Pasang Dorje who beamed ecstatically, rubbed his tummy and exclaimed "Ah, brandy!"

The entire expedition was together at Rungneet Tea Estate outside Darjeeling in early March. For several of the team it was their first time to the Himalaya and the view across to Kang-chenjunga took their breath away. Neil was excited and shouted "Come and see the Sherpas Jacko" then immediately led me to their cook house. There was the usual haze of eye-searing smoke, a smell of spiced cooking, the close packing of squatting figures, and the smiling faces of some dozen Sherpas. One of them stirred a pot of *tsampa*, his long black hair glistening in the light of the cooking fire. His face was familiar. It was Lobsang, the Namche trader I had last seen twelve months before crossing the Nangpa la on his way to Tingri Tzong in Tibet. So this is the moment once again I thought—the return to the Himalaya and back to old friends. It is always the same, and the start of great adventures, as Neil, John and Joe were to discover.

Following a ten-day trek out to the Yalung valley, we eventually established a base camp which we had to abandon because of problems with avalanche and an icefall. A second base camp had to be found.

In 1905, a Swiss expedition led by that strange, demonic man Alaister Crowley visited the Yalung valley with intent to climb Kangchenjunga. Climbing up the slopes on which we now hoped to force a route to an ice couloir, they were avalanched. Lieutenant Alexis Pache and three porters were swept into a crevasse and killed. All four were buried on a rock knoll called Pache's Grave and finally it was there where we put the tents.

Ferries to the rock knoll began straight away whilst George and Norman established Camp I and Camp II. Second base was good, being a high perch and seemed safe from the numerous avalanches that crashed down from all sides to the glacier below. Just once, George Band was able to keep a tally by marking a paper as each avalanche descended. The average was one every fifteen minutes throughout twenty-four hours. None of us spent much time at base, but when we did it was a relaxing place with sparse grass and other vegetation becoming a welcome sight as the snows melted. There we could indulge in reading, writing, bouldering and collecting, when not organising the next day's carry. Norman sometimes brought out his survey equipment and George, a geologist, added to his rock specimens. Many years after Kangchenjunga, I was surprised to receive a letter from my old friend Alan Brindle in the Entomology Department at Manchester Museum. On the Garhwal Expedition in 1952 and the Snowman Expedition in Nepal, I had collected insect specimens for him. I did the same on Kangchenjunga. On 16th May 1974, nineteen years after the climb, I received the following letter:

"Dear John,

You may remember giving me some insects you took in the Yalung valley near Kangchenjunga years go. We could not do much in naming them since, apart from butterflies, naming foreign insects tends to be a specialist's job. I have an assistant who looks after the beetle collections we have here and he is particularly interested in such beetles as Scarabs. Some time ago he sent off some Scarab beetles to a specialist in Austria for naming, and included some of those from the Yalung valley. The specialist, Petrovitz by name, has described some as new species, amongst which are some from your specimens and he has named them *Aphodius jacksoni*—naming the species after the collector—i.e. you. I hope you do not object to a beetle bearing your name—it is, after all, a method of ensuring your name goes down to posterity, even if only with beetle collectors...."

I was delighted for such is my only claim to fame!

George and Norman, after a fine piece of route finding established Camp I at 19,000 feet and then crossed the ridge above (called the 'Hump') descended an ice tongue and placed Camp II on an horizontal shelf.

At about this time Joe set up his eating record for the expedition. He made several carries to 21,800 feet when stocking Camp III with essential food, oxygen, and equipment. The journeys had improved his acclimatisation and his appetite increased. For breakfast one morning he ate almost three quarters of a pound of cheese, lubricated it by swallowing the contents of a bottle of tomato ketchup and followed this gruesome mixture by eating a couple of Mars bars. I think the record is that he kept it down for over half an hour whilst on his way up the ice slopes to Camp III.

Charles and Norman using closed circuit oxygen made a speedy reconnaissance of the upper icefall above Camp III and reached the Great Shelf, initially our prime objective. There they set up Camp IV at 23,500 feet. This was at the foot of a steep snow gangway rising to the saddle between Kangchenjunga and Yalung Kang. Without delay, Charles and Norman descended to base camp and called us all together for a briefing on an attempt for the summit. It was an exciting time and I remember we were all quiet wondering what our future held.

Just a tip-tapping of a typewriter in Charles's tent was evidence that at least a part of that future was being put to paper. At the briefing, each of us received a copy.

Tom Mckinnon and I with eleven Sherpas were to carry supplies from Camp III to Camp IV on May 18th. The following day we should take some 500 Pounds of equipment, tents, food and oxygen, to 25,500 feet and establish Camp V. Charles and Neil with four Sherpas would follow one day behind so that from Camp V, they could pick up a tent and food then place it yet higher on the mountain—final Camp VI. With Charles and Neil would be Joe and George, the first summit team. Tony and Norman constituted the second summit attempt party and would follow yet one more day further behind with Tom and I in support.

Top Camps and a Storm

Camp IV was on an open ice platform swept continuously by high winds of forty to fifty knots that blew from Central Asia.

Tom and I felt pleased with our carry when we arrived at 3 o'clock in the afternoon and set up the sleeved Meade tents in brigade. With the sleeves of the tents linked together and fastened, the four tents made one long tube. This was good for strength in high winds and very sociable too for it was possible to get from tent number one to number four without going outside. Sherpas love to get a stove going to brew tea and this is good for everybody. Not only does it warm the tent and the body but the tea helps to prevent dehydration. Strong cold winds rattled the tent walls continuously as we drank, wrote letters and prepared ourselves for the night. I was feeling particularly happy that a letter from Eileen was received at Camp III just before we left. Gave me the news that she and our son John were going to cool Kalimpong as a change from the heat of Calcutta. All was well. The view of Jannu before we turned in, my last for several days, was of giant cumulus clouds boiling up from the Yalung valley then billowing round the knife edge ridges at 25,000 feet.

Years ago there was a radio parlour game, where, among many things, the contestants were asked to say which was the most disappointing day or night of their lives. Some of the players found it difficult to decide. I have always known mine. I enjoyed the ascent to Camp IV during the day but found my goggles icing up a lot. The exhaust valve of my oxygen mask was frozen and exhaled air jetted out of the side of my mask onto my goggles. Water vapour froze immediately. At times the climbing had been steep and exposed and rather than stop, which would have been dangerous for the others, I had flipped my goggles on to my forehead until the terrain eased off. Perhaps at no time were they on my forehead for more than thirty minutes and I had often had a full day without goggles whilst climbing in the Swiss Alps. But at that height with the increased concentration of ultra-violet the short time was enough. During the night my eyes felt like red hot coals and streams of hot salty tears poured down my face.

Sleep was impossible. Most of the time, I knelt in my sleeping bag placing cool objects to my eyes, hoping against hope that I would still be able to see in the morning and thereby still help with the carry to establish Camp V. It was a dreadful night.

The Sherpas also were feeling the effects of the previous day. Because of the increasing cold and greater altitude they were coughing and groaning, and Tom also slept but little. For all it was a trying time. A biting cold wind blew snow and stinging ice particles at us in the early morning, increasing the difficulty of arranging our loads. It was a late start but all of us moved off on the carry. Tom who had the first rope worked tremendously hard all day. My own Sherpa, Phu Cheeta led the second rope, and I felt justified in following close behind, for though unable to see, I could at least carry a load. Stopping for a few moments at a whale-back of ice, I learned later that a Sherpa was vomiting on us from above. We seemed to go on, up, down and round for hours but always there was the friendly feel and link of the rope leading forward to our goal. Oxygen gave out a thousand feet below the Camp V, but it seemed a relief to breathe the cold external air. The snow cover became softer and deeper for a time and occasionally the first two ropes met together for a rest—talking little—then Tom would begin the slow but dogged plod upwards to Camp V. At last we crossed the bergschrund where a last steep ice-slope led to a broad ledge where eventually the tents were placed. We stopped at a point which Tom estimated at 25,100 feet and it was thought to be safer if I should stay rather than risk a slip on unseen ice-steps. The first two ropes climbed on. It was a lonely wait and I felt miserable at not being able to see and complete the carry. Sherpa Annallu was with us and oddly I remembered that two years before to the very day, he and Wilfrid Noyce had first reached the South Col on Everest—turning the 'key' that opened the 'door' to the summit of that mountain.

Sherpas rejoined us from above as the third and last rope of four came up to us still pressing on towards the campsite. I was still unable to see as we descended to the Great Shelf where at some time we came across Sherpa Changup who had the misfortune to lose his load. (This is Changup, father of Lakpa Thondup who was with Eileen and me in 1976 and whom we taught to ski.) He returned with us to the camp on the Great Shelf.

Once back at Camp IV, we found Charles, Neil, Joe and George plus the Sherpas who had already arrived. Sitting in the tent drinking a hot mug of tea, I could hear there was some anxiety as to the whereabouts of Tom and Sherpa Pemi Dorje. A search party found them in 10 or 15 minutes at the foot of the whale-back of ice. Pemi had been ill and vomiting, becoming dehydrated and Tom had stayed with him, secured him and safely brought him down. It had been a fine lead all day by the tough Scotsman and I wished that I could have helped him more. All three of us stayed at Camp IV with every intention of descending to Camp III the next morning but that was not to be. During the night a fierce storm blew up. Gusts of over 100 knots shook the camp and cold spindrift began to cover the tents. Hopes of reaching the summit seemed to be ending as it continued for the next three days. At noon on the second day, there was a lull in the storm and Tom and I took Pemi Dorje down to Camp III, from where he was quickly led down to base.

The others stayed on hopefully at Camp IV and finally on the third day the weather settled. Sherpa Tashi shouted excitedly that he could see Darjeeling, the peaks were clear. After a tiring struggle through fresh deep snow, Charles and his team arrived late at Camp V. Wisely they decided to rest throughout the next day, chipping and melting ice then drinking much liquid to prevent dehydration. A strong wind blew masses of powder snow off the mountain and in the evening the wind dropped, clouds settled over Nepal and they watched the last rays of the sun lighting up the great gendarme and summit of Jannu. The next day after a magnificent carry, Charles and Neil with their four Sherpas, set up the final Camp VI at 26,900 feet on the steep snow of the Gangway. Sirdar Dawa Tenzing had moved as strongly as ever and one of the other Sherpas, a young lad then, was Ang Norbu.*

---

*Twenty-one years later Eileen and I taught Ang Norbu to ski with Lakpa Thondup. He was then minus his toes and one or two fingers lost on Annapurna with the Japanese. We visited his home in Pangboche once more in 1988 when he reminded us of the wolf-hunters of Pangboche.

To the Summit

In the Meade tent that was Camp VI, Joe and George made hot drinking chocolate, ate a meal of tongue and meat bars, then slept for a while using sleeping oxygen. The morning of the 25th was fine. Tom and I with the remaining three fit Sherpas, again carried to Camp V.

There was no oxygen, but we must have been well-acclimatised for we moved well and, most important, enjoyed the movement as well as the remarkable mountain views of east Nepal rising from the cloud base at 22,000 feet. We felt particularly fortunate as we were able to see two small figures, Joe and George leave Camp VI and begin to make their way up the steep gangway. For once, it was sunny and warm and we couldn't hear the dull roar of the wind as it rushed across the rock crest of the 'Five Treasures'. We lost sight of them when they made their way across the rocks to the ridge, but felt there was every chance of the expedition reaching the summit. Later we learned that they had linked snow ribs where possible, and after several rock pitches, one a hard severe at 28,000 feet they had reached the summit at 3 p.m. Though but a few strides away they stopped five feet short of the top keeping a promise made to the people of Sikkim, to whom the mountain is sacred.

A hundred miles away as the crow flies, across a cloud layer, they could see Everest, Lhotse and Makalu. Tibet spread broadly to the north, and beyond the south summit of Kangchenjunga lay Darjeeling. It was late, oxygen was soon finished, progress was slow, and whilst they descended to the tent, the last rays of the sun bathed the Hog's Back in golden light. Evening shadows crept up the mountain and we at various camps looked anxiously for them, it was a relief when Tom shouted excitedly over the walkie-talkie set that he could see two figures on the Gangway. Although the outcome of the day was still unknown, at least they were safe. The following day, George and Joe descended to Camp V where they were able to tell Charles of their success. This good news was wirelessed down the mountain and whilst they descended further, I went up to Camp IV with cocaine eye-drops for Joe. His mask also had leaked, icing up his goggles and he too spent a painful night going snowblind. I stayed at Camp IV to keep check on the upper part of the mountain and late in the afternoon, was able to call Charles and tell him, that two figures were descending to Camp VI. This was Tony and Norman who had made a successful second ascent of Kangchenjunga.

Everyone was off the mountain by 28th May. Six weeks it had taken to go from base camp to summit—just two and half days to get down!

Sadly on return to base, we learned that cheerful, likeable and hard-working Pemi Dorje had died there of cerebral thrombosis. On the day that Camp V was established, he must have exhausted himself and with being sick probably became badly dehydrated. He was buried close to Pache's Grave.

Slowly, we packed our gear during the next few days, and Bhotias from Ghunsa, tough cheerful characters joined us and helped carry our loads down the Yalung glacier, and out to Darjeeling. Now the grass was a rich green, primulas sparkled near to clear snow-melt streams and a variety of bell rhododendrons added a richness of colour, which to eyes used to the glare of ice and snow, was a great delight. I collected a bag full of dwarf azalea leaves, so that months later the aromatic odour would bring back memories of a particularly happy and successful expedition. In Darjeeling, Eileen, our son John and I were reunited and with the others shared restful days and one or two hectic evenings with the French Makaulu expedition members.

Monsoon clouds obscured the mountains most of the time but before leaving Darjeeling, we did see Kangchenjunga again in the early morning.

At first the whole range was lit with a rosy glow, rapidly changing to a rich gold and finally a hard glittering diamond white. The huge massif was sixty-five miles away yet we could see every detail of the route above the Great Shelf. It seemed incredible that just a few weeks earlier, we tiny mortals had made footprints to within five feet of its virgin summit. Later, I was often asked by children what would have happened if the expedition had gone that last five feet. Nothing would have happened, I would say except we would have failed, because we would have broken our promise. I knew that none of us would ever forget those days we shared together and we don't. Almost fifty years later, we still have reunions and always remember our Sherpa companions without whom our ascent would not have been possible.

27

Sikkim:
Tenzing and a Sacred Valley

(1982, Updates to 1993)

"Twice more from Rungneet we saw the untrodden
peak. Once in the fading light, indigo and dark red and
again silvered by sunrise. It had lost nothing of its
power, though the invitation was no longer individual.
Now the mountain seemed to embody the spell of all
the high snows and hidden valleys that are waiting."
   –Charles Evans in *Kangchenjunga the Untrodden Peak*

In a year when Eileen and I drove overland to India, we at one
time left the caravanette in Delhi and took the train to
Calcutta. From Calcutta we flew to Bagdogra then travelled by
bus to Darjeeling and stayed for seven days at the Himalayan
Mountaineering Institute as the guests of the Principal, Group
Captain Amarjeet Garewal and his wife Elsie.

This visit, though short, recalled many pleasing memories and
a number of old friendships were renewed. The mountaineering
institute is sited on a western spur of Birch Hill at 6000 feet and
commands a grand panorama of the Kangchenjunga massif. In
1955 George Band and I as members of the team to make the

first ascent of the mountain had given a talk there on the expedition equipment. Whilst we were on the mountain, Eileen (plus our son John aged three) had stayed in Kalimpong with her friend Renee Wiggin and on several occasions, they had been guests of the H.M.I. through Major Nandu Jayal who at the time was the first Principal.

That brief visit to Darjeeling was a small but brightly shining facet of our overland journey to India, even though we hadn't, as we at one time hoped been able to trek out to Kangchenjunga. Patience is invariably rewarded and years later, we led a party of friends through Sikkim to the base of the south ridge of the mountain and to the Guicha la.

Memories and an Ethnic Evening

At the rest house at Yoksum in Sikkim, the bare wooden floor shook with the stamping of many feet and the walls vibrated because of joyful singing and the rhythmic beating of a metal pudding dish which served as a makeshift drum. Those of the party not singing or dancing with the Lepcha or Nepalese porters sucked happily at bamboo straws immersed in jars of *tombu*— fermented millet seed—and my mind took me back in time and distance to the Bhotia village of Walung Chung in the Tamur valley of Nepal. At Walung Chung, I had been introduced to *tombu* whilst at the house of the village headman, and my Sherpa companions too, had each been given a bamboo jar filled to the brim. I remembered too that as my Sherpa Ang Nyima glanced coyly at Sherpani Karmi, I had solemnly contemplated the consequence of "sipping cider through a straw".

Back at the rest house at Yoksum, I glanced suspiciously at John Noble but he was clearly content with his cider. Richard our aural surgeon and Mike Pepper, the optician concentrated on photographing the scene, and Shelagh Northcott, our nursing sister was safely conversing with my wife Eileen. That left Rani Puri, our Indian lady member who along with Bill Curtin, the concrete engineer, gyrated vigorously to the rhythm of the pudding dish. I soon knew that Bill was alright as he sank to the floor to take a fix, the inevitable fag with which he regularly punctuated each day. Only Rani, thoroughly enjoying this ethnic evening with hill people of the north of India danced on and worked off the calories supplied by *tombu*. It was the penultimate evening of our trek through Sikkim to the Guicha la and in two days time, we would be back in Darjeeling. The music, the *tombu* and the evening festivities had all been laid on by our porters.

Darjeeling (Dorje Ling—the Place of Thunderbolts) to Pemayangtse (Pemionchi)

To start the trek, we flew from Delhi to Bagdogra, the nearest airport to Darjeeling and then by jeep, climbed steeply for four hours. The road frequently crosses the track of one of the great train rides of the world, the famous 'toy train' which by switch-backs and loops, winds its way slowly from the plains at Siliguri to Darjeeling at 8000 feet.

At Darjeeling, we stayed once again at the Windamere Hotel (not a spelling mistake) where we had been twice before. A charming Tibetan family—the Tenduf La's run the hotel, which is now over 100 years old and is a perfectly maintained relic of the days of the Raj—old fashioned maybe, but comfortable, splendid service and good food. The mountain panorama from the road by the hotel is particularly good and straightway we were rewarded with views of Kangchenjunga, Jannu, Rathong, Kabru, Pandim and the lower foothills and valleys through which we would trek to reach the Guicha la.

From Darjeeling, it is usual for trek groups to travel by bus or jeep to Pemayangtse going via Gangtok, over the Tista river and back to Gezing. This is a long way round but enables visitors to see the capital city, to appreciate its spectacular setting and the superb views of the mountains. On this occasion, we preferred a more direct approach to Pemayangtse and early on the first morning, the jeep took us on descent of many thousands of feet, passing through areas of tea gardens and rice fields to the great Rangit river. Here we crossed the bridge, passed through the frontier post and into Sikkim. Still in transport, we wound our way through forests of cardamon, linked by lush green paddy fields, stopping occasionally in attractive Himalayan villages until at last, we reached Gezing to make a few final purchases. Another six kilometres took us to the luxurious Pemayangtse Tourist Lodge, which for me was a reminder that (however more slowly than Sir Douglas Freshfield suspected in 1905) the Himalayan tracks and resting places are changing. Not necessarily for the worse for the Himalayan peoples; but changing.

Half a mile or so from the lodge, built on a small knoll of mica schist is the Buddhist gompa of Pemayangtse, second oldest in Sikkim. Established in the 8th century by Padma Sambhava of the Nyingmappa sect, it is senior to all others in the country. For centuries, its lamas and scholars have made religious pilgrimage to Dzongri, the Onglakthang valley and the Guicha la, for the areas to which we were going are of great sanctity to the Buddhists.

Late in the afternoon, strong winds began to break up the high clouds, prayer flags (torcho) flickered and rustled by the gompa steps, from an enclave came the chant of a lama at evening prayer and the last light of the sun, lit the snows of Jubonu and the ice ridge of Tinchingkang. A young Sikkimese girl, a Buddhist scholar invited us inside the monastery and with quiet charm and courtesy showed us through the three floors—the last one of which contained an impressive elaborate representation of the Buddhist heaven. We returned again next morning passing many children and teachers on their way to school. They smiled at us broadly and shyly whispered "Good Morning" in English, then pressing their hands together added the greeting "Namaste". Beyond the prayer flags, the whole of the Kangchenjunga massif and the peaks above the Yalung valley were crystal clear, an omen for good weather during the next few days.

Yoksum and on to Bakim

Yoksum now is but a sleepy sprawling village, though once it was the capital of Sikkim and is still renowned as the place where the kings of Sikkim were crowned long ago.

Up on the ridge above Yoksum and well worth a visit is the

oldest monastery in the land—Dubchi monastery—but beware the leeches which on a warm wet day come out in thousands as we discovered on the return journey. To reach the village from Pemayangtse, we descended many thousands of feet, passing through small tidy homesteads, clustered by terraced fields of rice, maize and millet. Following crossing of the Rimbi Chu and the Rathong Chu, a final steep ascent had taken us to the holy ground of Yoksum. Here, at the forest rest house, we were informed that a party of Canadians, with Tenzing Norgay had departed earlier in the day.

Another group of American doctors on a physiological expedition were camping nearby. "Are the hills really becoming congested with trekkers," I wondered, but then I thought, twenty-six trekkers in an area of 3000 square miles of Sikkim can't really be termed overcrowding. Even so, it was clear that the Forestry Department were actively increasing the number of resthouses to benefit financially from the increase in tourism and so it was no surprise that we found another such building on arrival at Bakim. The trail from Yoksum winds through quite thick subtropical jungle, rich flora and fauna. Though October is not the best time for flora, the party was interested to see a variety of flowering plants, a profusion of tropical trees, and were frequently amazed to find the familiar Swiss cheese plants (*Mousteria*) growing like trees and often over 40 feet high. An hospitable Tibetan family invited us into their house for tea on arrival at Bakim and we knew that the next day, some twenty minutes further along the track, we would come to the last village on our journey to the Guicha la. This is the village of Tsoka—a small cluster of dwellings built by Tibetan refugees, who over thirty years ago by permission of the king of Sikkim, were allowed to settle and become the keepers of the king's herd of yak. The interiors of each house were set out in similar fashion to the homes of the Sherpas and whilst we drank butter tea and ate *chapatties*, Eileen and I were reminded of our days living with Sirdar Dawa Tenzing at Dingboche in Khumbu.

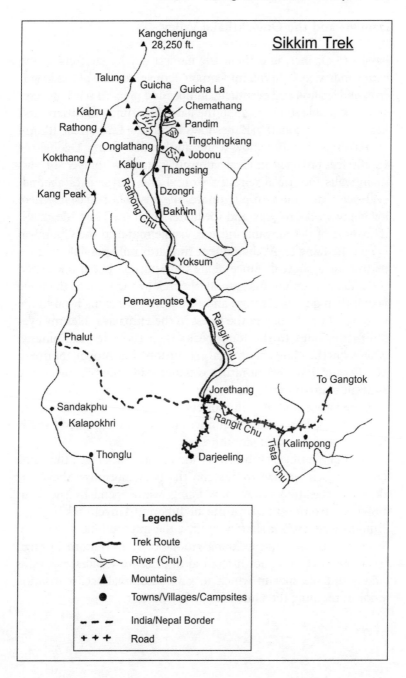

Dzongri and the Onglakthang Valley

Bakim to Dzongri is perhaps the hardest day for trekkers as the path winds steeply uphill into a more temperate zone of rhododendron and azaleas and eventually juniper and pine. At our luncheon stop, I was able to photograph the pale blue trumpet gentians and nearer to the Dzongri yak meadows found the Immortelle (Pearly Everlastings) looking snow-white and crystal sharp. Dzongri at 13,200 feet provides an ideal campsite. Chortens, (prayer shrines) mani walls (inscribed religious stones) and prayer flags abound, evidence that whilst on pilgrimage, the wise old lamas stay here for many weeks to pray and meditate. From the Holy Meadows, the whole of the Singalila ridge is visible round to the Chumbab la and the Kang la. At the present time it is only possible to get a permit for a short distance along the Singalila but if and when the Indians open up this ground, the trek by the ridge to the Kang la and then out via Dzongri and Pemayangtse (having been to the Guicha la) will be one of the finest in the Himalaya. I let my eyes follow the ridge to the Kang peaks then the ridge of Koktang, where on the Kangchenjunga expedition, Joe Brown, Norman Hardie and I in deteriorating weather had failed to reach the summit. Further north, Rathong and Kabru were draped in masses of hanging ice and at a line of chortens on the ridge above the Dzongri yak huts, Kangchenjunga, up to now obscured, finally revealed its five sacred summits.

Beyond the ridge, far below us and to the east, flowed the Parek chu in which we had to descend the next morning. Above the deep-cut glaciated valley, now being overdeepend by the swift flowing torrent, the summits of Jubonu, Tingchingkang and Pandim were etched sharply against the intense blue of the sky. It is unfortunate that trekking groups rush away from Dzongri after one brief night, for it is an ideal place for exploratory walks and a suitable spot in which to gain additional acclimatisation prior to reaching the Guicha la at 16,500 feet.

Kangchenjunga and the Guicha la

It proved to be a steep descent to the Parek chu and we finally crossed the glacial torrent by a bridge of rough hewn logs to reach the open grazing flats at Thangsing. A clear night and severe frost covered our tents with a glittering skim of frozen crystals. Blue smoke from the many wood fires of our porters rose vertically into the air in the anticyclonic conditions and it was some time before the morning sun melted the frost and sufficiently dried the tents for packing. This valley, through which flows the Parek chu is more often called Onglakthang after the Onglakthang glacier which flows from Forked Peak and the Dome, and a few hours walk above Thangsing, you arrive at the Onglakthang campsite. It is usual for camps to be taken at Onglakthang which is a sheltered spot by the left lateral moraine of the glacier. Tents are pitched some fifty yards from a moraine lake and near to a stone yak-hut minus its roof. I am quite sure that this campsite is used to please the porters and the trekking companies and not the trekkers. In my mind there is no doubt that if a party wishes to have the best of this mountain area and to enjoy the ascent to the Guicha la to the maximum, it is better to continue further up the valley to Chemathang (Chema—sand, thang—a plain). This is a flat and sandy floor of an old lake at 15,250 feet beneath the great west wall of Pandim.

On the way from Thangsing to Onglakthang, we again passed by many mani walls and saw other evidence of the sanctity of the area. Yak laden with rucksacks and camping gear passed by us and went on down the valley and soon Eileen and I were delighted to meet our old friend Tenzing Norgay, with his party of Canadians. There was no mistaking his red shirt and white flat cap as he came towards us but the look of surprise on his face when he recognised us was really amusing. Though he had heard there was a British party in the valley, he had no idea we were with the group. For fifteen minutes or more, we chatted about the mountains of Snowdonia and of friends and before we parted, I reminded him that in May of the following year, we would have the Everest reunion at the Peny Gwryd and would look forward to seeing him there as well. We also talked of Kangchenjunga and he could see I was thrilled to be once more at the base of the mountain and able to talk about the climb to his Canadians. The site of Camp V at 25,500 feet was visible and then further up the Gangway, I pointed out to him and the trekkers where we had Camp VI. The rest of the route to the summit was also mainly in view and memories flooded back.

That night at Onglakthang campsite, a few wisps of snow heralded the coming of winter and in the morning the sky was overcast. This was only our sixth day out from Darjeeling and it reflects credit on the group that on the next day all reached the Guicha la at 16,500 feet despite so little time for acclimatisation. It was a hard nine hour day for most and it is significant that we met up with three other trek groups of which no member reached the Guicha la. This trek would be much improved if two extra days are taken up in the mountains, where after all, everyone has travelled many thousands of miles to be. The two days can easily be taken out of the jungle walking on the return journey, where the days are easy and unnecessarily short. Extra time in the mountains would not only provide for greater enjoyment of the trek but also add considerably to the safety factor by giving people an increased opportunity to acclimatise to altitude.

Because of the overcast, visibility was not as good as on previous days and whilst walking from Onglakthang to Chemathang, we again passed by walls of mani stones and tumbled down shrines. Buddhist prayer flags attached to tilting sticks, rustled quietly in the light breeze. Mountain choughs "chak chakked" sharply as we trudged along the grassy ablation valley then for several miles we threaded our way through massive erratic boulders that littered the ridge of a huge and steep-sided lateral moraine. It is rugged and remote environment, a very special area of high cirques and hanging glaciers of rearing precipices and stark and awesome mountains—a paradise for the trekker and geomorphologist and the mountaineer alike.

The Guicha la seemed a desolate little spot and above it large tilted slabs of schistose material slanted up towards Guicha Peak. I scrambled up them for some 500 feet or so to take photographs

of the pass below and to obtain a better view of the peaks around—
Pandim and Tinchingkang to the east, Forked Peak and Talung
to the west and above me, beyond Guicha Peak, the massive ridge
leading to the five summits of Kangchenjunga. Everyone felt it
to have been a most rewarding journey to make and huge smiles
spread across the faces of Eileen and Bill, for whom it had been a
very special goal.

For me, it had been a special thrill on the ascent from Chemathang to look across to two 20,000 feet peaks climbed by Joe
Brown, Norman Hardie, Phu Cheeta and me during the acclimatisation period of the Kangchenjunga expedition. The rock spire
and the snow pyramid stood out clearly and once again, I could
hear in my mind the excitement as during the climb, each of us
pointed out possible lines of ascent on the massive south-west
face of the 'Five Treasures'.

Two days after reaching the Guicha la, we were down below
the alpine pastures of Dzongri and well on the way back to Darjeeling. The trek had been sound, the weather good, our companions
could not have been better and it had proved to be a memorable
return to Kangchenjunga.

Addenda

Subsequent to this trek, we returned once more. Twelve years later,
we again reached the Guicha la. At Yoksum, Bakim and Dzongri,
additional trek lodges had been built and a new roof placed on
the yak-hut at Onglakthang. We also placed a camp nearer to the
Guicha la by stopping at a yak *karka* just beyond Chemathang.
A supply of water was a long way away and not easy to obtain
but our friend Chewang Motup Goba soon sorted out the problem.
We also lengthened the journey by two days which enabled us to
visit the H.M.I. base camp and Silver Hut below Frey's Peak and
mighty Rathong.

The camp on the way to H.M.I. base camp is at Bikbari. This
was a first class addition to the trek and good for extra acclimatisation.

Because we had perfect weather on reaching the Guicha la, all the mountains were clearly visible. Simvu and Siniolchu stood out particularly clear against a cloudless deep blue sky and the Zemu Gap (Zemu la) felt to be but a stone's throw away. It was whilst ascending to the la in the 1930s, that John Hunt of Everest, came across footprints leading up the snow slope to the pass. Were they the footprints of a Yeti? Later he always felt they were. Finally the Windamere Hotel in Darjeeling is as quaint and charming as ever. Das still owns the best of the photographic shops and the mountaineering museum at the H.M.I. is not to be missed.

28

A Curious Trouser Button

(1954)

Stan was looking puzzled. He and I had just found a trouser button at a gap between two rock pinnacles.

"I don't think the 'snowman' wears trousers, Jacko," he exclaimed.

"No, some climbers have been here before, Stan". The implications were clear. Contrary to our thinking, we were not making the first ascent of the mountain and I put the button in my pocket. Climbing on we soon came to the last hundred feet of hard snow-ice that led to the crest of Kang Cho Shar.

"Watch the rope doesn't snag on those loose rocks," I shouted.

Within minutes I had brought up my two companions and we traversed the corniced ridge to the summit.

Kang Cho Shar is a peak rising to the north of the Nimagawa la, the pass that links the Chola khola with the Nimagawa valley and the upper Dudh Kosi. It is one of several mountains in Nepal considered suitable for climbing by trekkers and as such is given the misleading title of "trekking peak". It is a name that can give a false impression of standards of difficulty and I think most mountain people would favour a name like: "adventurers peak". To climb them, a down payment must be made to the Nepalese government and a special permit obtained, but it is not required that a liaison officer be taken. This reduces the expense of an ascent but rightly it is stressed that all who attempt to climb such a mountain should have, and know how to use, the necessary climbing equipment.

When Stan Jeeves, Bill Edgar and I climbed Kang Cho Shar, it was long before trekkers went to the Everest region. We made the ascent to gain a clear view and better idea of the complicated maze of mountains, valleys and glaciers around us in Sola Khumbu. Already the pattern of weather was changing following the cold winter months and each morning a yellow heat haze filled the valleys that stretched south towards the terai and hot plains of India. Yet each afternoon there was a fresh fall of snow which usually melted away before the following morning. That is why we let the sun dry and warm the rocks before we began the climb. First we sorted out the stretches of loose and shattered material before we came to firm and solid rock where we traversed several pointed pinnacles. That is where we found the trouser button.

At the summit it was forgotten when afternoon clouds began to rise up from the depths of the Chola khola. Flecks of snow began to whisper among the summit rocks and very quickly we took a panorama of photographs picking out the main peaks and valleys around us. In high spirits we returned to the campsite at the Nimagawa la, eight and a half hours after leaving.

Several months later, back in Britain, I returned the button to the owner. It was Charles Evans who had 'lost' it the previous autumn whilst making the first ascent of Kang Cho Shar with Dawa Tenzing.

Our second ascent leaves me with the memory of a neat climb in cheerful company and of a curious find of a trouser button.

Thamang Drums

The Thamangs are an ancient Nepalese people that have settled over a wide expanse of that country. You meet them south of Kathmandu or to the east as for many days you journey across the grain of the country and eventually turn north up the Dudh

Kosi to reach Everest. An itinerant group of Thamang musicians met us at the village of Thosi when we journeyed to Sola Khumbu on the Snowman expedition. They beat drums of various sizes and one blew a small curved reed horn of strident tone reminiscent of a Scottish bagpipe, and its sound the sweeter the further you were away. The next day the setting for their music was superb. We struck camp in the early morning and ascended to a pass above the village at a height of 9000 feet. The cool clear air of the mountains was refreshing. In the valley looking back to Thosi we could see cattle and sheep grazing, as local people hoed tiny terraced fields ready for growing crops of maize, millet, barley and sugar cane. Ahead of us was another similar fertile valley and in the distance beyond the valley, partly misted and seemingly floating on a lilac tinted smoke, rose the snow and ice mountains of Himachal—the Abode of Snow. Houses in the valley looked different to those seen previously, almost like the mountain chalets of Austria and Switzerland. Gabled roofs of low pitch were covered with wooden slats on which were laid large flat stones to weigh them down. Much wood as well as stone was used for building and the white-washed outer walls, spacious wooden verandah and solid construction helped to increase the similarity of appearance to alpine houses. The musicians having come with us, stopped at the top of the pass and the sound of their drumming slowly died away as we descended into the valley.

I again heard Thamang drums when we returned from the ascent of Kangchenjunga and went to the Gurkha regiment at Jalapahar outside Darjeeling. It was the most exciting drumming I have ever heard. Charles Evans and all the team had been invited to a Nautch dance. No womenfolk were allowed. A Gurkha regiment is made up of many different types of Nepalese people such as Limbus, Nawars, Thakals, Rais, Bhotias, Mangars, Sherpas and also the Thamangs.

There were several Thamangs here. Some were drumming, some were dancing dressed as women. It was strange and new to some of us but there was nothing queer about the evening. This was a men's regiment letting off steam, drinking rum, beating drums and initially going through ritualistic forms of dancing. Tenzing

Norgay of Everest pointed out that the finest looking big bosomed young 'lady' was a great soldier holding the highest decorations for bravery in battle. The night progressed. More and more fiery rum was drunk. The smoky room got hotter, the drumming more and more insistent in its rhythms. We all began to dance. Wilder and wilder we whirled around on the hard planked floor. Drums beat yet stronger the sound seeming to seep into every fibre of the body, blood pulsing in unison, pounding to the brain. Dancing, whirling, chattering, laughing, our clothing became soaked with sweat; and the Thamang drums beat on, throbbing through the night. It was almost dawn before the drumming finished and the Nautch dance ended. When we departed, our Gurkha hosts seemed well-pleased with our obvious enjoyment of the night.

29

Nangpa la: A Kind Act and an Amber Bracelet

(1976 and back to 1954-55)

E ach time I have camped in the vicinity of Namche Bazaar, the tents have been pitched in an old yak grazing field outside and above the village. This is near to the Sagarmatha National Park centre and museum. The view from the tents looking across the Namche glacier bowl to the massive wall of the peak Kwangde is really very special and makes the extra pull up from Namche at the end of a long day from Lukla or Phakdingma well worthwhile.*

Sherpa Lobsang used to live nearby and on one occasion, because we knew each other well, I asked if he was in the village. No one seemed to know where he was. Always in the past our meeting had been full of incident and promise, a time of interesting and memorable events. Our first time was in the Imja Khola when he helped me to barter with a Tibetan trader for a knife

---

*This camping area is now taken up by a large chorten and a spendid museum built by Lakpa Sonam, the Sherpa photographer.

and scabbard. The remarkably ornate scabbard turned out to be made from a butter tin from one of the first Everest expeditions of the 1920s. A great find; but our most extraordinary meeting was on the Nangpa la, a high pass to the north of Namche.

La is a Tibetan word. It has the same meaning as the French word 'col' or the Welsh word 'bwlch'. La is a pass, a saddle, a crossing point over a mountain chain, a means of travel from one valley to another. It can be a way of access for trade, a means of escape or a lead forwards to new horizons. The Nangpa la is a trade route from Nepal to Central Asia, a way of escape from one ideology to another, a watershed, and at the time of my story, for a small group of nomads it was the way back to their country, Tibet. At 19,050 feet it is the highest trade route in the world, but after a winter of being marooned in Nepal, it was for the Tibetans, the gateway to home. I have mentioned before that whilst hunting the Yeti, Ralph Izzard, Bill Edgar and I made a journey from the upper Dudh Kosi to the Bhote Kosi and went on to the Nangpa la. The evening before reaching the pass we placed our tents in a secure position on the glacier, and were intrigued when a group of Tibetan nomads arrived. Settling in for them meant clearing the ground, moving boulders. Sweeping away angular gravel, and creating snow hollows into which five or six people could huddle together and sleep. At each place, a curve for the hip and a hollow for the shoulder was formed. Each of them was wearing the *chuba* a long woollen tibetan smock made of wool and hide. The men, women and children, then settled down to sleep, wrapping blankets around themselves. Their pack frames and V-shaped carrying baskets laden with trade goods were then used to make an extra wind break against the chilly night wind. The snowfall during the night must have been very welcome and in the early morning quietened the sound of the elements as well as insulating the sleepers from the seeping searching cold of the early hours— the coldest time. When we began to move, they too, wasting no time on cooking, packed quickly and clattered past our tents over the glacier ice. Children sucked pebbles of sun-dried cheese. All moved with a steady purposeful plod to the head of the pass marked by a curving spray of bamboo rods festooned with dozens of fluttering prayer flags. There we joined the Tibetans and took in the view which for us was of a new land, the country of Tibet, but for them it was their home and the promise of reunion with friends and families.

Briefly, I have written before of the dying Tibetan woman and of one of the kindest acts I have ever seen in my life. I can tell it again, but more fully, for in the following year I was able to hear the end of the story. Shortly after the arrival of the Tibetans at our glacier camp the previous evening, we were also joined by a Sherpa. I was pleased to see it was Lobsang from Namche Bazaar. Being a trader he was carrying an enormous pack of goods, matches, cigarettes, trinkets and many felt Australian bush hats. These are the hats that the Tibetans form into headgear of great charm. Having recut and re-shaped them, they decorate the felt with threads of red, silver and gold, then line the hats with Siberian mink. Lobsang was still with us when we reached the top of the pass. An aged and ailing Tibetan woman lay on a bundle of rags, seemingly being left there to die. Now that the nomads had brought her within sight of the country of her birth, this was apparently all they thought was required of them. Though it seems hard and cruel, as with the Eskimos of a similar barren land, the custom was a way of life prescribed by the harshness of the land itself, but Lobsang was not prepared to accept the situation. When the Tibetans crossed the glacier and disappeared from sight into a country we were forbidden to enter, he picked up the old woman and placed her on the top of his pack. His was an incredible feat. We sat and watched by the fluttering prayer flags as Lobsang slowly paced his way into the distance and out of sight. He was on his way to Tingri carrying her to the promised land. Remember, he was at over 19,000 feet carrying a pack of some 80 Pounds. And added to it now was the weight of the Tibetan woman. What did he carry at that height—twice 80 Pounds? or 160 Pounds? or was it more? It could scarcely have been less. What eventually happened?

I had to wait a year to find out. In the Yalung valley of north-east Nepal, it was a pleasure to meet Lobsang for the third time. He told me he had made good trade in Tibet the year before and life had been good to him during the months between our meeting. "What of the old woman?" I asked. "Ah yes," he replied "I carried her to Tingri* and when I last saw her she was still alive and happy with her own people." Clearly Lobsang was more concerned with the present than the past and this incident on the pass to Tibet was to him of little significance. For me, it was the most remarkable of many memorable moments I had at the head of the Nangpa la.

Another one concerns an amber bracelet I obtained there, and several thoughts I had later about its possible origins.

With Dawa Tenzing, Eileen and I had just reached the summit of Gaumukh-tse "Look there at the first and second steps on the north ridge," I said quietly. I remember Noel Odell last year when I ran the 'Mountain Medicine' symposium at Plas-y-Brenin. He was sitting back in his chair and telling us all of the moment he last saw Mallory and Irvine on the second step at 28,000 feet. "I'm glad I have got that on tape" I thought. "And look there," I continued. Seeing where I was pointing, Eileen looked across to the west ridge first climbed by the Americans in 1963. "And there"—it was the south-west face, Bonnington's route clear from Cwm to summit.

"Where is the Nangpa la?" asked Eileen, and I knew she was remembering the amber bracelet I had taken home after the Snowman expedition. "It's over there beyond Cho Oyu," I pointed to Cho Oyu but of course we couldn't see the pass. The nearest Eileen ever came to being there was a day or two later. From Lake Mosumba, she was able to look up at the 'unnamed' pass by which I had crossed to reach the Bhote Kosi and the Nangpa la many years earlier. But what of the bracelet I obtained there? Eileen knew I had often conjectured about its origins and the possible ways in which it had eventually reached that remote part of the world.

It was a circular bracelet and I got it from a jolly rosy cheeked Tibetan girl at the Nangpa la in exchange for an empty round tin and a silver rupee. She didn't want the rupee, just the empty, and

---

*Tingri is 18 miles north of the Nangpa la.

to me, valueless cigarette tin. It was a fair swap for from the chuckle in her voice and the light in her eye, I could tell that as a trader she thought she had made a good bargain.

What of the amber and where did it come from? I will never know but from the moment I saw it I knew that I wanted it, because of the associations it might have with people and places in the distant past.

In the middle of the second millennium much trading took place between the people of the Mediterranean lands and those far to the north in the countries we now call Norway and Sweden. Along the shores of the Baltic Sea the golden fossil resin we call amber had long been gleaned at ebb tide by the hard-working, peaceful neolithic farmers whose low houses of turves and stones were built nearby. Already by the year 2000 B.C. this precious commodity had been used for barter with the tall trading Beaker folk from the Iberian peninsula and had found its way into the North Yorkshire moors where it was traded for jet. It was centuries later that the amber trade route developed across Europe where it persisted for a long period of time. Perhaps at that time some early traveller to the shores of the Skagerak traded goods of bronze, or beads of faience for the amber bracelet. How did it then make the journey along the river valleys of Central Europe, over high mountain passes, perhaps to stay awhile as some ornament or charm for an inhabitant of that great religious centre of the Alps —Val Camonica? Did it some centuries later find its way into the hands of a Cretan sea trader, who in turn at the port of Tyre or of Sidon passed it over to a Syrian merchant? It is possible to weave a fascinating pattern of its movements and conjecture as to its eventual passage to the high pass in Central Asia.

Possibly a Macedonian soldier of Alexander's army picked it up from a dusty road at Persepolis, dropped there as the people fled. For it was at Persepolis, after a drunken festival, that Alexander's army burned to the ground the palace of Darius, King of Kings. Later the same army skirted the mountains of Western Turkestan eventually reaching India via the Khyber pass. Was the same Macedonian soldier still with them—and the bracelet too? Slowly, exchanging hands many times, it may have travelled further to the east and eventually from the valley of the Indus to the land of Kashmir or over yet higher passes to Chang Thang—north Tibet. Perhaps for long periods of time it remained within one small area but eventually and always, the ambient charm would attract and be the source of barter. Finally, one cold and memorable day, on the roof of the world I bartered for it too and gained it for a cheap modern tin. Did the lump of amber, picked up on the Baltic shore then shaped and re-shaped, traded and re-traded take almost 4000 years to reach the Nangpa la? Certainly, within a few short weeks it had made the journey from that cold remote pass in Central Asia, back to a small village in northern Europe. Often since then in our home in Cymru (Wales) I have held it and felt its sensuous smoothness, looked at it and enjoyed its electron glow against the light. Always I have sensed something of its past. What I imagine may, or may not, have happened, but what does remain indelibly is the memory of the jolly Tibetan girl wearing the bracelet on the high pass in Central Asia and the tangible proof, the truth, that it got there somehow!

Postscript

Eileen and I have been back to Sola Khumbu and Everest many times, and not so long ago at Thame we were able to look along the Bhote Kosi—the valley that leads to Tibet. On another occasion we revisited the Changu la (Renjo pass!) and looked up the valley towards the Nangpa la. However, we have not been able to go to the pass because after the invasion of Tibet by the Chinese, access has been closed to travellers. But that is a small thing. The real tragedy is that no longer are Tibetans able to think of it as a gateway to and from home. It is the reverse, for instead it is their way of escape from tyranny, and of attaining freedom from persecution and the oppression of an invader who has killed over one sixth of their population.

Despite such terrorism and tragedy, I shall always remember the Nangpa la because of a jolly rosy-cheeked Tibetan girl, and witnessing the kindest act I have ever known.

Index